WHITEY

The Rise and Rule
of the Shoprite King

Niel Joubert

Tafelberg

Tafelberg,
an imprint of NB Publishers,
a division of Media24 Boeke (Pty) Ltd
40 Heerengracht, Cape Town, South Africa
www.tafelberg.com

Cover design: Nudge Studio
Cover image: Shoprite Holdings Ltd
Typography: Melanie Kriel
Translator: Linde Dietrich
Proof reader: Angela Voges
Proof reader: Gillian Warren-Brown
Indexer: Anna Tanneberger

Set in 12 on 17 pt Adobe Garamond Pro
Printed and bound by CTP Printers, Cape Town
First edition, first impression 2022

ISBN: 978-0-624-08789-2
Epub: 978-0-624-08790-8

Contents

Foreword by Johann Rupert

'Business giant of world stature' could indeed also have been an apposite subtitle for this book. Whitey Basson exhibited a unique flair for retail that is hard to explain. The Germans talk of *'Fingerspitzengefühl'*, literally 'fingertip feeling', which refers to intuitive flair or instinct. In his masterpiece *The Talent Code,* Daniel Coyle describes how exceptional talent is acquired and grown. Hours and years of practice, of trying and trying again . . . eventually leading to a unique, almost indescribable talent and intuitive feel.

Over the years that many of us had the good fortune to work with Whitey, his curiosity, enthusiasm and passion for work were an inspiration. His distinctive attention to detail was just as impressive as his ability to see the bigger picture. Retail is certainly not for amateurs!

Successful individuals do not take chances when they take risks. When Whitey embarked on challenging business moves, he was always fully aware of the risks that were attached to the deals. His masterly moves were calculated and resulted in enormous wealth for his shareholders. Furthermore, as a job creator, he was second to none. South Africans from all income groups are still benefitting today from his ability to offer fresh food at low prices. James Wellwood Basson understood *every* facet of his business.

Whitey has been particularly fortunate in having a marvellous marriage partner. Annalise regularly had to fill the role of both parents when he spent long hours at the office or was absent on business trips. Their four wonderful children testify to their success as parents.

My hope is that *Whitey* will be widely read as an example of what a boy from the rural parts of South Africa can achieve.

An international businessman of stature!

Author's note

I met Whitey Basson for the first time on a cold winter's day in 2019. Our meeting took place over lunch at Mont Marie, the restaurant on his farm with the same name outside Stellenbosch, which is situated just above his 'home farm', Klein DasBosch. I had flown down from Johannesburg to Cape Town that morning and was due to return the same evening. Hence I had arrived with only the clothes on my back, my cellphone and a notebook. The purpose of my trip was to persuade Whitey that I was the right person to tell his story.

Both the conversation and the red wine flowed freely, so much so that I completely lost track of the time. I had to rush to the airport if I were to catch my flight, but Whitey insisted that I have a braai with him at Klein DasBosch that evening, sleep over at the farm, and of course also meet his wife Annalise.

I tried to protest: the ticket was booked, I had to attend a meeting in Johannesburg early the next morning, and besides, I hadn't brought any clothes along. But one doesn't easily say no to Whitey, and he quickly made a call to change the booking. That evening, Whitey, Annalise, Mont Marie's owner and chef, Pieter Vlok, and I braaied, chatted and became better acquainted. I left for Johannesburg with a bit of a headache the next morning, but it disappeared fast when Whitey sent word: it's okay, let's write the book.

I would discover later, during one of our numerous interviews, that in Pep's early days he and Renier van Rooyen, founder of Pep Stores and Whitey's great mentor, used to assess prospective employees by inviting them for a meal accompanied by (lots of) wine and observing how they conducted themselves . . .

Our first interviews took place over two days in January 2020, but the Covid pandemic thwarted our momentum. We started conversing regularly online in September and resumed our face-to-face conversations early in 2021 at Klein DasBosch (and at Mont Marie).

Thus the book is primarily based on interviews, phone conversations, emails, WhatsApp voice notes and text messages between Whitey and me over a period of close to three years. The same applies to Whitey's school friends, contemporaries at Wilgenhof, colleagues at Pep and Shoprite, employees of Klein DasBosch, and friends and family.

In addition, I relied on newspaper reports, magazine articles, television interviews (many of which can be viewed on YouTube), Shoprite's annual reports (1987–2017) and an exceptional collection of scrapbooks with material about Whitey from 1954 up to and including his retirement in 2016, which were compiled and maintained by Annalise, Whitey's secretary Anita and his media team. They contain a wealth of material that includes photos, letters, email correspondence, notes, newspaper clippings, advertisements and speeches.

A tribute book that was compiled by Shoprite colleagues and presented to Whitey on the occasion of his retirement also provided many anecdotes and other information. All the sources are indicated in the text or in endnotes.

My heartfelt thanks to Whitey, for our many hours of conversation during which he shared his extraordinary story with me. So, too, to Annalise for her hospitality and hard work behind the scenes to get us over the finishing line, and to Anita, for all the arrangements. And thank you to everyone at Klein DasBosch who always welcomed me with open arms. Chef Pieter, your hospitality at Mont Marie was at all times gratifying after long hours of work.

To Erika Oosthuysen of NB – thank you for your patience and encouragement throughout this lengthy process. To Riaan de Villiers, the editor, for his labours in converting my text into better, more concise Afrikaans as well as a story that flows nicely, and also for our phone conversations, which invariably re-energised me to continue working. To Linde Dietrich, for her English translation and sharp eye, and all the other people who worked on the book – from cover design and proofreading to printers and marketing.

To my family, thank you for your support over three years during which I regularly had to spend evenings, weekends and holidays behind my computer. Especially my wife Janrie, who frequently had to take out and entertain our children, Daniël and Nieke, on Saturdays and Sundays. Thank you as well to my mother Landa, my father Daniël and my two sisters, Nelia and Jana, for your support. I love all of you.

Whitey Basson is indeed a South African business giant and the king of retail. Moreover, he is also irrepressibly and unforgettably human. I hope this book does justice to his life story, interwoven with the story of Shoprite and its people.

Niel Joubert, September 2022

Introduction:
The making of a legend

OK Bazaars had been the pride and pace-setter of South African retail since it was founded in Johannesburg in 1927. But as South Africa and its shoppers changed, OK gradually ran into difficulties.

In the mid-1990s, South African Breweries (SAB), owner of the majority stake in OK since 1973, was at its wits' end and decided to get rid of the millstone around its neck. Intense negotiations followed between SAB and a team from Shoprite, a younger chain that had been swallowing the highly competitive retail sector from below, bit by bit and without much fanfare, for the past twenty years.

Although he always had his finger on the pulse, the power behind Shoprite – Whitey Basson – spent the last few days of the negotiations in a hotel in Durban, 'away from the fire'. But he was still pulling the strings, for by that time he was a master negotiator. He had cut his teeth at Pep – in the art of negotiation as well as that of retail – and perfected his skills at Shoprite with the acquisitions of Grand Bazaars and Checkers. Then came the OK deal, which was closed on 3 November 1997. The following morning, newspaper posters trumpeted: 'Whitey Basson buys OK Bazaars for R1'.

Up until then, Whitey had been relatively unknown and Shoprite relatively small. Though financial journalists had gradually realised he was achieving something special in the retail sector, the reports were for the most part still tucked away in the financial sections of newspapers and in specialised financial magazines. But that changed overnight. The names 'Shoprite' and 'Whitey Basson' were on everyone's lips. Whitey's friendly face, blond fringe and mischievous smile appeared on the front pages and covers of nearly every prominent paper and magazine in South Africa – the architect of the 'bargain of the century'.[1]

'The purchase price sounds low, but OK is losing R20 million a month, and it will be the most expensive buy of my life if we can't return the group to profitability soon,' he told *Sake-Beeld*.[2] The acquisition was indeed a risk, and both Whitey's reputation and Shoprite's future were at stake.

'The takeover of the loss-making OK by Shoprite Holdings is going to be a big challenge for Shoprite,' Sake-kommentaar stated.[3] 'Shoprite, with Mr Whitey Basson at the helm, is well regarded after the struggling Checkers was taken over and transformed into a very profitable group within a relatively short time. All eyes are now on Basson and his team to see whether they can perform another miracle.'

The prestigious magazine *Leadership* dubbed him 'the R1 man'. 'What type of person buys OK Bazaars for R1? Supermarket supremo Whitey Basson, who is always in search of a win-win situation. But Basson's mission is inspired by more than just pure capitalism.'[4]

Marcia Klein of the *Sunday Times* asked Whitey why he bought OK when others preferred to steer clear of that challenge. He gave the kind of reply that would later be known as a 'Whiteyism': 'Some of us prefer blondes, and some brunettes . . .' He added: 'OK is a company that has been bankrupt for numerous years. It's like a man with a Ferrari who cannot get it serviced.'[5]

The glossy magazine *De Kat* described Whitey as a 'supermarket cowboy who saddles up winning horses'.[6] The journalist also quoted a saying that has since become legendary: 'People say the softest part of Whitey Basson is his teeth.'

De Kat continued: 'There are several reasons why he manages to pull off what heavyweight businesspeople before him have been unable to do. He is known for negotiating people to exhaustion, and notorious for not letting sentiment stand in the way of business. He is competitive as well, with a bloodthirsty zeal that probably gives opponents sleepless nights.'[7]

Little by little, parts of Whitey's story emerged – a remarkable individual who took over a hotchpotch of small stores in the Western Cape in 1979, with the single-minded goal of becoming the largest food retailer in Africa. Notwithstanding his success and heavy work schedule, he remained a family man and a down-to-earth boerseun.

Renier van Rooyen, the legendary founder of Pep and one of Whitey's greatest mentors, said simply: 'There is no other retailer in the country like him.'[8] When he acquired OK, analysts wondered again whether this time Whitey had not bitten off more than he could chew. But he and his team set to work quickly and decisively, and within a year OK had been returned to profitability. The turnaround was a phenomenal achievement.

Not content with resting on his laurels, Whitey took on new challenges. He expanded early into the rest of Africa, before the rest woke up. He was intent on 'arm-wrestling against the best in the world', and even made a short-lived foray into India. Shoprite has become the largest retailer in Africa and one of the 100 largest retailers globally. In the process, the company has created jobs and other opportunities for thousands of people. While many still do not realise it, today Shoprite is South Africa's largest employer after the state.

Whitey's renowned judgement did not fail him when it came to Steinhoff either. He warned his long-standing business partner Christo Wiese against Markus Jooste and his furniture group and prevented the integration of Shoprite into Steinhoff, which would have resulted in disaster. When Steinhoff collapsed, Shoprite was safe, largely thanks to Whitey who had for years opposed a merger between Shoprite and Steinhoff.

In 2017, Whitey finally walked away from the company he had built up. He sold nearly all his shares in Shoprite and is now very wealthy – a solid billionaire.

Much earlier, after having resided for years in Cape Town's northern suburbs, he and his wife Annalise had moved to a farm outside Stellenbosch, which they transformed into a show estate and where their four children grew into adulthood. The Shoprite 'family' and many other guests were hosted there at large-scale events.

Nowadays Whitey produces a limited quantity of select wines on the farm with the help of the winemaker Jan 'Boland' Coetzee. But a leisurely retirement does not seem to be on the cards – besides still creating jobs on numerous farms and in other enterprises, he assists promising young people to start new businesses. He occasionally grants interviews (and switches off the unnecessary lights once the television teams have left), and the government asks him for advice behind the scenes. Yet he has always remained something of an enigma.

Who is Whitey Basson really? Where does he come from, what motivates him, and how did he turn Shoprite into Africa's largest retailer? This extraordinary story began just after World War II, on a farm in the Swartland region of the Western Cape.

PART ONE

FORMATIVE YEARS

1

Son of the Swartland

Wellwood is a hard-working boy, tries his best and has progressed beautifully. We expect a bright future for him.

– Miss LK van Tonder, Standard 1 report,
Porterville Preparatory School

When he was just five years old, James Wellwood Basson invited the farm manager's daughter for a spin in the farm bakkie. It was parked on a slope and they went hurtling down the hill, landing up in an irrigation ditch. Cool and unfazed, the young Wellwood climbed out, behaving as if this sort of thing happened every day.

Of course, there were repercussions, recalls his elder sister Juel, 'But driving a bakkie, *that* he could do!' – as long as you turned a blind eye to the rather unfortunate destination, of course. She recounts this incident to illustrate the sort of charmed life her little brother seemed to lead, and that, even as a youngster, he displayed an unusual degree of self-possession and self-confidence – something that became a hall-mark of the prankster-turned-businessman throughout his trajectory to become a kingpin of South African retail.

She believes his attitude stemmed from their father being besotted with his little laatlammetjie, whose shock of blond hair later gained him the nickname 'Whitey'. 'My dad regarded him as something special and spoilt him rotten. It had a significant influence on his development,' says Juel. 'He walked early and talked early, and had a lot of self-confidence from an early age.' Today, Whitey sees it slightly differently, saying simply, '[My father] devoted a great deal of time to me. I was brought up almost as an only child.'

Perhaps this was precisely because Juel, the eldest, and younger brother Jan, had to do without their father during their formative years as he was away fighting in the Second World War. By the time Whitey came along, however, their dad was home and settled into a new life as a farmer and politician. Whitey says even though his father didn't speak much about the war – in fact, he was very private about his war experiences – 'the war had a huge influence on me'. Having enlisted in 1939, Jack Basson was discharged in 1943 with the rank of captain.

Whitey explains his father's officer status: 'Before the war, my father was working at Silberbauer as an attorney. The firm made a large donation to the British War Fund and could recommend an officer on account of that. He spent a long time in Italy, and also in Africa. He and General Jan Smuts were very good friends. Smuts brought him back to South Africa, and he was then detached to Military Intelligence at the Castle.'

When he was discharged from the army, Basson decided against resuming his career in law and bought the farm DasBosch, some twenty kilometres south of Porterville in the agricultural district of Vier-en-Twintig Riviere at the foot of the Groot Winterhoek Mountains. There he set about farming wheat, citrus and grapes. A while later, he also became involved in politics, representing Smuts's United Party as a member of parliament.

About two years after settling on DasBosch, Jack and his wife Maria, or Maude, welcomed their laatlammetjie into the world. Assisted by their family doctor, Maude gave birth to him on the farm on Tuesday 8 January 1946.

So how did it happen that someone named James Wellwood Basson was born on a farm in the staunchly Afrikaans-speaking Swartland region during the mid-1940s? 'Well, the birth part was easy – the name was the difficult part,' quips Whitey, whose sense of humour goes hand in glove with his razor-sharp wit. Later, Wellwood proved to be a bit of a mouthful for his predominantly Afrikaans-speaking platteland mates, so, on account of his hair colour, Whitey it was. (Years later, the name caused him embarrassment when he stood for election to a school board in Welgemoed. The candidates' names were displayed on a board, and he was 'James Wellwood'. Since no one knew who this candidate actually was, he did not receive a single vote!)

The origin of his rather unusual baptismal names is related to politics. He was named after a close friend of the Bassons, Scottish immigrant James Wellwood Mushet, who served in parliament alongside Jack as a fellow United Party member.[1]

Mushet was a wealthy businessman and politician who had come to South Africa in 1889 at the age of eighteen. Among other things, Mushet served as a minister in Smuts's last cabinet before the latter's election defeat in 1948.[2] Mushet and his wife Alice were childless, and James Wellwood regarded the Bassons' new arrival as his own son. The rich Scot wanted to bequeath his entire estate to the boy. 'You know, this was big money, it was millions of pounds in those days,' Whitey says. But Jack Basson balked at the idea. 'My dad was a man of firm principles. There was no family connection with Mushet, and he believed it wouldn't be good for me to inherit such a vast amount of money.' Mushet lent Jack the money to buy DasBosch, and Jack and Maude decided to name their youngest son after their good friend.

* * * *

In a primary school composition titled 'Die Plaas Dasbos',[3] which has been preserved to this day, Whitey wrote: 'The farm Dasbos comprises

2 700 morgen. It is located some 96 miles north of Cape Town. The farm is situated in the Swartland area of the Cape Province. The closest town to the farm is Porterville, about 12 miles west.'

The farm teemed with animals. Whitey also wrote about a budgie named Opel, the 'most important pet' on the farm: 'The cat, is the favourite of the owner's wife, but Opel, for other reasons, is not very fond of the cat.' Although many pets came and went over the years, everyone's favourites were the two jackals named Blits and Simson. While it was 'quite pleasant' to have them on the farm when they were younger, Whitey wrote, they killed so many chickens when they grew older that they had to be put down. 'Pets are very important on the farm, as without them life would otherwise be rather dull,' he added.

Juel still remembers the time Whitey got his own dog, a Boxer. 'It was a farm dog, but from early on he used to smuggle the dog into his room at night and let him sleep on the bed, which my mother refused to allow. And when Mom became aware of it, there would be a big war as she chased the dog off the bed. But as soon as the house was quiet, he would lie down on the floor next to his dog and pull the blanket from the bed. There they would sleep peacefully until one of our parents discovered him on the floor when they went to bed. From early childhood, he would always make a plan!'

In his composition, Whitey wrote that social life in the district was generally quite boring. 'The people of the district are very hospitable, but the social life of the town cannot be compared with that of a place such as Paarl.'

Regarding 'future plans', he wrote: 'The farm will have to become more modernised because the labour problems are worsening. Machinery will have to replace labourers. The most important plan for the future is to try and save on repair work. Most of the repair work will therefore have to be done on the farm.'

Juel also recalls that even in his childhood Whitey thought differently about things. She recounts: 'Grandpa Nel once visited us and was digging with his spade in our vegetable garden. He told Wellwood, who just stood there watching him, that instead of being so lazy he should rather help a bit, to which Wellwood replied as clever as could be: 'No, Oupa, when I'm big, I'm going to have a little spade made for me that works with a machine, so that I can do other things.'

It was a carefree, largely rural life, but Whitey realises he was privileged to have grown up in a well-off home with a well-educated father and mother who could offer him all kinds of opportunities. 'I believe that I had an advantage over some of the other children in the area,' he remarks.

* * * *

Whitey's paternal grandfather – Jan Hendrik Basson, or 'Oom Jan' – was a prominent Swartlander. Whitey relates that he was part of the start of Sasko and Bokomo, 'but was actually a farmer'. He played a leading role in the wheat industry for many years and was inter alia the 'father' of several new wheat varieties.

Born in 1890 on the farm Bakensvlei in the Moorreesburg district, he farmed for 32 years on Anyskop and for 25 years on Driebos outside Porterville. Later, he sold both farms and moved to Moorreesburg. He was chairman of the Moorreesburgse Koringboerekoöperasie (Moorreesburg Wheat Farmers' Cooperative) for 32 years, and chairman of the Moorreesburgse Koöperatiewe Handelsvereniging (cooperative commercial society) for 18 years. In addition, he was a founding member of Bokomo and served on the board of directors at the age of 28. He also served on the board of Sasko from 1931 until his retirement in 1963, for the last number of years as deputy chairman.

Whitey's maternal grandfather was Hendrik Nel, who joined General Manie Maritz's commando during the Anglo-Boer War and 'experienced remarkable adventures and mortal danger'.[4] Before the war, at sixteen years old, he had studied at the old Victoria College in Stellenbosch, which later became Stellenbosch University.

At the age of nineteen, Nel and a friend, Careltjie van der Merwe, decided to run away and join Maritz's commando, which at the time was based on a farm near Rietfontein in the Agter-Hantam. Right until the end of the war, he stayed with Maritz on commando, crisscrossing Namaqualand in their guerrilla campaign against the British forces.

'I think he was the only bloke in Manie Maritz's patrol who was literate,' says Whitey. 'So he kept Maritz's diaries. There was plenty of speculation about Maritz's exploits, but the truth was recorded in the diaries. My father kept them in his study, but unfortunately, they were destroyed in a fire at our house in 1975.' Grandpa Nel was charged with high treason and sentenced to death, but received a pardon. He subsequently did his articles at the law firm Bisset and Hofmeyr and became an attorney in Calvinia, where he later set up his own practice, Nel & Lawrence.

According to Whitey, in time his grandpa Nel became wealthy and was a founding member of the North West Board of Executors, which would later become part of Syfrets Trust. Nel and his wife eventually moved to Somerset West. However, after being brutally attacked on their farm one evening, they spent their last years in Stellenbosch.

* * * *

Whitey's parents were married in Cape Town on 25 April 1936. They had met at the University of Cape Town (UCT), where Jack studied law and Maude education. According to Juel, their parents were both highly intelligent people who had a major influence on the lives of the three children. 'My dad taught all of us how to play chess in early childhood. And he never wrote out a speech – just jotted down a few points on the back of his cigarette box. He was an excellent speaker.

'He also read a lot. His favourite book was a biography of Napoleon, a weighty tome that he practically knew by heart. We grew up with shelves filled with books in our home. Mom used to say jokingly: "While they were still reading only *Die Kerkbode* in the Swartland, we were reading Shakespeare."'

When the general election of 1948 was round the corner, Jack was 'constantly away from home, holding meetings across the Cape Province', Juel recounts. 'This was where his political career started in earnest. He was a member of the Provincial Council and he defeated PW Botha in a constituency in Parow and Goodwood.'

According to Whitey, his father was a straightforward person, very honest, and loyal to his political party. 'He was a true team player. He was farming when General Smuts asked him to stand for election as a member of the United Party in Sea Point, a seat he retained for many years.' Jack won the constituency for the first time in 1958 and retained it in 1961, 1966 and 1970. Colin Eglin, the leader of the Progressive Party, lost to him on two occasions. In 1974, when Eglin did capture the seat, Jack was no longer a candidate.[5]

Whitey continues: 'In those years my dad was one of the longest-serving parliamentarians, and although he received offers from the NP [National Party], he remained a member of the United Party. He always used to say he had only one set of principles – "I don't have another set in my top drawer, and that's it." But he was liberal in his thinking. He viewed the NP as traitors who had been on the side of the Germans during the war.

Although the tensions between 'Sappe' (supporters of the United

Party) and 'Natte' gradually subsided, Whitey still experienced the antagonism on a personal level. 'We were called jingoes – in other words, Afrikaners who were more English than Afrikaans. In Porterville we were labelled as communists into the bargain. And I was punched at school because I was a Sap – one day my nose was even broken.'

Whitey and his dad would converse for hours on end. 'I could argue with him and was often exposed to foreigners and their thinking.' This was somewhat different from the standard Afrikaner household of the time, when people did not easily hold 'dissident' views that deviated from the norm. Children were seen and not heard, and did not question their parents, the church, or the government. On DasBosch, debating was encouraged and questions were answered frankly: an environment that was conducive to the cultivation of free thinking, which is essential for entrepreneurship. This may be why Whitey, from an early age, did not hesitate to challenge 'authority for authority's sake'.

Whitey also recalls that his mother and father taught him about thrift from early childhood. 'My mom tried to save wherever she could. And if someone would, for instance, ask my dad why he didn't buy a new car, he would say: "There are thirteen reasons. The first one is that I don't have the money, and the other twelve don't count."' Whitey evidently inherited his sense of humour from his father as well.

In fact, Whitey describes his dad as charismatic. 'He made very good speeches – world-class speeches. He was handsome, with blue eyes and blond hair, tall and lean, and very charming. And he could speak English as if he'd been born in England.' Whitey learnt from him what looking beyond the horizon involved. 'He was well-read, as was my mother. They stimulated me on other levels and played a huge role in my vision for my life – what I wanted to do and what I wanted to achieve,' he told Jak de Priester in the television programme *Reis na Gister*.[6]

Whitey and Juel concur that their mother was an 'exceptionally smart woman'. Juel relates: 'She was first in the Cape Province in matric at Good Hope Seminary, where she had been at boarding school. She came from a very well-known family – our grandmother was a Louw from Sutherland and a cousin of the poets WEG Louw and NP van Wyk Louw, who also grew up there. Although she'd studied education at UCT, when her mother died at a young age, she returned to Calvinia to live with her father on the farm.'

Whitey chips in: 'My parents supported me but would also disagree with me. My dad had a great deal of ambition for me, but my mother, on the other hand, was the one who would put a damper on things – don't do this or that – whereas my dad would always say, "Go for it". I was always very proud of my parents, but today I'm sad that I didn't devote more time to them.'

According to Whitey, they were a close-knit family who loved nature. 'There was the radio for entertainment, and for the rest it was you and your family, the farm and its people, and nature that kept you occupied.'[7]

* * * *

Whitey has been good with figures since childhood. In primary school pupils were given time off if they were quick at completing their sums, and Whitey and his pal Attie Dippenaar were always the first to finish. Then they were allowed to go outside, but before they could play, they had to water the hydrangeas in front of the school with manure 'tea'. 'Now you can imagine how we reeked of chicken manure every day, and that because we were so good at sums,' Whitey quipped. 'Today I wonder why I was so stupid – I could rather have stayed in the class-room by *not* being good at sums.'[8]

Whitey and his father also did sums together. Among other things, they made bets about how much grain per hectare the farmers of the district would harvest and what they would earn from it. Whitey often won a few rands from his father, and he remembers in particular the tricycle he once won in that way. 'My dad used to brag about me to the farmers in town. I then had to do sums and would always win a cooldrink or an ice cream,' he recounts.

His first introduction to retail was the day once a year when he and his father sat down with the owner of the local grocery store to go through the farm's account and settle it. 'Everyone on the farm could buy their groceries there. And then, every year when the harvest money had come in, my dad and Mister Hassim would sit down with the accounts for the entire day and go over the accounts for the year. And in that way, I saw what people bought, and it was always basically the same, and never more than two handfuls of the same goods.'

Whitey's father also helped shape his talent for retail in another way. On top of his farming operations and political activities, Jack Basson co-owned several bottle stores together with friends and partners. Whitey started working there over weekends and gained valuable experience in retail.

'Being a retailer is instinct,' he says today, 'and from my schooldays, I learnt by working in my father's bottle stores. This was where I acquired practical experience in retail. Today I can still walk into any store and estimate the turnover for you, and tell you whether or not it's going to succeed. I know stores like the palm of my hand.' He would continue working in the bottle stores as a student and later even owned a few.

* * * *

A classmate of Whitey's in Porterville, Carina Mouton, also remembers that he was a brainbox. 'When we were standard seven, we had to take bookkeeping as a subject. The teacher himself was rather unsure about the new subject, and when he wrote a sum on the blackboard, Whitey, who was sitting at the back of the class, put up his hand and said the sum was wrong. "So come and show us what it should be," the teacher said. Whitey took the chalk, erased a part of the sum and redid it. From that day on, Whitey and the teacher taught us bookkeeping more or less in tandem!'

But Whitey was not just brainy, he was playful too. One of his teachers, Miss Tinkie, recounts that she always had to make him sit right in front in the class, the 'sweet little fair-haired boy with a very mischievous streak'. Every time she wrote something on the blackboard, there would be a wriggling and a fidgeting behind her back. When she turned around, it would usually be Whitey who was up to some or other prank.

Juel relates: 'Whitey was never really naughty, but he was very mischievous. I couldn't bring a boyfriend to the farm without Whitey terrorising the guy to such an extent that he would throw in the towel and vamoose. He deflated tyres and bombarded cars with acorns, and when I tried to find some privacy in the garden with a boyfriend at night, he would jump out from behind bushes and photograph us with a flash!'

* * * *

The homestead on DasBosch looks very different today. But the two stone pillars that served as Whitey's goalposts for rugby games are still standing. 'This was where I learnt how to kick a rugby ball – me and my friends,' he recounts. Other games included swimming in the rivers and catching trout and Cape kurpers.

Whitey's best pals were the children of farmworkers – Esau, Baai and Dappie Tang. In fact, they constituted a little community. But there was also a dark side to this apparently idyllic existence: 'We were children in a Nat environment. So the coloured kids, my pals, had to walk kilometres to and from their school while we rode in comfort in the bus to school and back, with the bus about two-thirds empty.

'On our return from school in the afternoon, we would already be playing ball on the farm while they were still walking back, and the next morning we drove past them in the bus, and I would wave at them, at Esau, Baai and Dappie Tang. I couldn't understand why it had to be like that. My dad always used to say he couldn't really do anything about it because those were the rules of apartheid. He did pick up the kids as often as possible and drop them at school.

'It has always stuck in my memory, and that is why I was later very proactive in the coloured communities. They always got the short end of the stick. Things like that angered me from an early age – the principle of inequality that I couldn't understand. That injustice left a mark on my soul.'

* * * *

Whitey loved the farm life, but in his first years at high school he sometimes had to stay in the school hostel in town while his parents were in Sea Point. 'Then I would go to school in the school bus on Monday mornings and return to the farm on Friday afternoons.'

But Whitey was not fond of the hostel. 'The food was bad. The teachers had nice meals, but our food was skimpy – some evenings we only had bread and jam.' When a hunger strike was organised he was one of the ringleaders, and the food improved somewhat. He also regularly devised plans to go home earlier. 'I would just tell the hostel head that I felt fluish, or that I suspected I was getting mumps, then I would go home with the bus and stay with Oom Albert Louw, the farm manager, for about two or three days.'

One of the pluses of the hostel was that it was for boys and girls – and from an early age Whitey has had an eye for a pretty girl. In the evenings, when he had to lock the doors that separated the boys from the girls, there would usually be 'a pretty girl who had to lock the doors from their side, and I could at least give her a squeeze before we had to go to sleep'.

During school holidays, when parliament was in session, the three children would travel to Sea Point to stay with their parents. 'But I didn't like that very much because I didn't really have friends there. My friends were in Porterville.'

Whitey took part in athletics in summer and played rugby in winter – 'a bit of everything', as tends to be the case in a small school on the platteland. He recalls, though, that he ran hurdle races and once had to compete in a Boland competition, but he knocked over all the hurdles as he ran. 'It was because our athletics teacher had set our school's own hurdles too low,' Whitey says, laughing. 'Or maybe that was just my excuse because I had run badly!'

In those days, the motto displayed on a wall of the Hoërskool Porterville read: 'Een lewe . . . lééf dit!' (One life . . . *live* it!) In standard seven, Whitey would gaze at the motto while sitting on the floor of the hall and wonder how he would make money one day.[9] But his life would soon take a different turn – away from the farm, away from Porterville, and away from Afrikaans.

2

Learning from 'the English'

Be yourself, I told somebody, but he couldn't
because he was nobody.

— A frequent saying of Maude Basson's

In 1961, Whitey's relatively simple farm and school life was upended – he had to complete his high-school career at the elite Rondebosch Boys' High School in Cape Town. 'My dad said I had to go to Rondebosch to learn how the English thought and operated, as they controlled South Africa's business life.'

Since the NP's assumption of power in 1948 political power had largely been in Afrikaner hands, but the private sector (apart from agriculture) was controlled almost exclusively by English speakers. In 1981, a full twenty years after Whitey had gone to Rondebosch, there were still only four Afrikaner-controlled corporations with assets in excess of R300 million: Volkskas, Trust Bank, Rembrandt and Sanlam.[1]

Thus, the fifteen-year-old Whitey became a boarding-school pupil in Cape Town's southern suburbs, an area renowned for its outstanding schools. Although Whitey's elder brother had matriculated at Porterville, his sister had attended Rustenburg Girls' High School, just around the corner from Rondebosch Boys'. His boarding house was Canigou House. Though Whitey had a reasonable command of English, Afrikaans was still his mother tongue, and the shift to English – and the new lifestyle – was a significant adjustment.

'Porterville was small, and the competition was not too tough, so

I was able to do fairly well. But all of a sudden, I had to learn everything in English. At home we could speak English reasonably well but learning terminology from scratch in another language is quite hard. For example, when they talked about "oxygen" in the science class, I genuinely had no idea what they were talking about. So, doing maths and science in English was tough going.

'I worked very hard in an attempt to get back to the academic level on which I had been in Porterville. I think I never really caught up. I still did well academically, but didn't reach the level on which I'd been in Porterville, and that as a result of things being alien to me.

'This was a very difficult part of my life – suddenly I discovered a culture that was totally different from what I was used to. There were many other Afrikaans-speaking boys but, funnily enough, they were the most arrogant of all. When you change schools in the middle of high school . . . it's hard, you leave your friends behind, everything you know. You could just as well have moved to Australia. But Rondebosch inspired me to get to the top. In the end it was good for me, and I made good friends. But that thing of not being allowed to go out, of being forced to study for two hours every night, to go to church, and to do this and that, that wasn't really for me.'

* * * *

His contemporaries at Rondebosch remember Whitey's typical Swartland burr when he spoke Afrikaans, with an r-sound pronounced like a g. A classmate recalls how Whitey told them that his father was a 'gyk man wat gy in 'n Fogd Gelexy'. He was also as thin as a rake at school. Another contemporary remembers someone remarking: 'If Whitey was standing behind a telephone pole, we would only see his Adam's apple.'

Like at Porterville, Whitey took part in athletics and rugby. 'And keep in mind, even if you played rugby, the other guys had been playing together for years and now you pitch up there in the middle of your high-school years. So they won't even pass the ball to you. I started practising for the A team and ended up playing my first match in the D team.

'I played fly half. And I scored a fair number of points because I kicked well, but I never managed to get back into the A team. I was very good friends with them – now we laugh about it and I say, you bastards, you held on to the ball. Roy McCallum played centre at the time and the scrum half was Doughy Crisp – he would just throw the ball pass me to Roy.

'And I also ran without spikes at the first athletics meeting – everyone else had spikes. I didn't have a tracksuit either – just a rugby jersey with red and white stripes and 'Eendrag maak Mag' (Unity is Strength) or something like that on the pocket. I did get a pair of spikes later, but in Porterville you only really wore spikes if you were a Springbok.'

An activity that Whitey did take seriously was cadets. In those years the school cadet system prepared white boys for military service, and activities included rifle shooting, discipline and drill exercises. On many Friday afternoons he was the neatest and most smartly turned-out pupil on parade, and then he would be honourably dismissed for the day. 'How the rest of us envied his departing figure, cap badge glinting in the sun, belt and shoes polished to perfection,' recounts a classmate, Neil Veitch. 'Clearly, here was a man who took great pride in his appearance, in his school and, doubtless, in his country as well.'

Years later, Veitch asked Whitey what his motivation had been for such smartness on parade. 'Well,' Whitey replied, 'you must be joking if you think I was doing it for Vorster and Country. I was just so keen to avoid the parade and have the afternoon on my bed at Canigou!'

Rondebosch was an excellent school, and Whitey made good friends there, but he did not like what he calls the 'one-size-fits-all' approach. 'I found it very hard. We also had to study for a long time. I had to study for two hours every day because *everyone* had to study for two hours, but some might master the work more quickly than others. For the most part I would sit staring at the roof, pissed off, because I knew and understood the work, but then you still had to sit there and pretend that you're swotting.'

'So, I had no great love for my high-school days. And I always say, I never have to go to church again because I attended church every day, and even twice on Sundays. At Rondebosch I filled my entire quota.'

The loss of the carefree life in Porterville was tough at times. 'On Saturdays we were allowed to go to Newlands to watch rugby. We would often work as ushers, and at half-time we had to traipse down that moerse distance for roll call to make sure you haven't slipped away. That wasn't my style.

'On Sundays after church you could visit your girlfriend in your civvies. Early in the morning you would walk to church, which was far from the school, and all the way back again. At one o'clock we had lunch, and then we were allowed to leave. My girlfriend lived in Pinelands, so I had to walk down to the station, take the train to Observatory, and then the bus to Pinelands. I would visit her for perhaps an hour before having to take the same route back to make it to the school in time for supper at six o'clock.

'It was things like these that infuriated me later in my life. I have often said that I can't handle thoughtless decisions. That thing has been embedded in me since childhood – that I would say, hell no, what you people are doing now is simply not logical. Then they would ask, but what else can one do? And I would say, I don't necessarily know, but you should sit down around a table and perhaps decide that the pupils whose marks are above a certain percentage only have to study for one hour per day, or something like that. But simply treating everyone like foot soldiers . . .

'Mind you, it was much the same in the hostel at Porterville. But it made me quite rebellious against people who were not prepared to debate about something and look for other options or solutions.'

Although Whitey stayed in the hostel for a few months of the year at Porterville, at least he still saw his parents regularly. That was not the case at Rondebosch. Today, he describes this as a loss. 'We got only two weekends off per term. And the lack of contact with my parents was hard for me at that age. You had a tickey box from where you could phone them, and then you saw them a few times a year. On Sundays, they could at least take you out for the day. When my parents were in Cape Town they would come to see me, but it was just not the same.

'That is why I have a very close relationship with my children and try to see them as much as possible. It was tough for me during those two years, and later at university too, because I had little contact with my father at the time when I was going through puberty and had to decide, what the hell I was going to do with my life. And besides, my dad's attention was split among politics, the farming operations and his businesses. The only times we spent together were when we drove back to Porterville on my weekends off. Then we would eat a mixed grill at the Greek café in Paarl and continue our journey to the farm.'

But life as a boarding-school kid in the southern suburbs taught Whitey some valuable lessons. 'The advantage of boarding-school life is that it makes you self-reliant. At Rondebosch I also quickly got into a position where I learnt to fight for myself. I learnt to be hardegat – I'm not someone who let myself be bullied by the abuse of authority.'

In 1963 Whitey matriculated at Rondebosch with English Higher, Afrikaans Lower, Physical Science, Maths, Geography, and Bookkeeping and Commercial Accounting as subjects. After first considering following in the footsteps of his grandfather and father by studying law, Whitey decided he wanted to study medicine and was admitted at the University of Cape Town. But before embarking on his studies he set off to enjoy a proper holiday, and that would steer his life in a completely different direction.

3

Taking chances in Matieland

It was December 1963 and the young Whitey, having just finished matric, was having a whale of a time holidaying in Strand. And he was head over heels in love with a 'very pretty girl'. He was due to return to Cape Town the following year, 1964, to study medicine at UCT – 'probably because the doctor in Porterville, Dr Charlie Frank, drove the best-looking cars'. But the holiday romance would turn these plans upside down and have an enormous influence on his life.

The reason for his sudden change of course was simple: he wanted to extend his holiday in order to spend more time with his new girl-friend. His medical classes at UCT were scheduled to start quite early in the new year, before most of the other faculties at Stellenbosch. In any case, he had never really been sure about his first choice of career. 'My mom never actually wanted me to study medicine. She said I didn't like blood – I don't know why – and I wouldn't be able to handle it.' Consequently, he decided to study towards a BCom at Stellenbosch University.

There were also other reasons why he changed universities. His sister and brother-in-law lived in Stellenbosch, and Whitey knew many other people there. 'Many people from our town sent their children there, so I had that connection as well.' Whitey had to scurry around to find a place in a residence, but fortunately he had good contacts. Juel was married to James Starke, who played flanker for the Springboks in his day. He was also a Rondebosch old boy and had studied at Stellenbosch, where he played for the Maties' first rugby team for many years and therefore came to know Dr Danie Craven well.[1]

Besides his legendary rugby activities, Doc Craven was also the residential head of Wilgenhof, the oldest and most sought-after men's residence at Stellenbosch. 'I was late with my applications, but James helped me, and via his connection with Doc Craven I was placed in Wilgenhof.'

Whitey registered for a BCom in Accounting, or BCom Acc – the degree one required to become a chartered accountant (CA). 'I didn't even understand properly what BCom Acc was. Nor did I really know what a CA was. In fact, if I'd known what a CA did, I wouldn't have continued my studies!'

His parents, however, supported his decision. 'My grandfather was involved with Syfrets Trust, so we had grown up with finance, figures and business. We didn't find it strange if someone were to study finance or accounting – I just hadn't given much attention to these subjects at high school.

'My dad gave me R1 500 when I went to university,'[2] Whitey related years later. 'He told me that was my money for three years; from now on I had to fend for myself. I invested the money with Oom Boeta Smit and I then started playing with my interest. My parents were not poor, but I wasn't just given everything I wanted either. In my child-hood we used to go to Strand for the summer holidays. One year my dad said I wasn't getting any pocket money because I'd been naughty. So I painted my old toys and sold them to other children. That's how I earned my own pocket money for the holiday. I also worked on the farm for pocket money.'[3]

On a sweltering day in January, Whitey's mother dropped him off at Wilgenhof. That same day Whitey acquired another interesting nickname. 'We had a Wolseley 610 with those little fold-down tables, it was a brownish grey colour, with burgundy seats. So we drove in at Wilgenhof, and I told the senior students: boys, I'm just dropping off my suitcases, I'll return later, my mom and I are quickly going to have lunch. Then they asked me: what is your name? I said I'm Wellwood Basson, but you can just call me Whitey. It was then that the seniors decided: you rock up here as cocky as can be, so we'll just call you Butch.'

Whitey was actually not cocky at all, says Schalk Coetzee, who was at Wilgenhof with him. They were not roommates but attended classes together and were virtually inseparable. 'The seniors might have called him Butch because he came from Rondebosch Boys' and his dad was a politician. But to us he was always Whitey.'

Whitey did not concern himself with student politics. He was at Stellenbosch to get a degree and to enjoy student life. 'I never stood for any social positions, such as house committee or any other committee.' Although Whitey never failed a subject, he did not work himself to death either. He enjoyed his student life immensely, so much so that 'if I could go back to Wilgenhof today, I would do it all over again'.

Coetzee recounts: 'We would also bunk occasionally. As you know, it's hard to get up early in winter. It's cold, dark, the rain starts pouring down, and then you would just snuggle down again in your bed. We weren't academic giants, but we managed to do okay.'

Whitey relates that Coetzee once sat next to him during a test for which Coetzee was not very well prepared. 'When there was about half an hour left, he poked me with his elbow and said: *we* – and by that he really meant me – need to move our arses because we won't finish in time. He had been copying from my test paper all the time!'

Wilgenhof is close to Stellenbosch's downtown area, which was home to the renowned watering hole Tollies. Whitey, Coetzee and their friends were regular customers. 'Tollies was fairly close to Wilgenhof, so you would walk into town quickly, but then walk back at a much slower pace. We would go drinking there often and had good times, but never drank so much that we made fools of ourselves. We always observed a degree of moderation, but we enjoyed ourselves thoroughly.'

Whitey says jokingly: 'Any student who refused to acknowledge Prof. Nic Olivier, the owner of Tollies, as an influence in his life would be a hypocrite. His classes started in the late afternoon and would last until the early hours of the morning …'

Wilgenhof forged strong ties among its residents, and Coetzee and Whitey have been friends to this day. It was also at Wilgenhof that Whitey and Christo Wiese first crossed paths. Wiese had started studying at Stellenbosch a year before Whitey arrived. At 21 he was relatively old for a first-year, and a few years older than Whitey. But Wiese, too, came from a Sap family, and the two quickly became friends. They soon realised they shared similar world views.

In the early 1960s the university was a leading Afrikaner institution with a conservative ethos and a Christian-national character. Wilgenhof was more progressive than the rest of the campus. At Die Plek (The Place), the men not only partied with gusto but also exchanged ideas and debated.

Wiese was actively involved in student politics; Whitey less so, although he supported Wiese. 'Christo and I were very good friends at university, we were both what they called "bloedsappe" (staunch United Party supporters), and we would cover for each other – although I took most of the shots since he was on the students' representative council,' says Whitey. 'We were all on the list of people the police had files on. Of course, so were all other non-conformists,' he recounted in a later interview.[4]

Whitey has never liked politics. 'As a young boy I soon realised most politicians were only in it for their own gain, and that it wasn't about the party, the country, or what we were moving towards. My dad was caught up in the United Party, and in favour of a surrender of power, but on a structured basis. His party, however, made the classic mistake of moving too far to the left, and they started attracting fewer and fewer votes. I developed an aversion to politicians, because the politician was the same guy who was chairman of the pigeon club, the baking society and the CSV (Students' Christian Association). And if he hadn't yet blotted his copybook too much, he would try to become chairman of the church council too.'

Whitey received an additional nickname at Wilgenhof. He had played rugby up to his matric year but then ruptured a lung and had to stop all participation in sport. 'So they called me Butch "*Long*" Basson as well. Christo still calls me "Uncle Butch" sometimes. When that happens, I know he is in a good mood, but when he calls me "Whitey", I know that today he is full of nonsense.'

According to Wiese, he and Whitey had much in common and soon became friends. 'We both came from the platteland; both of us were also bloedsappe – and proud Wilgenhoffers who drew inspiration from the values of Die Plek. And both of us had an eye for pretty girls. Of course, Whitey claims that he did much better than me in that area,' teases Wiese today.

Whitey acknowledges that accounting has helped him in the business world – it is referred to as the 'language of business' for a reason – but in his view it is 'stupid to spend hours doing calculations and adding things up'; today computers can do that in the blink of an eye. 'I was interested in the taxation side and the legal part, but not in the accounting principles. In fact, I didn't like accounting at all. Also, computers have changed everything. A good friend, Jan Calitz, who later became a director of one of the big life insurers, lectured us in interest calculation, and that was one of the worst things we had to do. I could never understand why you had to learn formulas by heart – they could just have given you the formulas and then you could use the right one for your answer.

'Later, when I was at Shoprite, I phoned Jan Calitz one day and said to him, I'm sending you a financial calculator from Hong Kong that costs a few hundred rands at Shoprite because that entire half year I spent in your interest calculation class, where you wasted my time, one can now do by pressing a few buttons,' he says jokingly.

One of Whitey's mentors was Prof. Giel Loubser, who lectured them in taxation. 'I liked the logic of taxation. And we always had debates in Prof. Loubser's taxation class. I was very fond of him, he was a really good guy, a brilliant person, and I can thank my lucky stars that I could attend his classes.'

Loubser was a partner at Brink, Roos & Du Toit, which subsequently became PricewaterhouseCoopers (PwC), where Whitey would also work later after completing his studies. 'I will always remember him as the man with the bright eyes, few words, and a sweet smile on his face when he had you cornered. I think I went to work for him at Brink Roos because he gave me 2 out of 20 for one question in the final arithmetic class. I learnt so much from him that he even delegated me to present a few of his extramural classes,' Whitey wrote to Loubser's wife years later.[5] Loubser also taught him that there is only one correct answer.

'But then I also had some lecturers who reminded me of the letter my friend Leon Frank's dad had written to his school principal in Porterville years ago: "Never mind, in three months' time you people will be rid of him and he of you, thank God!" But I learnt a lot. I remember I once got an "onvoltooid" (incomplete) from one lecturer. Luckily, my dad thought they were referring to a building that hadn't been completed.'

* * * *

Whitey's hard-headedness also manifested itself at Wilgenhof. 'We had to move out when the old boys came to stay there during holidays, when former residents came to attend reunions, or when the university presented winter schools. So I said, but what am I supposed to do with all my clothes? The guys tried to prevent me from getting into an argument with Doc Craven. I just felt it wasn't fair to everyone – what about the bloke who lives in Pretoria, where should he go with all his clothes and his stuff? We weren't offered any other options. I don't like things like that. I've never been able to do things that are forced on me. And I didn't like people who couldn't think or argue logically.'

But Doc Craven did listen to Whitey. 'Eventually arrangements were made that suited most of the people, so it turned out well. People may be scared to challenge things – the status quo, and the way things have always been done. But in this case compromises were made, we found a solution, and things were done differently after that.'

In between the studies, the girls and Tollies, Whitey also solidified his experience in retail. His father's main bottle store was in Tyger Valley, in Bellville, and he regularly worked there over weekends.

* * * *

An undated letter written to Whitey during his student days by his mother Maude has been preserved. The heading reads 'Dasbos', Porterville, Sunday evening. Writing in Afrikaans, she started off by addressing him as 'My dearest Whitey', but after news about the farm she switched to his baptismal name:

Wellwood, I am seriously worried about your reckless way of life nowadays. I have again found a summons for speeding in the post. Where do you intend to get the money to pay for the repairs to your car and all the other fines on top of that?

Pappa and I expect so much of you, but lately you have been living like someone who doesn't care about anything. You can't carry on like this throughout your young life, where is it going to end? – and we won't always be there to protect you.

Your father was quite upset about your long hair the whole way home, and rightly so. The long-haired creatures are always involved in all scraps. You must please have your hair cut before I see you again.

I am sending the summons on to you, you are completely throwing away your good name with such unnecessary things. You must also make time and maintain your car thoroughly yourself. I don't have any more money for cars, and you know yourself that Pappa won't help you either. No, my child, you need to choose your friends properly, and stop the never-ending chasing after girls – how much happiness has that brought you up to now?

. . . I must conclude. I am sending you the letter by tomorrow's post because the summons is for Thursday . . .

Look after yourself . . . Much love, Mammie.

* * * *

For his part, Whitey believed that if you were a student, people should at least cut you some slack. He put it like this: 'Christo used to say that if you're a Sap and you come from Upington on top of that, you get only one chance at Stellenbosch. I, on the other hand, was of the view that if you come from a smaller town like Porterville and you're a Sap, you ought to get two chances.'[6]

On 8 December 1966 he was awarded a Bachelor of Commerce degree (BCom Financial Accounting).

'Then I asked: what does a guy do now? And they said, now you can become a CA. And I thought that sounded nice because I could be a student for longer, or at least a semi-student.' He was also accepted to serve his three-year articles with the distinguished auditing firm ER Syfret & Co. in Cape Town.

4

Whitey finds direction

In 1967, with a degree behind his name, Whitey embarked on his articles at the Cape Town auditing firm ER Syfret & Co. later known as Ernst & Young. This was also the year in which compulsory military service was introduced for young white South African males. Whitey sidestepped conscription, however, and was able to start working immediately.

'I never went to the army because my dad said he wouldn't send me. He used to say he'd devoted the best part of his youth to defending South Africa and fighting the Germans while the blokes in the Ossewa-brandwag were blowing up bridges at home. If PW Botha's son were to do military service, he would send me too. So, I never went. Luckily or unluckily, I had ruptured an alveolar sac in a rugby match at school, and a doctor subsequently certified that I was unfit for military service.'

In order to qualify as a CA, you had to complete a training period of three years as an articled clerk at an auditing firm, obtain a postgradu-ate qualification in accounting, and pass your board exams. Clerkship amounted to three years of 'earning a pittance and swotting hard in the evenings'. After his studies, Whitey's friendship with Christo Wiese continued, and they would play poker with friends on Friday nights. For a year Whitey lived on his own in a small flat in Bellville. After that, he shared a flat with two friends, and later he moved back to Bellville where he again shared a flat with two friends. It was a two-bedroom flat, 'so one of us always slept in the lounge'.

Whitey still recalls his first day at ER Syfret: 'I was the youngest clerk, and around eleven in the morning my head asked me to fetch the tea from the kitchen and pour it into the cups. It was a culture shock for this boerseun, but I soon became adept at serving tea.'[1] At least this role did not last long.

Whitey was still rebellious and did not let himself be dictated to unquestioningly. He did not waste his time on trivialities either. On a certain audit, the audit clerks had to inspect the clock cards. They had to check whether everything was correct and that the cards had not been tampered with.

'And then I became annoyed and told the partner – I'm not cheap labour. I'm actually expensive labour, and your job is to teach me! From tomorrow morning I'm no longer doing that job. I couldn't stand it when someone was bullied to do things. You were expected to just accept it meekly without being allowed to discuss it. I've had that contrary streak in me since childhood. I always questioned and challenged things . . .'

He tells about a rude farmer from Villiersdorp who treated the clerks and auditors from their firm badly. One day Whitey told him: listen, our farm is bigger than yours. And then he took his bag and walked out, and told his bosses he was no longer doing that audit. 'I was nobody's skivvy. I had no intention of doing things that I felt were not right for my career.'

Whitey also had good mentors during his articles. 'I was fortunate enough to do my clerkship under Laurie Albertyn, the chairman of the company. He was a very good chap. I reported to Tom Wixley, who later became chairman of Ernst & Young. He had come first in the CA exam, so I worked under two top-notch men.

'I enjoyed it a lot, as I was given a fair amount of freedom. Laurie and I frequently had discussions about shares. He also gave me bigger jobs than the other guys, who remained stuck with the donkey work for longer than I did.'

Whitey, confident as ever, knew he would pass his final CA exam – he had no concerns on that score. 'So, about six months before the end of my articles, I asked them: Well, what now?'

By that time Whitey was already doing the full audits of large companies, including Irvin & Johnson and Truworths. He then requested that the firm come up with a concrete plan for how his career would develop over the next few years, otherwise he would resign.

'I asked the partners, what will my position be going forward – will I become a partner? They came back to me and informed me they didn't make anybody partner before a certain age, which was then still quite a few years in the future for me.'

Consequently, he approached Giel Loubser, his taxation professor and also a senior partner of Brink, Roos & Du Toit. Whitey had conditions, however: 'What mattered was not my salary but the experience I could acquire in working for them. I felt I wasn't getting sufficient exposure to all parts of business, including taxation. We then agreed that I would do a certain number of big audits, and along with that a certain number of smaller audits, the ones where one did the audit on all levels, such as even completing a farmer's tax forms as well.'

Thus, Whitey was able to continue learning from the brilliant Loubser. Moreover, the offices of Brink, Roos & Du Toit were in Bellville, close to where Whitey was living at the time. During the same week in which he completed his board exams, he resigned from ER Syfret and joined Brink, Roos & Du Toit as audit manager.

One of his big clients was MCB Switchboards, with Seymour Reyke at the helm. This company was part of the Alwarvo Group, which included Alwarvo Furniture. Alwarvo Holdings was declared insolvent, however, and Reyke wanted Whitey to go into business with him and buy MCB Switchboards.

'I was mad about Reyke – he was a successful businessman, and I learnt a great deal from him. For instance, he always pooh-poohed the accepted advice that you shouldn't do business with crooked people. Because half of all people were crooked, so you could only do business with half of them. So, rather do business with everyone, but just be alert.

'But I was still a youngster, with no money. He offered to help me borrow money from the bank, but my dad put a stop to it. He said Seymour was too crafty for me, and that I shouldn't become his partner.'

This lost business opportunity prompted Whitey to do further introspection about his future. 'I was tired of advising other people, doing their tax and examining internal controls and making recommendations. It was easy work; every day you would walk out, put your papers in your briefcase and go to bed because it's not your problem, it's the client's problem, and tomorrow you carry on again.

'I actually became a bad auditor because I became too involved in the clients' businesses. I would go into their workshops and say, but look how you're doing it, shouldn't you rather do it this way? And that is not what you should do as an auditor. You can advise them on tax, internal controls and so on, but not about the operational aspects.

'I also had a big problem with forms, regulations and corporate governance. Whenever I wrote a letter, it first had to be signed off by the audit partners. But Giel Loubser and Piet Aucamp's English was worse than mine, and they would change my English. I would get angry and say, no man, that's stupid. Just read it and then we'll send it off.'

Whitey increasingly enjoyed visiting his retail clients. 'Because my father owned bottle stores, I grew up with buying and selling. I happened to know something about retail and liked my retail clients.'[2]

* * * *

50

One of Brink, Roos & Du Toit's clients was a fast-growing clothing store group called Pep Stores, which had started in Upington in 1955. The company was run by Renier van Rooyen, a legend in the making in South African business history.

To the surprise of many who had expected Whitey's university friend Christo Wiese to pursue a career in law or even in politics, Wiese joined Pep Stores as company secretary after his studies. Wiese and Renier both hailed from Upington. Wiese's father had invested in Pep Stores from the outset, and Renier was married to Wiese's cousin. They had big plans for Pep – they intended to expand the company considerably and to list it on the Johannesburg Stock Exchange.

Whitey's auditing firm decided to appoint him as Pep's audit manager, and he reported in this role at Pep's new head offices in Kuils River. This was arguably the biggest turning point in Whitey's life.

It was a dynamic young company, and soon he was devoting more and more attention to Pep Stores. 'In order to familiarise myself with Pep I went through the books and financial statements as bookkeeper and auditor, but also started looking at the company from a management perspective,' Whitey recounts. He and Renier van Rooyen hit it off from the outset. Whitey had met Renier previously through Giel Loubser, but they were now working together for the first time.

'He was a charismatic person, an incredible entrepreneur, and one of the best retailers I've ever met. We gradually started spending more time together because he wanted to list his company and had other dreams as well. The existing management wasn't really adequate – it was more focused on operational aspects. But I increasingly started giving attention to the broader business.' A close friendship developed that would strengthen further over the years.

* * * *

In December 1969 Whitey obtained his Certificate in the Theory of Accounting (CTA). This gave him admission to the final examination conducted by the Public Accountants' and Auditors' Board, provided he was registered with the board as an articled clerk. He received a letter on red paper from his sister Juel. A translated version reads:

My dearest Boeta

I first wanted to phone, but then decided to rather use one of my very special 'red letters' to address you.

I understand that you have officially passed your exam. I was shocked (no reflection on your intelligence) but am immensely happy for your sake.

No doubt this is the start of a long and glorious career; I hope.

Much love, Juel

* * * *

In May 1970 Whitey passed the board exam, and on 18 November 1970 he qualified officially as a chartered accountant (CA). At that point he considered becoming a partner at Brink, Roos & Du Toit. But then Renier asked him to join Pep as financial director. Encouraged by his father, who believed he would benefit from gaining a few years' practical experience in an existing business enterprise, he decided to accept the offer.

'I told them, that's great. I was here as auditor and it was nice, but I'm not going to stay long. And then I ended up having to work so hard that I never got a chance to leave!'[3] joked Whitey. His happy-go-lucky attitude was indeed a thing of the past. After matric, he had more or less gone wherever the wind had taken him. At Pep he was to find his direction, and his dreams would start taking shape. In the meantime, there was another turning point as well – this time in his personal life.

5

Whitey meets his better half

When Whitey was doing his articles, he met his future wife. Anna-lise Spies, who hailed from Kuils River, was studying occupational therapy at Stellenbosch. But at the time they met, they were both in other relationships. 'He was still engaged to the girl for whom he had exchanged Ikeys for Maties, and I was dating one of his friends. His friend warned me to be very wary of Whitey, but he didn't provide reasons. However, I suspected it was because he was quite a ladies' man,' she relates today.

The beautiful Annalise immediately caught Whitey's eye. After all, she had been named 'South Africa's prettiest first-year student'.[1] This snippet appears in an article in *Die Byvoegsel*, a supplement to *Die Burger*, which has been preserved in a family scrapbook. According to the article, Annalise wanted to qualify as an occupational therapist so she could help people with physical and mental disabilities. Besides subjects such as psychology, sociology and physics, her training included weaving – and woodwork to boot. At the time she was making a coffee table, she said excitedly, and she was doing it without any assistance. She designed and made most of her clothes herself, and did not have a steady boyfriend. 'I'm still too young for a steady relationship,' she told the journalist.

But Annalise was instantly drawn to this fair-haired man. 'Whitey had an attitude,' she recounted with a smile years later,[2] 'and I like challenges. He is cautious about showing people how he feels about them. This makes him attractive to the opposite sex.'

What also attracted her was his strong personality and his ambition, and that 'he has always had a zest for life. Because that which he enjoys, he does wholeheartedly. He knew exactly what he wanted to do and how he had to go about achieving it. He was always the centre of any gathering.' Whitey broke off his engagement, and he and Annalise soon became a couple.

According to Annalise, in those days she was rather quiet and reserved. 'My first meeting with Whitey's parents at their farm in Porterville was quite a shock to me. I grew up in a home where we didn't talk much. Children never spoke at the table, nor in the company of adults. My sister, Carin, drove to the farm with us for the baptism of Whitey's brother's first baby.

'But here everyone talked at the same time, and argued about politics, food, religion and so forth. No one spared anybody's feelings. I disappeared in the company. Afterwards I had to hear that Whitey's father was disappointed I was his girlfriend and not my sister!' Annalise related. 'But Whitey helped me to come out of my shell. He gave me self-confidence and taught me to take a stand.'[3]

Her father was initially not in favour of her relationship with Whitey, but she paid little heed to his opposition. 'I didn't know what his real concern was. He was a diehard National Party supporter, and Whitey's dad was an MP for the United Party. My dad might just have felt that our worlds were too different.

'At one point I did start thinking my dad might be right, and we decided to break off our relationship. But Whitey had already asked me long before that to accompany him to his class dance, and I then decided to keep my promise. He convinced me that we were indeed right for each other. And the rest is history. Whitey conquered my dad with his charm, and from then on there was only one road ahead.'

By then Whitey was already working very hard – at the auditing

54

firm during the day and studying for the CA exam at night – and they didn't see much of each other. On Sundays they would usually go to visit some of his father's friends in Sea Point. 'They were all successful businesspeople from whom Whitey wanted to learn as much as he could. He wanted to know everything about running a business successfully,' Annalise says.

They became engaged two and a half years after their first meeting, on Annalise's 21st birthday, and after another year and a half, on 7 August 1971, they were married in the Vredelust Dutch Reformed Church in Bellville. The wedding was not an extravagant affair. 'The reception was in the civic centre in Bellville, with a band from Strand that I had known for years,' Whitey recounts. 'Everything was very beautiful. Annalise made her wedding dress herself, as well as the bell-shaped wedding cake.'

The thriftiness also extended to the honeymoon. For the first few days, the couple went to the Drakensberg. Annalise contracted laryngitis and had to stay in bed, but Whitey decided that since he had already paid for the stay in the hotel, he should make the best of it.

'He went horse-riding during the day and participated in the rest of the activities the hotel offered their guests,' Annalise recalls. 'After that we joined his parents in East London where his father was attending a congress, and from there we went to visit friends of his parents in Port Elizabeth for a few days. And for the most part we stayed everywhere for free!'

In 1972 Annalise came second in the *Cape Argus*'s Bride of the Year Competition. The paper described her as 'a slim, attractive girl with golden brown hair', with 'a terrific flair for arts and crafts', who was married to a 'fair-haired handsome man'.

After the honeymoon they moved into a tiny flat in Bellville. Annalise started working as an occupational therapist, and Whitey at Pep

Stores in Kuils River. 'It was a rather miserable two-bedroom flat,' Whitey relates. 'The one bedroom was so small you could barely squeeze a single bed into it. And the kitchen was green and dark. It was actually not a bad block of flats – in the heart of Bellville, next to a river. We lived there for a year and a half. We lived mostly on Annalise's salary so that we could save money for a house of our own.'

For entertainment, they attended Willie Muller's auctions in Bellville over weekends. 'It was interesting to watch how people bought junk. We came to know Willie well. My name was Bonnievale Furnishers, and Willie used me as a "ghost bidder". This was also where we bought most of the furniture for our flat,' Whitey says.

In the meantime, Whitey still worked in his father's bottle store in Tyger Valley on Saturdays, and Annalise started pitching in. Later, Whitey bought two bottle stores of his own with Mike Kovensky of Aroma – one in Bothasig and one in Paarl, both of which were managed by Mike. The experience also encouraged Whitey at a later stage to start Shoprite's liquor division, Shoprite LiquorShop.

After a year and a half, they had saved up enough money to buy a house in Welgemoed, where they would live for the next twenty years. 'My dad always said, you buy the smallest house in the best neighbourhood,' Whitey states. 'Welgemoed was the most expensive area in the northern suburbs. It was a three-bedroom house on a nice stand, on the corner of Da Gama and Diaz Streets. We built on over the years as our need for more space increased, since our children were born during the time we lived there.

'I had set myself the goal of being debt free at 50,' he continues. 'I never wanted to run the risk of losing anything as a result of debt, and that went for business as well. I was always averse to incurring debt, and I'm not talking about ordinary debt such as credit cards. Accordingly,

I've never in my life bought a luxury item on credit – for instance, I paid cash for every car. I probably lost out because of that – if I had incurred debt, I could perhaps have done better with certain things. But when it comes to certain types of debt, I am risk-averse.'

* * * *

Whitey and his family's lives were intertwined with those of the 'Pep family', as Annalise calls it, from the outset. 'On Sundays we would all get together socially at Renier's house in Durbanville. We braaied, played tennis, did the washing up together, and laughed. There we learnt the importance of having a good, comfortable relationship with your colleagues.

'Whitey always used to say that Renier, when he appointed a new person, wanted to interview the individual's wife or husband as well, because to be a good employee you needed to have a stable home life with someone who supported your career. Fortunately, I have known nothing else because Whitey operated on the same principle from the start. Work and the family tied for first place – it was a dead heat,' says Annalise.

Whitey and Annalise had clarity on their respective roles from early on, and had a good understanding. Annalise stopped working during her first pregnancy and decided she should support Whitey in everything he did. 'Even if it meant that the business came first and the children and I second,' she recounted later.[4] 'From the start, our approach was: I look after all of you, and you look after the children,' Whitey adds.

This agreement is also the reason they are still happily married. 'We respect each other,' says Annalise. 'It was important to me to help him reach the top of the ladder. Being Whitey's wife, and a mother to our children, is a full-time job. Had I not been prepared to support him, it would probably have handicapped him.'[5]

PART TWO

THE PEP YEARS

6

Birth of a retail giant

*You must select a market, know the product you are selling,
and you must believe in what you are doing. You have to be
single-minded and prepared to work day and night.*

— Renier van Rooyen[1]

Whitey's story is inextricably linked with those of Renier van Rooyen,
the legendary founder of Pep Stores. As mentioned previously, Whitey
first encountered Renier when he worked for Brink, Roos & Du Toit
and took over the Pep Stores audit.

'Renier was one of the most impressive businessmen and retailers
I'd ever met,' Whitey recounted years later. 'He had the ability to
take a new idea and transform it into a profitable business. He was a
brilliant man, a very good marketer, and he had this passion to supply
people with affordable clothing – not cheap, but affordable. And he
knew his market.'[2]

In 1955 Van Rooyen and a friend bought a small general dealer
in Upington called The Bargain Shop. It dealt in a variety of goods,
from household goods to clothing and even donkey carts. In 1959 he
opened his second store, Upington Volksklere. He soon realised he
should concentrate on selling clothing, shoes, blankets and bedding
at discounted prices in self-service stores where customers could select
what they wanted from among the stock. He called his new stores
BG Bazaars, and by 1965 there were four branches in the northern
Cape Province.

Van Rooyen wanted to expand further, but for that he needed capital. There was great interest among friends and family, and in 1965 he founded Pep Stores (Pty) Ltd.[3] But he had a distinctive precondition: if you wanted to invest in his business, you had to be prepared to work for the group. And if you wanted to the work for group, you had to be prepared to invest in it. This deterred prospective investors, and in the end he raised only R50 000 of the R250 000 he had hoped for.

Van Rooyen often used the word 'pep' to encourage his colleagues. He also wanted a short name that would be easy to remember and sounded good in both English and Afrikaans. John Lee, a supplier and later a director, came up with a list of suggestions, and Van Rooyen immediately liked the name 'Pep'. The first Pep appeared in De Aar, in a former BG Bazaars outlet. In December of that year a Pep was opened in Kimberley and, only a week later, another one in Postmasburg.

Pep Stores soon acquired a reputation for providing reasonable clothing at low prices. Van Rooyen's philosophy was: 'We don't sell cheap clothing; we sell clothing cheaply.' The low prices found favour with consumers in lower-income groups, and growing numbers of customers supported the new stores.

In the meantime, Christo Wiese had joined Pep Stores in a full-time capacity after his legal studies at Stellenbosch. Stoffel Wiese, Christo's father, was an investor and also served on the board of Pep. In 1965, while Christo was still studying at Stellenbosch, he himself had invested in the business – R5 000, half of which he had borrowed from his father. It had always been the plan that he would join Pep Stores after obtaining his law degree.

Wiese had worked at Pep Stores earlier during some of his university holidays but when he joined Pep in 1967 on a full-time basis, he was company secretary as well as second in command. He was also responsible for the recruitment of staff. But his biggest task was finding premises for new stores, and he had his hands full.[4] Pep grew briskly. By 1971 there were 115 branches in the Cape Province, but Van Rooyen was dreaming of a countrywide chain of stores. 'There was never any doubt in Renier's mind that he would become one of the largest retailers in the country,' says Whitey.

Van Rooyen and his team converted Pep Stores into a public company and issued 350 000 shares valued at R1,50 each, which were sold privately. Van Rooyen stated that the group wanted to establish 50 branches annually over the next four years. Pep Stores also intended to list by the middle of 1972.[5] Accordingly, Van Rooyen was looking for a chartered accountant to prepare the company for listing, and he knew just the right man. On 1 November 1971, at the age of 25, Whitey took up a full-time position at Pep as financial director.

7

A baptism of fire

We don't sell rubbish – at a given price our wares are of a good quality, a fact realised by our customers – poor people are not stupid – they cannot afford to be.

– Pep brochure, 1972[1]

A mere two days after joining Pep, Whitey underwent a (literal) baptism of fire. Early on the evening of 3 November, Whitey and Tom Ball, head of manufacturing, were at work at Pep's head office when a devastating fire broke out in the warehouse. 'Tom and I had to go through and review all the stock results,' he recounts. 'It was donkey work, but it was important and someone had to do it, and we didn't want to appoint an additional person. Tom and I were still sitting there working when Mr Mouton, one of the property managers, ran in and said there was smoke in the warehouse.'

Whitey and Ball dropped everything and rushed to the warehouse. When they opened the doors, there were smoke and flames everywhere. 'We then saw the fire running along the shelves. We were actually stupid; with the rapid entry of oxygen through the open doors, the fire jumped literally twenty, thirty metres into the air and the asbestos roofs started cracking. So all we could do was to get away from there. The fire brigade arrived quickly, but the entire place was ablaze.'

After having made sure everyone was safe, they set to work salvaging whatever they could and ensuring that the remaining goods were not looted. 'Many staff members came in to assist, and Annalise brought us

James Wellwood Basson, aka 'Whitey', was a bright and diligent learner.
Here he is at thirteen years old and in Grade 8 at Porterville High School.

Above left: Whitey's parents Maude and Jack, with a bag of shopping, in Adderley Street in Cape Town in 1938. They had a huge influence on Whitey's life and taught him from an early age to look at the world differently.

Above right: Whitey was, and still is, a crack horseman. Here he is riding at Porterville's agricultural show in the early 1960s.

Whitey's sister, Juel, could never take a boyfriend to the farm without Whitey terrorising the guy to such an extent that he would throw in the towel and vamoose. The Springbok rugby player James Starke, however, stuck it out and married Juel in 1960. Here Whitey plays photographer on her wedding day.

Whitey with fellow residents of Wilgenhof during his second year at Stellenbosch, 1965. He is in the longest row, fourth from the right, with light hair and spectacles.

4 St jacohofS
Kroningslaan
Bellville.

Geagde HEER,

Graag versoek0 ek hiermee die hand van u
DOGTER in die huwelik.

Whitey and Annalise on their wedding day at the Vredelust Dutch Reformed Church in Belville, 7 August 1971.

At the top is the note Whitey typed for Annalise's dad to request his permission to marry her.

The 25-year-old Whitey in his first office at Pep Stores. He took up a full-time position as financial director at Pep in November 1971.

The first board of directors of Pep Stores after its listing on the Johannesburg Stock Exchange, 1972. *From left:* Renier van Rooyen, Johan Greyling, Frank Weetman, Basil Weyers, Christo Wiese, Whitey, John Lee and Tom Ball.

Whitey with his children in December 1983. *From left:* Nikki, Cornell, Mari and Adrian.

sandwiches late that night,' Whitey recalls. Van Rooyen was in Durban at the time. 'I was scared stiff because Renier was not there. Everyone was half-falling over their feet. I then realised I would have to assume leadership.'

In fact, Whitey had already started working at Pep in the evenings earlier that year. 'From about six o'clock, after my day at the auditing firm, Tom Ball and I would work until ten, eleven o'clock at night. And the next morning I would be off to the auditing firm again. I didn't want to leave my work with them unfinished – I had to complete my audits before moving to Pep. So, for about three or four months I actually worked for Renier for free in the evenings. My principle was: you don't leave something half done, you finish what you started.'

On the night of the fire, Whitey and other employees risked their lives to save as much as possible – stock, equipment and company documents.[2] The fire, which was suspected to have been caused by an electrical short-circuit, swept through the entire Cape warehouse and head office and caused enormous damage. The loss of goods was estimated at about R1 million, which was big money in those days.

Whitey snatched one or two hours of sleep before getting cracking again early the next morning. 'David Newham, a property developer, came with me to look at new warehouses because things weren't standing still – the Christmas stock was coming in. The following morning we inspected a number of places that could accommodate us and then opted for Meyer & Ferreira's warehouse.'

Renier had arrived in Cape Town in the meantime and signed the contract for the temporary warehouse. Whitey felt proud that he had managed to get the wheels rolling again in such a short time. 'That afternoon at three o'clock we received the first deliveries that were intended for the burnt-down warehouse. Just half a day later we were in operation again. This was absolutely vital for us because our entire stock for the Christmas season had been destroyed – there was nothing left.

'The first delivery was from a bloke who delivered socks, someone with whom everyone was usually gatvol because he was always late with his deliveries. But then he happened to be the first one to deliver, and we were overjoyed at the sight of him!'

Pep's culture was that no one was afraid of getting their hands dirty. And everyone pitched in. 'All of us, including Renier, packed goods to ensure that our stores would receive their stock. It was wonderful having Renier there because we received, for example, thousands of shirts, and there was no time to worry about details. Renier would just take a cursory glance at the merchandise and say what should go where.' Luckily, a fair amount of merchandise had already been dispatched to the stores before the fire, and the group also had other warehouses. The buildings and stock were insured. Van Rooyen would observe later that Whitey 'deftly handled' the insurance claim.[3]

The company recovered swiftly – in the year ending February 1972 they doubled their turnover to R22 million, and earnings per share rose by 52 per cent.[4] With the crisis averted, the Pep team could once again give their full attention to the listing on the Johannesburg Stock Exchange.

'It was an unlisted company, with Renier as majority shareholder, so the systems were not in place in a way I would have liked or would have been comfortable with,' Whitey recalls. 'So we instituted a range of systems and introduced internal controls I had seen at other big audits, such as at Truworths. My major job was getting the books and the accounting systems in order, and getting the listing finalised.'

Whitey also soon discovered that at Pep, being the financial director meant you did whatever was necessary. With a typically humorous twist, he said: 'You might have to see to it that the cars got serviced, that there was toilet paper in the bathrooms, that there were ballpoint pens for the storeroom clerks. If the company had needed someone to tap dance, you may have had to do that too. And then, if you had the time, you also had to keep an eye on the company's financials.'[5]

Meanwhile, Whitey had to focus on another big task as well: concluding the takeover of Budget Footwear. It was the first takeover of many, and Whitey relates that he was rather nervous. Budget Footwear was the largest shoe manufacturer of its kind in the country,[6] it was his first takeover deal, and on top of that he had to work with partners from Ernst & Young where he had been an audit clerk only a few years before.

'So I had lunch with the management and auditors of Felt & Textile [Budget Footwear's owners] in the company's dining room. There were a lot of people around a big table, waiters with white gloves, and the most delicious food. Then they started telling jokes in turn, going round the table, and in those days the big shots knew the best jokes. I almost prayed that I wouldn't be asked to tell a joke because the ones I knew wouldn't have been appropriate. I was wearing a blue shirt and was sweating so much that it was wet almost to my waist. But fortunately, they didn't get around to me,' Whitey recounts.

He was sharp when it came to the financials, however, and keen to make his mark. 'I was able to spot things others failed to see. I then did a reconciliation of the purchases and sales and depreciation of fixed assets, and things didn't quite tally. So we quickly made a better deal.' He bought the factory for considerably less than they would have paid originally.[7] 'Renier was very chuffed with me,' he recalls. The transaction was finalised in 1971. And on 6 June 1972, Pep Stores was listed successfully – a big event on the South African bourse.

Though Pep Stores already boasted 163 branches, this was clearly only the beginning because the parts of the country with the highest population numbers and most buying power still had relatively few stores. Investors were eager to share in the growth of this retailer that knew how to reach the dormant black consumer market. On the opening day the share started trading at R2,75, rose to R3,50, and closed at R3,30. Close to 400 000 shares were traded. Van Rooyen and his investors who had taken a gamble seven years before in Upington were suddenly much richer.[8]

The group, which had been built up by a bunch of platteland traders, was to some extent changed by the listing. The young Whitey, however, was in the right place at the right time. He was learning from the best people in retail and enjoying himself immensely. 'I enjoyed it a lot. I learnt a great deal, and as financial director I had to transform all the Pep Stores systems from an accounting perspective. Many people at the branches were angry with me because I put many new systems in place, but Renier always said: I trust Whitey.'

In September 1973 the Johannesburg Afrikaans Chamber of Commerce invited Whitey to deliver a speech at the Course for Retailers. The topic was 'Stock control measures for profit'. He concluded his speech with these words:

> . . . I have now spoken for a long time about the wonderful effect of good [stock]control and the impact it has on profits, but I would feel guilty if I were to leave here tonight without telling you that I believe no matter how good your control may be, you must always remember that in order to make profit from stock – you have to sell it. You should therefore exercise your control in such a way that your end goal is to sell stock. I would like to emphasise once again that you must provide your customers with what they want and not with what you think they want.
>
> Thank you very much.

This speech is indicative of Whitey's customer-centric mindset, something he learnt from Renier and would later perfect at Shoprite. He also learnt from Renier that you should surround yourself with the best people. And Pep had a relatively young and strong team of senior managers.

'Tom Ball, who was then still head of manufacturing, was excellent, with an eye for detail. Frank Weetman was one of the best marketers, or sales managers, with whom I've ever worked, and Basil Weyers, head of purchasing, had all the experience in the world. I also relied a great deal on one of our operational divisional managers, Stephen le Roux.'

Whitey tells about their visits to the branches: 'Before Christmas, Renier, Frank Weetman, Oom Basil Weyers and I would drive up to George and visit all the branches in the small towns. Frank used to drive the car – a big black Mercedes. By that time Renier was famous. One night we arrived late at our accommodation in Swellendam. The kitchen was already closed, but when they saw it was Renier they opened it again and we were served an excellent mixed grill. Annalise always used to say Renier walked about like a movie star – people would greet him without knowing who he was. He was a good-looking man, jovial, and brimming with self-confidence. And he always knew exactly what went on in his stores.'

Renier van Rooyen was a trader in the true sense of the word, something Whitey would take to heart and emulate. Also, he was quick at making decisions and quick to swing into action. 'He wanted to do everything on the same day. Once he bought a car in Cape Town and sold it in Worcester that same day because the car wasn't fast enough to get him to Durban in time for his next appointment.

'I learnt an extraordinary amount from Renier. I asked him to teach me everything about business, and especially the clothing trade. I enjoyed every moment and was able to gain all the practical experience in the clothing trade at the side of a man who knew what he wanted and how to achieve it. I couldn't have asked for a better teacher. I'm happy with my academic qualifications – but if I had to choose today between what I achieved academically and the experience and knowledge I acquired under Renier van Rooyen in the business world, I would choose the latter without hesitation,' he later told *Pep Nuus*.[9]

He also told the paper that every six weeks he returned to his family farm – to DasBosch – where he would traverse the area on horseback or on a motorbike and seek out unspoilt nature. Then he became philosophical: 'I can't say whether I would have been a good or a bad farmer if I had to farm permanently. But it gives me a second level of interest, and also helps me maintain contact with my background, my family, and with those deeper life truths that will always have great significance for me. Not forgetting those things is very important to me. On the farm I get in touch again with the realities of life – realities that help and stimulate me to keep my head in the bustling world out there where moral values so easily get drowned out by the siren call of materialism.'[10]

Whitey's responsibilities at Pep expanded. His initial plan had been to spend only a few years at Pep before starting his own business. But Wiese, who felt Pep Stores had 'lost a bit of its charm as a family business' as a result of the listing, decided in 1973 to leave Pep Stores.[11] Another reason was that he thought Van Rooyen was a better number one than he was. Pep Stores was at that stage known as 'Van Rooyen's Express', and Wiese was not cut out to be a number two. With Wiese gone, and Van Rooyen increasingly withdrawing, the company suddenly needed Whitey more.[12]

8

Whitey gets power of attorney

A business does not succeed because it is big or long established,
but because there are men in it who live it, sleep it and dream it,
who believe in it and who build great future dreams for it.

— Renier van Rooyen[1]

The early 1970s was a time of incredible growth for Pep, so much so that the company was generating cash that it could not reinvest. This was a problem many businesses would have loved to have. The question was: how would Pep keep its momentum and grow further?[2]

Whitey believed they were able to manage their existing stores more efficiently. 'For the first time in our history we know how many items we are selling, in every branch and per customer,' he told the *Financial Mail*. He was confident that the quick reporting from branches kept him abreast of changes in buying habits and customer preferences. 'What is important, is that all those involved are personally committed to improving the company's performance – an asset that cannot be quantified. It is to this commitment (as well as targeting the low-income groups with low prices) that the company's remarkable growth can be attributed.'[3]

According to Whitey, every business has an internal culture, and at the time Pep's culture was one of 'platteland people who weren't necessarily highly educated or qualified, but who had enormous passion, and who were very loyal to Renier and the company. In those years we were constantly tackling new things, with fresh ideas and new people – nothing stagnated. But this is where it becomes difficult because if you grow bigger, would people still retain that passion, and how do you motivate them?'

It was an important question; with Wiese gone, Whitey's role at Pep Stores gradually changed from a purely financial to a more operational and strategic one. Whitey himself also wanted it that way. 'I was tired of the statements and the figures – things you do afterwards. I wanted to create the future and not merely record it in the books,' he remarks.

He rapidly became Van Rooyen's right-hand man. This role would become increasingly demanding and entail more responsibilities, as the listing had put extra pressure on Van Rooyen. 'Analysts and journalists were suddenly combing through everything and scrutinising every move. Renier was a retailer, but after the listing the expectations were different. He was more of an operational man, but the playing field had changed,' Whitey adds.

In 1974, in a sudden and unusual step, Van Rooyen withdrew from the management of Pep Stores and gave Whitey unlimited power of attorney over the company. A translated version of the procuration reads:

I, the undersigned, Renier van Rooyen, hereby nominate James Wellwood Basson, a shareholder of Pep Stores Limited, to act as director in my stead during my absence or if it is not possible for me to act as director, and to perform any act at any meeting or other place or institution that I would have been able to perform as director of the company Pep Stores Limited and any of its subsidiaries on which I serve as director, and I ratify and confirm any act performed by the said James Wellwood Basson in pursuance of the abovementioned power of attorney. Thus, done and signed at Kuils River on this 29th day of October 1974.

Whitey was only 28 years old at the time. 'I had many mentors,' he says, 'but Renier was the best retailer I ever worked for. He did spectacularly well with Pep Stores, and he was a retail legend, but when I took over in 1974, he started doing things that were not his style and shifted the responsibility for many things, basically everything, on to me. You don't just give away your power of attorney, do you?'

According to Whitey, Van Rooyen realised that his older friends were dying, and his energy and commitment started waning. In fact, he was just 'burned out'. 'Renier had worked incredibly hard all his life, from poverty to wealth, and I think he was simply exhausted.'[4]

Having been given this power of attorney, and with Van Rooyen devoting less and less attention to the daily operations, Whitey effectively took over the retail division of Pep Stores in 1974. He was in charge of acquisitions as well, and Tom Ball managed the manufacturing division.

In the past Pep's people always used to say, 'we don't sell cheap clothing; we sell clothing cheaply', but according to Whitey it was merely a slogan – one that people didn't necessarily believe. Consumers often associate cheap products with poor quality. While this is not necessarily true, in retail, customer perception is everything. 'We had to give people reasons why we were cheaper, and then *show* that we were indeed cheaper,' he says.

By the end of 1974 Pep Stores had 296 outlets countrywide and Pep was a household name in South Africa's rural areas (where about 70 per cent of its stores were located), and particularly among coloured and black consumers (who were responsible for about 70 per cent of the company's turnover). Pep was doing well, and its directors knew it. The cover of the annual report at the time featured a picture of a high mountain peak with the words: 'Getting to the top with both feet on the ground.'

The company's spectacular progress, and the 'cheek' of the group, prompted the financial media to ask when the bubble would burst and the directors be brought down to earth. 'Wellwood Basson, Pep's 28-year-old financial manager, says ruefully that Pep management is aware that many people expect a decline as dramatic as Pep's rise,' read an article in the *Financial Mail*. The magazine quoted Whitey as saying: 'We leave the surmising to them and go on doing our own thing.' In summary, the article concluded, that Pep was in a healthy state, had a future, and was not a flash in the pan.

Meanwhile, Van Rooyen did not like being at the mercy of suppliers and wanted Pep to manufacture some of their lines themselves. But manufacturing and the factory system would become a touchy subject between Whitey and Van Rooyen. 'Renier and I had our ups and downs, at times quite bad,' Whitey recounts. 'We seriously disagreed about the manufacturing industry – my view was that we should stay away from it.'

The acquisition of Budget Footwear in Durban was the first step in Van Rooyen's plans to integrate the business vertically by manufacturing his own goods. He believed this would reduce costs and protect the business against stock shortages. Pep continued to expand its manufacturing interests, and within three years it was producing a quarter of its own requirements itself.

Whitey and Van Rooyen were two strong personalities and they were increasingly at loggerheads, especially when it came to the company's business model. 'I was always of the view that we had to focus on retail, expand to the rest of Africa, and concentrate on our strengths. And our strength was not manufacturing – it was buying and selling,' says Whitey. The group also built a blanket factory at Butterworth in the Eastern Cape. In the 1970s the area was part of the 'independent' Transkei and the South African government encouraged firms to establish industries there, as part of an economic decentralisation policy aimed at job creation in the homelands.

Pep Stores utilised attractive tax incentives from the Xhosa Development Corporation to set up the blanket factory. Among other things, these included loans at a very low interest rate, low rental charges for factories and housing, tax breaks for employing black workers, and rebates on goods that were manufactured in the region.[5]

According to Whitey, however, the Butterworth factory was a 'total disaster'. He explains: 'I saw manufacturing as a simple sewing house that didn't have to produce complicated clothing but rather items such as panties and petticoats. But then we started with blanket factories, for example. We got good tax deals for manufacturing in the Transkei, but I said we couldn't let ourselves be led by tax structures and things like that. The tax structures won't be favourable forever, and you can't forget basic economic and business principles.

'So, I thought it was a bad idea. Capital, labour, land and entrepreneurship are the four important economic factors, and Butterworth didn't comply with much of that. The standard of the clothing wasn't good enough either.'

Whitey became gatvol because building or buying factories meant big money. 'Each time we then had to have another rights issue to finance another factory. But a factory guzzles capital, and your return on capital is low.'

Whitey relates that Renier did everything he embarked on 'very enthusiastically'. 'On one occasion he took hundreds of people on a tour to look at the manufacturing industry in the Eastern Cape, which started with a three-day conference in East London followed by a trip to Butterworth, but I refused to go along.' Van Rooyen was not very happy with him. 'But I couldn't stop myself from intimating even in the inner circle and top management that I disagreed with this strategy.'

According to Whitey, some of his peers held the opinion that Pep should manufacture everything itself, as this was cheaper and better. But he did not agree. 'Tom Ball and I were happy with the sewing houses, the piece-job factories where we produced simple items. And our policy was that we should never manufacture more than 60 per cent of a specific style or line. 'If you don't buy that 20 per cent or 30 per cent of goods from outside, you have no idea of what is happening in the market, what sells and what doesn't, and what your rivals are doing.'

Besides the blanket factory, there was also a manufacturing unit that produced pyjamas and other clothing. 'But, figuratively speaking, the one leg of the pyjama pants would be two inches wide and the other six inches, and the fly was at the back. And all the blankets started fraying.

'Once I was walking up the stairs and Jimmy Fouché came up to me with a pair of pants that looked as if it had been designed for a two-year-old, but it was intended for a child of ten and the one leg was narrower than the other. Then I exclaimed: "One day I'm going to close down these damn factories!" Renier was coming down the corridor at the same time and said: "Whitey, would you mind informing me when you do that?" At that point we were both pretty gatvol with each other about this manufacturing business.'

After obtaining a law degree at Stellenbosch, Jimmy Fouché – a grandson of a former state president with the same name, and later a director of both Pep and Shoprite – started working at Pep in 1973, first as trainee branch manager in Somerset West, and then as branch manager in Stellenbosch, Bredasdorp and Montagu. The rule at Pep was that you had to gain practical experience and get to know the business on the floor. 'You must know where the cash register is,' says Fouché.

But he was soon transferred to the property department of the company, where his tasks included identifying new premises for Pep. 'Then my base was Pep's head office. The office set-up was fairly informal – we constantly liaised with one another to and fro. But I would be on the road in search of new premises, and then back at the office to deal with the paperwork and administration,' relates Fouché.

'I didn't see much of Renier and by that time Christo had left for the Cape Bar, so the guys I worked with were Whitey and Tom Ball. Then I started renting premises for stores, and I had to work closely with the financial people – to figure out, why would a specific branch work? What would our turnover be, what would we pay in rent, and then I would discuss it with Whitey and Tom.'

According to Fouché, Whitey's attitude was always that you should focus on what you are good at and then do that very well. 'Whitey always used to say: reflect a bit on what it is that you want to do – what is the market you intend to target?'

He also tells of a prank they played on Whitey one evening. A team of senior managers from Budget Footwear had come from Durban and it was decided they would go out for dinner, to the nearby Harlequin Steakhouse in Parow. 'Generally, each one would pay his share of the bill. But that evening we had a slap-up meal and plenty of drinks, and when it came to an end, everyone stood up in unison and said, Good-night Whitey, sleep well and see you tomorrow! So, he was stuck with the bill for the whole party!'

The economical Whitey did not find this funny at all, but the next morning everyone dropped in at his office and paid back his share. Fouché adds: 'Whitey isn't a reckless and extravagant person, and he has never been flashy. This was also the example he set, to create that culture and mindset – that you don't waste money, and that you must keep that instilled in your people.'

'What did I learn from Renier?' muses Whitey. 'That a firm's culture is one of the most critical success factors. And along with it, that you must appoint the right people.'

9

Takeovers and turnaround attempts

Audited figures mean nothing if you don't understand the business.

– Whitey Basson

A smallish clothing boutique chain called Papillon was the first strug-gling business Whitey had to turn around. But the attempts to transform this caterpillar into a butterfly would soon suffer their first setback. 'The first step in turning the business around was to close its head office in Johannesburg and move it to the Cape,' Whitey recounts. 'We found premises that were within walking distance of Pep's headquarters in Kuils River, and that worked well.'

The move to Cape Town entailed a huge furniture removal truck having to pick up machinery, fabrics and the patterns for the season's fashions in Johannesburg and transport the goods to the Cape. 'The youngster who drove the truck then decided to pay a visit to a girl he knew near Potchefstroom,' relates Michael Lester, a colleague of Whitey's at Papillon. 'Along the way, the road changed into a narrow gravel road that ran over a very narrow single-lane bridge. Needless to say, the truck with all our supplies tumbled off the bridge, and our fabrics and patterns went down the river.'

Whitey and Leon van Niekerk, who had been appointed to help bring about the Papillon turnaround, hurried to Johannesburg and went with Lester and every available Pep regional manager to the accident scene. 'We spent hours on the bridge trying to sort out the mess, and almost everyone got sunstroke,' Lester recounts.

Back in Cape Town, Whitey had his work cut out for him because Papillon had been underwater even before the season's fabrics and patterns had gone downriver. According to Whitey, he had been overseas when Renier had acquired Papillon, and the latter had only told him about the purchase on his return. 'And he said I'll be happy, because it was bought at the NAV (nett asset value). But when we did the sums properly, we saw that the NAV was minus and Papillon was in fact bankrupt.'

'Mr Van Rooyen announced on 6 June 1976 that Pep's takeover bid for Papillon, a firm with 14 fashion boutiques, has been successful,' an article in *Pep Nuus* read.[1] 'The stores are all situated on the Rand and in Pretoria. The group has more than 220 employees and their own factory that supplies about 60 per cent of their requirements. The turnover for the year ending February 1976 was R1,8 million . . .'

The plan for Papillon was that it would continue trading as an independent group. The Pep team were optimistic about Papillon's prospects – they anticipated that the group 'would still expand enormously in future . . . and that they could make as big a breakthrough in the clothing market for the higher-income group as Pep Stores had made earlier in the lower-income group'.[2]

The article painted a rosy picture, but the initial adversity was not limited only to the supplies that had landed in the river. The founder of Papillon was Jael Mankowitz, and at the time of the takeover he was still in charge. Just before the takeover Mankowitz had ordered a lot of fabric in Japan, and they had been unable to stop the order. 'Every month thousands of rolls of this material would arrive. So we made all kinds of clothing we could with this material. I think it took us two or three years to get rid of the stock!'

But Whitey enjoyed it, so much so that he even helped to distribute pamphlets. Since there was no money for advertisements, they had to resort to 'knock and drop' – in other words, pamphlet distribution – in residential neighbourhoods and particularly at women's residences. 'Papillon was a nice business. It was exciting, sort of an after-hours job, which gave me great pleasure.'

Papillon was Pep's first step towards a more affluent market. The concept was simple. They purchased the fabrics, manufactured the clothing themselves, and sold it in small boutiques at prices that were lower than those of Foschini and Truworths. They also devised and designed the fashions themselves, although some ideas were 'borrowed'. It was rumoured, for instance, that Whitey once passed a girl in the street who was dressed in a striking cat suit. He stopped her on the spot and asked whether she would be so kind as to walk into the nearest store, buy anything of her choice, and give him the cat suit so that the design could be copied. Whitey also used to say he had to 'feel' the clothing because he had to 'test' the fabric.

'Also, we only sold certain sizes. At Pep we had more sizes because Renier always said people complain if they can't find their sizes. And then I said one day with my big mouth, if we're going to stock those sizes at Papillon, we'll be bankrupt within a year because those people aren't my customers.'

This did not go down well, and Whitey and Renier started bumping heads about other aspects of Papillon too. Whitey wanted to turn Papillon around, but Renier thought Whitey was spending too much time on Papillon. 'I told him: if you or someone else can manage the business better, then do it. So we got someone else, who really messed it up. For instance, previously the sales ladies who worked in the stores were mostly younger girls, and one just made peace with the fact that many of them wouldn't turn up for work on Mondays. But then they started appointing older ladies, and culturally it was a wrong move,' says Whitey.

Only four years after Van Rooyen acquired Papillon, Pep Stores got rid of the boutique chain, which had expanded to 43 stores in the meantime. Some were closed and the rest were sold. Where possible, the premises were sublet. Papillon's sales amounted to less than two per cent of Pep's total retail sales, and the closure did not have a significant impact on the company.[3]

The impact on Whitey was more substantial. 'It was the only business I walked away from that had not become successful and profitable,' Whitey says. 'I'm still a bit sad about it because I enjoyed it very much.' Papillon was modelled on fast fashion for a more affluent market, which did not quite fit into the Pep philosophy. For a while Whitey had forgotten his philosophy – that you should focus on what you are good at. But he would not make the same mistake again.

* * * *

Half Price Stores was to be the first large struggling retail chain Whitey had to take over and turn around. 'It was my first big takeover, where I really learnt how to negotiate,' Whitey relates. 'And, secondly, I learnt that you needed to understand the business and examine the figures carefully. Audited figures mean nothing if you don't understand the business.' Jimmy Fouché was also part of these negotiations. 'During the acquisitions Jimmy was my right-hand man and knew exactly what was going on,' Whitey adds.

A few years earlier, Fouché's future at Pep had still been uncertain. 'When I joined Pep, Renier said he didn't really want guys with degrees because they didn't last long. Except if they were financial people, then he wanted the formal qualifications,' recounts Fouché. But Whitey told him he should hang in there – there were many opportunities at the company.

Whitey confirms this: 'Renier wasn't always very good with guys with degrees, and they tended not to last long.' And Jimmy was on the same trajectory. 'Then I said, I'll take Jimmy and he will make it.' So he took Jimmy under his wing. 'He sat close to me – I had a door sawn open between my office and his, so we knew what was happening in each other's offices.' Fouché would eventually become Pep's company secretary and a director of Shoprite.

According to Fouché, 'Whitey used to involve himself in everything and was very interested in the operational side of retail. He always knew what was happening on the shop floor. He didn't sit in an ivory tower.' That was also the case with the investigation into Half Price Stores. Whitey, Frank Weetman and Stephen le Roux travelled across the country to determine whether the stores were worth their while, and what they were prepared to pay. Whitey recounts: 'I drove an old Audi Renier had said I should use, with R2 000 in my pocket for fines. Among the three of us, we visited all the Half Price stores in South Africa.'

Although this clothing retail chain was much smaller than Pep, it had long been a thorn in their side. The stores of the two groups were often located next to or opposite each other. This led not only to price wars but also to a fierce rivalry that would sometimes degenerate into physical confrontations. 'From time to time we had put out feelers for Half Price Stores,' says Fouché. 'Our branch managers always used to keep an eye on our competitors on the other side of the fence, usually further down the street. Half Price Stores was actually just based on the Pep concept. When we displayed something in the window, they would follow suit.'

The staff of the two companies had no time for each other, and the hostility was evident during Pep's takeover of Half Price Stores in 1978. In fact, Half Price Stores' employees did everything in their power to thwart Pep's bid. The acting managing director, Hugh Ashby, said his employees saw themselves as the David 'taking on Goliath'. And at times they would literally come to blows. In one case, the manager of Pep's Claremont branch appeared in court for having assaulted two Half Price employees who, according to him, had 'spied' on his store by writing down prices outside his store windows. The manager, Gert Prins, ended up admitting he had boxed the Half Price manager's ears and then 'planted' the notebook in a flower pot next to the entrance of the store.[4]

According to Ashby, merging with Pep was 'inconceivable' to many of his employees. And Whitey describes Sam Stupple, the founder of Half Price Stores, as a nuisance. 'I realised he had got hold of Pep's information somewhere. He would phone me out of the blue on a Monday or a Tuesday, and then he would say he saw that this product had done well, or that one had done badly, but he wasn't mentioning products in alphabetical order, he was talking exactly according to the computer numbers. So I knew he was sitting with our sales figures in front of him – and that someone was providing him with the information.

'So I told one of the buyers, let's throw Sam Stupple a dummy and let on that we're going to start selling food. And he fell for it hook, line and sinker. The next moment, he was buying rice from India and you name it.'

But in 1977 Half Price Stores was in trouble. The company, with its 144 branches countrywide, suffered huge losses and was put under judicial management. The Pep team were confident that they could save the company and return it to profitability. But an intense battle lay ahead.[5] In April 1978 Whitey and his team submitted their first

offer of R1 million. It was not accepted. A month later they increased
the offer to R2,4 million. Half Price Stores' creditors were still considering this bid when Scotts Stores from Durban unexpectedly entered
the picture.

While smaller than Pep, Scotts was still one of the country's leading
retailers and intent on expansion through diversification. Half Price
Stores was the perfect way in which to achieve their goal. This was the
start of one of the longest and toughest takeover battles in South Africa.
Pep and Scotts would repeatedly try to outmanoeuvre each other and
up their bids for Half Price Stores.[6]

Some of the largest creditors were Philip Frame's Consolidated Textile Mills and Anglo African Shipping. Whitey then drew a line in the
sand: 'I went to see them and said, don't waste everyone's time. Tell
me now whether you will support me or Scotts, but I'm not going to
plod on like this.'

A report in the *Cape Times* referred to a 'secret deal' with the liqui-
dators, but Whitey denied this. In the event, Pep did secure the support
of Anglo African Shipping, to whom Half Price owed the most money,
as well as that of most of the other creditors of its subsidiaries. Scotts
Stores did not increase their bid, but a group of employees of Half Price
Stores – with Ashby's support – opposed Pep's bid. This process reached
a stalemate. On 20 July 1978 the Cape Town Supreme Court had to
decide whether or not Pep's last offer should be accepted.

Scotts, who had earlier thrown in the towel, were now up for the
contest again and once more increased their bid. Both Pep and Scotts
got back into the ring and did their utmost to outwit each other. The
offer on the table was raised several times, which prompted Judge Gerald
Friedman to protest that he was not an auctioneer. 'But then it turned
into an auction anyway,' Fouché recounts. Both companies eventually
offered 45 cents in the rand for Half Price. Owing to different stock

valuations Pep's total offer was slightly more than that of Scotts, and the bid conditions also differed in some respects.[7]

'Dave Scott from Scotts Stores then went to Renier,' Whitey relates, 'and wrote down on a piece of paper what he was prepared to pay for Half Price, plus a proposal for a deal from which both he and we would gain.' It worked like this: He would offer 65 cents in the rand – 20 cents more than the bid that was on the table at that point. Pep would pay him half of the difference – in other words, ten cents in the rand – and he would walk away.

'They came to me with this, and I said: "There is no way I'm getting involved in a deal of this kind. Because the creditors and the families that worked for Half Price were entitled to get the maximum the market was prepared to pay. So, I'm not going to enrich Scott at the expense of others. We're bidding against Scott cent for cent, and he has to take our punches." Renier conveyed the message, and the next day they walked away.'

The court also found that the objections of the group of employees were invalid, and ultimately Pep emerged victorious from the contest. The final purchase price was about R3 million, much higher than the R1 million Pep had offered only a month before. But the battle was over, and Pep could look ahead knowing that one of its most trouble-some rivals was now in its stable.

Half Price Stores was initially still operated under its own brand, but was eventually fully integrated into Pep Stores and all the outlets were converted into Pep branches. As Whitey and his team had promised, they turned around the Half Price stores that had not been closed, and by December 1978 they had returned to profitability.[8] 'But I still had to sell rice for a while, as it kept arriving on the ships from India!'

* * * *

In 1978, after a four-year break, Van Rooyen returned in full force. The disagreements between him and Whitey intensified. 'He felt much of what I'd done he would perhaps have done differently, and he then tried to overturn it,' says Whitey. 'Although we always remained friends, relations between us were more strained for a while. He treated me like a son and we were very attached to each other, but people could see at that stage that we were quarrelling, and that we didn't see eye to eye on a number of things. '

Whitey realised something had to happen. 'And at a point I told him I couldn't work with him any longer, that I had a lot of respect for him, but that he and I were now going to create bad blood between us. I didn't feel like it any more. It was his company that he had started, and he took the final decisions, and everything I'd done he now wanted to reverse.' Whitey wanted to resign in order to preserve the relationship between him and Van Rooyen. He admits that Van Rooyen had an 'enormous influence' on his life. 'He taught me how to paint, if I can put it like that. He taught me the art of retailing, and that probably helped me the best.'[9]

For a considerable time, however, Whitey had been thinking of going into fast-moving consumer goods such as food retail, and he and Van Rooyen discussed this. Whitey was keen on starting a new venture, and Van Rooyen encouraged his entrepreneurial zeal.[10] 'He said he wanted to back me, and his proposal was that we do it together. The plan was to be partners – I help him, and he helps me.'

Whitey began scouting around for opportunities and did his home-work about the retail food industry. He went to Germany and Italy and eventually collaborated with the Italian company PAM Supermercati with a view to bringing a low-cost, limited-assortment business similar to Aldi or Lidl to South Africa.

Whitey and Pep were on the verge of entering into a partnership in this regard when luck intervened. Back home in South Africa, a golden opportunity would present itself. A tiny company in the Cape Peninsula came on to the market. The Rogut family had fallen out among themselves and wanted to sell their business. An acquaintance phoned Whitey and said: 'There are eight stores for sale here with the name Shoprite. Are you interested?' The blank canvas of Whitey's masterpiece lay before him.

10

The acquisition of Shoprite

*We had a board meeting, and it was decided that
since I knew the difference between peas and baked
beans, I would manage the food division.*

– Whitey Basson

Shoprite had been founded by the seasoned retailers Barney Rogut and
Basil Geller. The first Shoprite had opened its doors on 17 November
1966 in the old Gaiety Cinema in Wynberg and sold mainly groceries.[1]

The rest of the merchandise consisted of a hotchpotch of products,
mostly clothing, but also blankets and white goods, curtains and rugs,
kitchenware, toiletries, garden equipment, electrical appliances, toys,
sweets, stationery, shoes, motor spares, and a variety of haberdash-
ery items including women's hats. There was a limited assortment of
perishable products on the shelves as well – 'potatoes, onions, sweet
potatoes and cabbage', Whitey recounts. Shoprite catered for some
of the needs of 'one-stop customers' and was more of a general dealer
than a grocer.

Although Whitey's idea was rather to start 'convenience stores' anew,
with a smaller instead of a broader range of goods, he was also realistic.
'I realised it would be better and faster to buy something that already
existed than to establish something from scratch.' And, as luck would
have it, this was something that was already established and for sale.

'Martin Shane, the chairman of Dougson Holdings, a clothing company, had heard I was interested in food stores, and he then let me know

about these guys at Shoprite, and would I be interested in talking to Barney Rogut?' Rogut was an experienced retailer who had cut his teeth at Grand Bazaars. As a young boy he applied for a position as messenger at the company. He was initially not the favourite candidate, but after declaring himself willing to do 'anything and everything', he got the job and never looked back.

Whitey recounts: 'He worked his way up in the company until, later, he even had a considerable interest in the Grand Bazaars group. But with the listing of Grand Bazaars Barney had a huge falling-out with Manual Sachar, the founder of the group, and according to him he walked away with only the clothes on his back.' It was then that Rogut and Geller launched Shoprite. 'I felt that if I could do it for somebody else, I could do it for myself,' Rogut remarked in an interview with the *Cape Times* in October 1979.

The concept proved popular, and Rogut and Geller soon opened the second store, in Lansdowne, where the head office would also be situated. By the time they sold to Whitey, there were eight stores in all – in Woodstock, Brooklyn, Goodwood, Milnerton, Lansdowne, Wynberg, Bellville and Paarl.

Whitey got the bargain of a lifetime. The group's annual turnover was about R10 million. The business was very profitable, and the cash flow was good.[2] On account of their disagreements, the family was eager to sell. And unlike Whitey's earlier takeovers, the acquisition of Shoprite went off reasonably smoothly.

'I met Barney at the attorneys, we started talking, and after a few days I knew I wanted to buy the company,' Whitey said. 'It was just so good a buy that I couldn't refuse it.[3] We paid Barney and Geller R1 million each, but there was R1 million in the bank, so actually we only paid R1 million for the entire business.'

Whitey and the much older Rogut – who would stay on in senior management – immediately took a liking to each other. Both of them were zealous and ambitious and believed in hard work. It was the start of a friendship of many years, and Rogut would be in Whitey's circle until his retirement in 2004. The two of them nearly went into business on their own, without Pep in the picture. 'Barney had many ideas, and he became annoyed with the people at Pep. His proposal was that I buy his partner's 50 per cent, or that he sells the whole company, but to me and not to Pep Stores.'

They had already started arranging financing at the banks to buy Shoprite on behalf of Pep and have sufficient operating capital with which to expand the business. 'Then I told Renier, I'm actually being very stupid now because the deal has been brought to me, and the guys don't want to have anything to do with Pep in any case. But I was working for Pep at that stage, and I went to him again and said, it's the bargain of the century. If I hadn't been so decent, I would have resigned and bought it myself.'

While Whitey wanted to 'do his own thing', he also realised that a partnership with Pep would hold many advantages. Furthermore, he wished to stand by his promise to Renier that they would 'do it together'. They then agreed that Pep would buy Shoprite, but that Whitey could buy 25 per cent of Shoprite's shares at the original valu-ation – in other words, for R500 000. But the finer details of this deal, which was settled with a handshake, still had to be approved by Pep and therefore had to go through all the company's processes.

'There were many discussions, and lots of meetings, and the matter went to Pep's board, which in turn referred it to a subcommittee. After months the subcommittee said it wasn't their policy to hand out shares in unlisted companies, and that Barney and I had to take up shares in Pep itself.' Whitey was not happy with the decision. He told Renier this was exactly what he had not wanted – he wanted an independent company that would be able to list independently one day. In the event, the shares in Pep were never offered to him either.

'This was contrary to the decision Renier and I had agreed upon, and I was very angry with him for not having carried it through. But I think it was partly out of his control. So I just let it go, and when Christo subsequently took over from Renier, we concluded an agreement in terms of which I would get a percentage of Shoprite's operating profits.

'But Christo, savvy dealmaker that he was, put a limit on it. After two years I had already exceeded the limit, and from then onward my bonus structures only grew with inflation – but the profits went through the roof.' In the first year after the takeover the profit amounted to R600 000, on an investment of just R1 million.

Whitey continues his account: 'I was sorry that I hadn't bought Shoprite myself, but I did well enough not to regret it for too long. I was just very gatvol – our board was dominated by directors from Senbank, Sanlam and Federale Volksbeleggings. That's why I still believe outside directors only immobilise a company if they are incapable of entrepreneurial thinking or don't know the company well.'

Pep Stores eventually bought Shoprite for R1,9 million in May 1979. 'Messrs Rogut and Geller, who were the only shareholders in the company, will stay on in the top management team, while the 301 permanent and 148 part-time employees are retained too,' *Die Burger* reported. Though Geller would depart before long, Rogut would continue playing an important role at Shoprite and in Whitey's life.

Although Whitey did not own Shoprite, it was his business and he could run it as he saw fit. He was itching to put the boardroom politics behind him as soon as possible and focus his attention on that which mattered to him – getting to know Shoprite better, expanding it, and making it very successful.

PART THREE

SHOPRITE'S EARLY YEARS

11

Learning on the shop floor

If you look after the pennies, the pounds will look after themselves.
– Whitey Basson to a friend.[1]

'In the beginning, after Barney Rogut broke the news to us that he had sold the company to Pep, this laaitie walked in and I thought to myself, my God, he can't run the organisation,' recounted Selwyn Schiff, who was Shoprite's sales manager at the time.

'But we clicked immediately and when he said, "Stick with me and we'll go places," I trusted Whitey instinctively.' Schiff would eventually become operations manager and a close confidant of Whitey's.[2]

The 'laaitie' was eager to learn, however, and Rogut's training school was Shoprite's shop floors. 'Just imagine', says Jimmy Fouché. 'Whitey is now the boss, but he's learning from Barney – a sort of self-imposed apprenticeship.' Whitey says he knew precious little about supermarkets at the time. He knew retail well, of course, but food retailing was a different kettle of fish.

Initially the plan was that Barney would stay on at Shoprite for six months but, 'gatvol and stressed', he decided to resign, and Whitey found it hard to cope. He was engaged in a major restructuring and expansion programme. He put sales under the control of two regional sales managers – Selwyn Majmin and Selwyn Schiff – and purchasing under the control of two purchasing managers – Jackie Reiser and Harry Rogut, Barney's brother.[3]

One evening Whitey paid a visit to Barney, and his passion and determination had a contagious effect on his old teacher. 'He then said he wanted to come back,' Whitey relates. 'He was very emotional, and so was I.' Barney was soon permanently back at his post, and from that time on the two of them were virtually inseparable.

'Barney was a wonderful person. I still remember the first day he and I walked into the stores. He had to teach me everything about food because I didn't *really* know the difference between baked beans and peas. So we went from store to store, me with my little blue shirt with "Shoprite" on the chest and my Crimplene trousers, and I had to watch and learn.

'And we got to a branch where there was a sidestack display – a bunch of tins stacked on top of each other at the end of a shelf, but none of them were marked. In those days nobody scanned yet, and every tin had to get a sticker with the price on it. I thought I was clever and said to Barney, "Just look at this. What should we do now?" Barney took two marking guns, gave me one, and said: "Now you and I are going to mark them because the customers will be arriving soon and then everything has to be right." I'll never forget that.

'Barney never wasted his time on trifles. He was a practical guy, and he taught me that if you want to get things done, you must just *do* them. Let's get the job done. And your first focus is on your principles and your core business. No sideshows were allowed,' Whitey relates. Barney would also teach Whitey that you had to watch every cent because every saving could be passed on to the customer. This was the foundation on which Shoprite had been established and Whitey was to build – the promise of the lowest prices.

'One day one of the auditors stood there counting packets of chewing gum, and Barney went up to him and said: "My boy, just take a calculated guess, because by the time you're done counting, there is no more profit in it for me."'

96

This thriftiness was something Barney had been learning since childhood in a poor household. 'Barney used to tell me they couldn't afford fresh bread and always bought bread that was past its sell-by date.' The mindset of frugality extended to everything at Shoprite. In the early days, for instance, they did not pay for cleaning services. 'We would just clean our own toilets ourselves, and the stores too, when it was quieter.'

Shoprite's head office consisted of five small offices that were situated above its store in Lansdowne Road on the Cape Flats. To reach the offices, you had to walk through the store and go up a flight of cement stairs. But you also had to get your timing right because the storeroom was at the top as well; the sliding chute through which boxes were sent down to the store was in front of the stairs, and a box could land on your head.[4] The lean operation also meant that if anyone phoned with a complaint, there was a good chance the phone would be picked up by a manager. It was a steep learning curve.[5]

Whitey would take a different route through the aisles every day to see what was happening in the store. 'Every year the government increased the sin taxes in the budget, so we would purchase as many cigarettes as we could beforehand and make a big profit on them,' he recounts. 'But there wasn't enough storage space, and at times our offices would be crammed with cigarette cartons stacked up to the ceiling.'

In addition to his other qualities, Barney was a shrewd negotiator. 'He always said, you don't need to write anything down if you never lie because if you tell the truth, you don't have to remember it. He taught me that you don't negotiate in case lots, you negotiate in single tins, for the seller would be more inclined to give you a discount of 20 cents per tin than R2,40 on the whole case.

'It was little things like that he had learnt over the years and that he taught me in turn. They might sound pointless, but you were learning from a man who started out with nothing – who knew how I should do my pitch, and how you approach sales directors and a bunch of MBAs. Barney always had a very humble demeanour and would butter people up, but most of the time he walked away with what he wanted.'

Barney was not scared of trying new things either. 'I have the greatest respect for what he achieved because he taught himself retail, and I could trust him to take care of the nitty gritty while I was occupied with other matters. We also had one big thing in common, and that was that we strove to create jobs and to avoid retrenching people. Barney had a huge influence on me, because I was still quite young when we bought Shoprite from him.'

Had Whitey listened to the 'experts', the Shoprite of today would not have existed. At the time Shoprite started, the market was dominated by three large groups – Pick n Pay, OK Bazaars and Checkers. Many analysts questioned Whitey's acquisition of Shoprite and believed the smaller retail group would struggle to make headway against these three.[6] He quickly realised he had to box clever against the 'big three'. The strategy was not to challenge the stronger rivals head-on, but rather to target a segment in the food market that was still underexploited at the time. This segment was the neighbourhood supermarket – smaller stores within walking distance in residential areas themselves.[7]

The strategy also involved limiting the assortment of goods slightly and not stocking ten different brands of the same product.[8] Whitey systematically started selling more perishable products as well. 'The first week we had fresh mushrooms on the shelves, we sold probably six packets. Today we sell millions.'

* * * *

The first Shoprite with Whitey at the helm opened in Albert Road in the old inner-city Cape Town suburb of Salt River on 30 April 1980. Barney was unable to attend the opening ceremony as a result of a back operation but sent Whitey the following letter:

Dear Whitey,
Well, your first 'Baby' has finally arrived. Now I hope I won't have to hear any more: 'Hell, Barney, ek is moeg van die rondmorsery. Wanneer gaan ons klaar kom.'

This is your big day, and I am very sorry I am unable to be present to share your joy. Please convey my apology and thank all our friends, associates and staff for the cooperation and wonderful teamwork spirit which I know prevailed throughout.

Heartiest congratulations to you and the 'Board'. I hope your only problem will be replacing broken windows on opening day.

I am thinking of you all right now. Do enjoy yourselves. I happen to know the caterer and she normally excels herself. [It was his wife, Haide Rogut.]
Kindest regards to all.
Barney

* * * *

An excited Whitey delivered an opening speech that abounded with wisecracks and jokes. Among other things, he paid lavish homage to Barney Rogut. But he was expected to be back at his post before long. 'Barney taught me quickly but not too fast, so to the members of the Pep board who are present this evening, you can report back to the chairman that I now know the difference between baked beans and peas, which I don't consider too bad for ten months' work.' Towards the end he also put Shoprite and his approach to entrepreneurship in a wider context:

> You would appreciate that opening new stores and facing competition, especially in the Cape, takes a lot of courage, and if you will bear with me for only a few minutes more, I will try and explain to you how I see the economy of the country and the future.
>
> I think we can take it for granted that the pressures on South Africa will increase, and that South Africa will not be excluded from the problems which face the Western world as a whole. The biggest of these are inflation, the rising cost of energy and the tremendous gap between the rich and the poor. These problems can develop into monsters unless we can handle them.
>
> The only way I can see us living in harmony and enjoying the country and its beautiful surroundings is to rely on people to solve these problems for us. In short, all the problems can be put under one umbrella and called the Crisis of Leadership.
>
> We can look at the solutions in two ways, one commonly known as 'zero-sum', which I am afraid so many people have been practising for too long a period. Now, zero-sum means there is only so much energy to go around. A fixed amount of prosperity, and a fixed amount of poverty, and to divide these fixed amounts so that the positives balance with the negatives. People tend to use this as an answer to survive, society uses it – individuals can only benefit at the expense of others. Rich versus Poor, White versus Black, Age versus Youth, East versus West, Consumer versus Producer.
>
> This style of life will only lead to tragedy. If you apply this zero-sum mentality to sports, you will see that in rugby there is no fixed number of tries to be scored or in cricket no fixed number of runs

to be made. There the contest is governed by the limitations of time and the potential of each player.

Now, gentlemen, look at the nations such as Japan and Germany who after the war did not waste time and energy on arguing how to divide the economic pie, but rather concentrated their talents and energies on making the pie grow. That is the second alternative to our problems.

These are the types of people and management that have been bred into Shoprite since Mr Rogut started it thirteen years ago. People who do not believe in zero-sum ideologies. What you see here tonight was created by the people of Shoprite. They intend to make the pie grow.

I would just like to reconfirm to Barney Rogut, the management and the staff my absolute dedication to Shoprite and its success, which can probably be summed up best in the epigram of the late John F Kennedy – 'A rising tide lifts all boats'. It inspires you to want to improve and more importantly, it inspires cooperation, so that we all have enough.

The opening day was a resounding success. The doors were even closed a few times as a measure to control the more than 6 000 customers who turned up.[9] About 3 500 customers per day kept the cash registers ringing over the first three days, and the store exceeded its sales targets by more than 70 per cent. Whitey had ambitious plans for further expansion. 'Our [business] models were always based on growing very big, very quickly,'[10] he confirmed later. He also wanted to give the company a sign that it was destined for greater things.

'Barney lived from hand to mouth in the business, so to speak, but I wanted to expand quickly and also signal to the employees that our intention was to go big. He and I shared an office, and I sat on his previous partner's chair. When you leaned back, you would just about fall against the wall because its hinges were defective. I then told him, we can't drive around in these old rusty cars full of holes any longer – all the cars used to belong to his brothers or sisters. We had two Volkswagens, a Valiant, a Datsun, and a few others. So I called an acquaintance at Motors Western Province who gave us a good deal on Volkswagens, and I negotiated all kinds of extras into the bargain,' Whitey recounts.

'I was very chuffed with myself and thought this would prove to Barney that I wasn't such a bad negotiator. We then had tea and discussed the deal, and Barney took another sip from his cup and asked: "So, Whitey, who's paying for the number plates?" I had forgotten about that! I then phoned again and asked if they could please also throw in the plates for free. On the whole deal the amount was negligible, but it just shows you how his mind worked and why he was so successful.'

In the early years they did not use security services to transport cash to the bank either. 'Each of us had a toolbox made of tin; we would split up the outlets among us and each guy had his route. You spend an hour or so in a store, place the cash in the toolbox and put it into the car, and nobody would suspect that it was filled with cash. Then you would drive to the central office and from there it was deposited. In that way we saved a hell of a lot of money.'

The Shoprite style was one of 'frugality and no frills', confirms André van Zyl, who moved from Pep to join Shoprite as company secretary and property manager. 'Shoprite sounded exciting, and it wasn't one meeting after the other, you were operationally involved. Our offices were not fancy. I moved over with my secretary, which was necessary due to the nature of my work, but this wasn't very well received because at Shoprite you would just do everything yourself.' He would end up working for the company up to his retirement 30 years later.

Shoprite was still in its infancy, but Whitey's young team had one common goal. 'We worked very hard, late nights and early mornings and over weekends – that was the lifestyle. It was hard work, but there was the end goal, and you didn't want to let your colleagues down. You didn't want to be the one who dropped the ball, for you relied on your teammates and they on you,' recounts Van Zyl.

'Naturally, one mostly remembers only the good things, but when we were under pressure, we would often butt heads as well. However, everyone was enthusiastic. There were also good incentives, in the form of bonuses and share schemes. And you knew where you stood with Whitey, and if you worked hard and used your brains, everything was fine. Everyone knew who the boss was.'

12

Cheaper on chicken

When I walk into a store, the manager has to know what his prices and his competitor's prices are on his top twenty products. And heaven help him if his competition is cheaper than him.

– Whitey Basson

As an inexpensive source of protein, chicken is a key product for retailers – particularly for a chain such as Shoprite, with its specific target market. Paying the lowest prices for chicken and passing the price benefit on to your customers is a major objective.

For Shoprite, therefore, chicken sales have always been a serious matter. 'Chicken was always very strategic for us,' confirms Whitey. 'If you wanted to poach a customer from Grand Bazaars, you had to be cheaper on chicken. And we were always the cheapest on chicken.'

In the 1980s Shoprite was still small fry while Rainbow Chickens, which had been founded by Stan Methven in 1960,[1] was one of the biggest suppliers of frozen chicken in the country.

'They controlled the price because they had so many chickens,' Whitey explains. 'When they had a surplus of chickens, Stan would dump them and the prices would come down, and if they had too few, the prices would go up.'

Rainbow set its prices once a week for the coming week. They were announced to retailers via ticker tape – at Shoprite, this played out in the company's head office. On Thursday evenings at six o'clock all the retailers would wait for next week's price, hurriedly place their orders, and then calculate their prices for the coming week. The other suppliers also kept more or less to Rainbow's prices.

The other heavyweight in the chicken market was County Fair. The company's founder, Des Lurie, was a good friend of Pick n Pay's Raymond Ackerman. 'They were golf buddies, so why would he give me better prices than he gave Pick n Pay? They were of course bigger than us, and bought more chickens,' Whitey relates.

Dave Finlayson, a contemporary of Whitey's at Rondebosch Boys', bumped into him again years later when he was working for the very same County Fair. Finlayson was visiting Shoprite's headquarters in Lansdowne, and he, too, recalls the cement stairs and the hundreds of boxes through which he had to negotiate his way to reach the tiny offices on the top floor.

Eventually he heard a familiar voice: 'Hey, Finlayson, come here!' There sat Whitey, surrounded by bags of flour and other stock. 'I didn't expect to find *you* here,' said Finlayson. After the usual 'how are you?' and 'what have you been up to?', Whitey explained that he had recently bought Shoprite and was going through the books. Finlayson informed him that he was now working for County Fair and selling chickens. Whitey remarked: 'You tell Des Lurie he should tell Raymond Ackerman we're going to become bigger than Pick n Pay.'

At that stage Shoprite was still small, and Whitey endeavoured to use smaller suppliers. He could negotiate better prices and more favourable terms in this way, and did not have to put up with a Lurie or a Methven. That was how he crossed paths with Laura Kotze (née Singer) of Golden Grove. 'She was a real go-getter. I told her, I'm small and you're small, so let's work together and support each other.' So Golden Grove supplied chicken largely to Shoprite and gave Whitey better prices. Like many other suppliers, Laura would grow along with Shoprite and build up a large business.

'The average Pick n Pay or OK Bazaars didn't care a hoot about running out of chicken, but Shoprite always had chicken in stock,' Whitey recounts. 'When I looked at the figures of the Bellville branch and they were not what we'd expected, I knew we had run out of chicken by eleven o'clock in the morning. In those days we didn't have cellphones, but we would put Johnny on the road with a truck full of chickens. He was only twenty minutes away from any Shoprite branch – ready to deliver chicken wherever it was needed. He was in contact with Laura via a walkie-talkie as well.'

It was also at this stage that Whitey began contemplating his own central distribution model, which was to become one of Shoprite's major competitive advantages years later. 'That was why we started our DCs [distribution centres], because the delivery from suppliers to the stores was too poor.'

First thing in the morning he would check the ads of all the retailers, and early on Saturday mornings Brian Weyers, head of marketing, would receive a call from Whitey about their single advertisement in the weekend papers. 'In those days we had a rule: never advertise chicken when the market [wholesale chicken prices] is falling because you can be priced out by your advertisements,' recounts Weyers.

Whitey explains it as follows: 'The chicken market moved in cycles – for instance, at a point there would be diseases and no chickens, and the prices would go through the roof. But at times when there was an oversupply of chickens, the prices went down. And you never advertised in a market like that because you didn't know at what price Pick n Pay had bought their chickens. You never knew how many chickens your competitor had, and what he had paid. So someone might be advertising chickens at R10 per kilo, for example, and you at R9 per kilo, and then another bugger comes and he sells at R7 per kilo.'

One morning, that happened. 'Pick n Pay undercut our chicken prices for the weekend,' relates Weyers. 'Whitey phoned me, incensed. I think he was in the bath, because after giving me a tongue-lashing, he exclaimed: "I'm so pissed off, I feel like punching a hole in the water!"'

Lower prices at Pick n Pay meant that Shoprite would lose customers. A supermarket group cannot give its competitors the slightest chance to woo their customers with lower prices. 'Once a customer has been in your store and you don't have what he wants, or if it's more expensive, he'll defect and go to your competitor,' states Prof. Nic Terblanche, a professor in the department of business management at Stellenbosch University and adviser to Shoprite. 'Whitey understood that very well.'

Whitey also explains how his customers had to watch their cents: 'Our customers don't look at the price per kilogram, but at whether the price of the whole chicken – R19 or R20 or whatever – fits into their budget. So people would scratch around among the chickens because they look for one they can afford. They don't give a damn about whether it's 10 per cent more expensive per kilo – all they want is a price they can afford.'

In his account of the negotiations about chicken prices, Whitey sheds rare light on the art of retail: 'You get, say, 10 chickens in a box, so if 20 boxes come in, you have 200 chickens. But we would weigh the box and calculate the average weight per chicken. In some stores you want smaller chickens because the average customer has only so much money. Then the chickens would be "cheaper". In other stores, the customer doesn't care.

'But at what point do you agree on the price with the supplier? Because we're purchasing large quantities, aren't we? When the average weight per chicken starts going down, you know you shouldn't do a deal because the supplier's demand is rising and he needs to slaughter earlier – let's say at 33 days, then 32 days, then 31 and then 30. And if the average weight per chicken goes up, you know he's not managing to sell all his stock and the chickens are staying with him a day or two longer.

'In that way you can see when the guy's stock is building up, and when he has less stock. And when you see a surplus is building up in the market, then you start negotiating. And you should never advertise when the prices start dropping, for you don't know how low they will go. All of that is important because the margins are low, but the volumes are high.' Indeed, by 2015 Shoprite was selling more than 400 000 chickens per day – about 150 million chickens per year.

According to Terblanche, Whitey was a brilliant businessman. 'What makes him exceptional is that he never deviated from the simple principle that you are managing cents. Your profit may be just a cent on a product, but if you sell a million of that product, you have a million cents. It's the supermarket mentality – volumes are everything, and you have to sell enough of a product to justify its place on the shelf.

'One thing Whitey taught me is that shelf space is their single biggest asset. As soon as an item has been packed onto the shelves, it needs to be sold because it is costing you money for as long as it is on the shelf. And every product is appropriate for the target market.'

But it was not only about chicken. Other staple foods such as rice and cooking oil were important too. A colleague relates that someone once proposed at a meeting that Shoprite should be the cheapest on all cheap products. On that occasion, Whitey cautioned: 'You should never be the cheapest on the cheapest products, but on the products that determine value.'[2]

Whitey divulges another secret of retailing: it is all about customer perception. Most people can only remember the prices of a handful of items, and these are usually the products they purchase frequently. By identifying your known value items – the items that determine value for your customers – and being cheaper on those products than your competitors, you create the perception that your prices are generally lower than elsewhere. At the same time, you are deepening customer loyalty to your brand.

And every cent does count. 'The guy who has nothing has to get by on his R100 for the week or month, and he can only buy what he can afford. He doesn't look at brands or at what he likes, he has to buy food with that meagre amount he has, and then price becomes everything. Our competitors didn't understand that.

'We had to do backhauling – that's when customers get to the cash register, and they are a little bit short. Barney and I spent thousands of rands of our own money in helping out people with 20 cents here and 50 cents there. But most people would leave the products they couldn't pay for in the baskets. Then our staff had to take the baskets and pack all those products back on the shelf. It was painful to see that. Many people don't understand it – what it means to genuinely have no money.'

Shoprite knew exactly what its key products were. 'I carried lines Pick n Pay shied away from, like certain types of maize meal, because Pick n Pay didn't want too many of our kind of customers – they were worried that it would scare off customers at the top end of the market. For the same reason, they couldn't advertise cheaper prices on certain other products either. But I also had to ward off Pick n Pay on the middle- to higher-income market, so that I wouldn't lose against them. There, too, we had to show that we were cheaper than them.

'And at the bottom end of the market I had to do things that were appropriate for that market, which were previously done mostly by spaza shops and OK Bazaars. And I didn't necessarily have examples to follow. People give you things that customers supposedly want – air conditioners and shorter queues – and don't take the trouble to ascertain what they actually want. I was privileged in that I knew my customers. I came from Porterville, and I knew what people with lower incomes really wanted.'

With these tactics and with customer needs in mind, Shoprite remained the cheapest in the perception of customers and slowly but surely captured market share from its rivals. As Shoprite grew and became more and more successful, its negotiating power increased as well. Today it is the single largest buyer and seller of frozen chicken in South Africa – more than 60 per cent of all frozen chicken in the country goes past its cash registers.[3]

13

Refining a winning recipe

We exist to provide value to our customers, which means that in addition to quality and service, we have to save them money. Every time Wal-Mart spends one dollar foolishly, it comes right out of our customers' pockets. Every time we save them a dollar, that puts us one more step ahead of the competition – which is where we always plan to be.

– Sam Walton, founder of Walmart[1]

Some existing Shoprite outlets were more clothing store than grocer, and the stores all looked different. 'Some stores had carpeted rather than tiled floors, and when you pushed your trolley over the carpet, it would create a sort of bubble in front of you,' Whitey recalls.

One of the first things he did was to make Shoprite more fit for purpose. He soon introduced standards for premises, the stores themselves, and what they should and could sell. 'Even the colour of the tiles on the walls and floors, the size of the shelves, etcetera have been standardised, and layout and departmental placement inside the stores conform to a uniform pattern,'[2] *Pep Nuus* reported in 1981.

Whitey's perfectionist streak manifested itself in the design, layout and construction of new stores. Every tile had to be perfect and create the right atmosphere. A contemporary, Louis Pienaar, worked for a firm that built the first new Shoprite, in Parow. 'The wall tiles of the butchery were supposed to have been white, but then Whitey thought it would look like a hospital and decided that colour had to be added.

It is still like that today. I subsequently joined Shoprite, and over the years my respect and esteem for him only grew.'[3]

The logo, too, underwent a makeover. The old 'S' was replaced by a symbol similar to the dollar sign, and the corporate colours were changed from blue and white to red and yellow. These decisions were not taken randomly, but were based on research that showed red was powerful and yellow was associated with 'discount'. The logo was also redesigned so as to be timeless and instantly recognisable to the consumer.

Whitey had commissioned an American market research firm that specialised in retail to conduct his initial market research. Besides the new logo and colours, the firm's recommendations included how the group should position itself, what its target market should be, and even how its marketing should be undertaken.

In November 1979 *Pep Nuus* described Whitey as Shoprite's 'young and energetic managing director', and quoted him as follows: 'We are not only going to double the current size of the group, but also aim to double the turnover of R11 million of the previous year by the end of next year [1980].'

Whitey also elaborated on the strategy of locating stores close to residential areas where there was a reasonable flow of passing pedestrian traffic. He explained it like this: 'In spite of the great strides made in South Africa in the building of modern shopping centres there are many trading areas which have been neglected, and our aim will be to operate mainly in catchment areas that are too small for the big chains. We believe that we can provide a service which is needed in these areas and that our expansion programme will benefit the shopping public.'[4]

Whitey studied the American retail giant Walmart carefully and paid annual visits to the United States to keep abreast of the latest trends in retailing and marketing. He appointed an American consultant as well. 'Darryl Fine, head of Shoprite's advertising agency, and I visited Bentonville, Walmart's headquarters in America, and they took us through the whole place – the stores and the warehouses. At that stage Pick n Pay and Checkers were getting the best premises for new stores, so we had to adopt the Walmart model.'

Sam Walton writes in his autobiography: 'Our key strategy . . . was simply to put good-sized discount stores into little one-horse towns everybody else was ignoring.'[5] Whitey and Shoprite would follow this example: 'Walmart started in smaller towns and moved into bigger urban centres as they grew. I said, we're not going to challenge Pick n Pay head-on in the main cities. Instead, we took Shoprite to Pietersburg, Hartswater, Vryburg, and places like that where we could make good profits without exposing ourselves to one guy – such as Pick n Pay – who had the ability to wipe us out.

'That was my tactic, to expand in the smaller places and move in from outside into the bigger suburbs and cities. We first did very good business in the rural areas before we took on the guys in the urban areas. At that stage they had better distribution networks than us and had been in retail for longer. The next thing they knew, we had become too big, and they could no longer wipe us out.' It would still take a while, however, before Shoprite achieved that position, and although the company was doing well and Whitey was enjoying it, the long hours and hard work were very taxing.

'It was a rush to open stores and build a successful business. But running the business was not stressful – I was crazy about it. I only experienced stress about how much I had to absorb, and the time I had at my disposal. And I had a lot to learn. I knew retail but knew nothing about food.

'So that was always where your tension built up, the worry about tiny mistakes that could cost millions. We always said, if we take Shoprite to a place, we'll get the customers. But when you open a new store, you do lie awake worrying whether it will be a success – you wonder whether the people will buy from us or drive a few kilometres on to Pick n Pay.'

Customer service was another important area. 'Today customers expect good service and expect and assume that companies pay attention to it, but that wasn't always the case.' Because of its customer-centric approach, good service became another focal point for Shoprite, which in turn improved customer loyalty.

'For a few years, if you wanted, say, Omo washing powder but couldn't find it at a Shoprite, the manager had to take down your name, phone number and address and deliver it to your home. And the managers had to do that in their own time. This put pressure on the managers and their staff to make sure that products like that were always on the shelves,' recounts Whitey.

* * * *

In 1980, the year in which Shoprite expanded so rapidly, something happened that gave Whitey and his family a huge fright. One Sunday, in the middle of the snoek season, Whitey, his elder son Adrian and his nephew went out on a fishing trip on his ski boat at Hout Bay. The wind sprang up and the boat started taking on water.

'When I got home that day, it felt as if my heart rate was much too fast. I called the physician Johann Rabie, who lived nearby, and he took me to the hospital right away. I was admitted on the Sunday evening and lay in Tygerberg's cardiac unit. I said goodbye to Annalise and the children – I didn't know if I was going to make it through the night,' Whitey relates.

Even under these circumstances, Whitey could not resist the temptation to play a prank on the hospital staff. He was not too happy with their customer service and decided to test them. 'So I ripped off all my monitors to check how long it would take them to discover that there was a problem. It took about twenty minutes before a whole team came rushing in to investigate. I told them: I died twenty minutes ago!'

Whitey's doctor was Pieter 'Budgy' van der Merwe, who happened to be a local of Porterville too. 'He was actually a paediatric cardiologist,' says Whitey. 'Then he said it was an atrial fibrillation – an irregular heartbeat, or arrhythmia – and not a heart attack.

'They couldn't really establish what had caused it, but according to the doctors it probably happened because I had become very stressed on the boat. I've had trouble with an overproduction of adrenaline all my life, which is why I could carry on working for days on end. But I never had heart problems again after that.'

In 1981 – just after he had taken over Shoprite – Whitey was also informed that he had ankylosing spondylitis – a form of arthritis that primarily affects the spine but other major joints as well.[6] 'My dad still took me to Groote Schuur Hospital. I suffered incredible pain. I could hardly use my one leg, and it kept getting thinner. There was a rumour going around that I had cancer,' Whitey relates.

'I read up extensively about the condition and found out that it is mostly prevalent in the East. So I went to a Chinese doctor for treatment, and subsequently flew to Taiwan. A Taiwanese friend who lives in America had organised it for me. There I was treated by the top Chinese muscle doctor. Miraculously, I recovered. I was still taking a lot of medication at the time. The doctor took it away on the Friday and started treating me. The following Friday I was playing golf, and I never experienced pain again.'

It is ironic that someone who considered studying medicine and is still interested in medicine was healed with 'Eastern' remedies. 'Look, it probably sounds like everything I don't believe in, but that was what happened. Maybe it was a coincidence that it disappeared in the same week. I still have the disease, but I don't have any symptoms – it's in remission. But the tests and treatment have also improved in the meantime.

'That was a very difficult time. I had just started Shoprite, I had young children, and I didn't know what the prognosis was.' Yet even this setback did not slow Whitey down.

14

Full steam ahead

The people from Pep I took with me to Shoprite and those I later appointed as well – the qualification that topped the list was that they had to be willing to walk through the fire with me.

– Whitey Basson

After the launch of Whitey's first 'own' store in Salt River, Shoprite expanded rapidly in the Western Cape. On 29 May 1980 the tenth branch was opened, in Grabouw. 'It was a sight to behold,' read the report on the opening day in *Pep Nuus*.

'Hundreds of curious customers, eager to buy, moved through the aisles between the rows and rows of neatly packed gondolas, with baskets, trolleys and arms crammed full of bargains, until there was hardly any standing room left. The tills operated at full steam under the deft fingers of select cashiers. And the shopping frenzy was contagious. But everything went off smoothly and without a hitch. The news spread, and the next day even more customers came. Shoprite has arrived in Grabouw and is here to stay.'[1]

For Whitey and his team of young comrades, the first years were an exciting challenge. This team included a number of confidants he had brought with him from Pep. According to Whitey, Renier van Rooyen told him: 'They don't have to be clever; they just have to support you because you're going to have a hell of a time.'[2] This group of Young Turks – all of them a few years younger than Whitey – included Braam de Klerk, Brian Weyers, Alex Wasserfall and Stephen Braudé. Whitey's philosophy at Shoprite was 'getting people who are hard-working, and on whom you can rely'.

According to Jimmy Fouché, one of Whitey's strengths was selecting the right people. 'There was a very successful meshing between the old Shoprite culture and the Pep people who moved to Shoprite with Whitey. They spoke the same language. Whereas Pep was at the bottom end of the market in clothing, Shoprite was in the same position in food. You had to give your customers what they wanted – meet their needs – and that was the role Shoprite filled in respect of groceries. They targeted the market below that of Pick n Pay, Checkers and OK.'

Another philosophy was that, even before the business was listed, employees could be given shares and therefore share in the profits. 'We enjoyed it,' Whitey recounts. 'We were a bunch of young guys who had embarked on an adventure – all of us with a good knowledge of retail and other disciplines we could apply. We were really just playing cat and mouse and bush war with our biggest opposition at that stage in the Western Cape. Each time you won something, you got that incredible adrenaline rush that told you, let's go for the next step.'[3]

Since his Pep years Whitey had been a strong proponent of recognising the essential humanity of one's colleagues and staff. 'At the time I joined Pep, there were barely 30 of us at the head office. We knew one another by name and lived like one family and were truly caring towards one another. Later there were so many of us that we couldn't do that any longer, and it seemed as if we didn't attach so much value to it any more.

'When I arrived at Shoprite with its eight stores and only a handful of people, there was again a sense of community like at Pep in the early years – I felt at home among Barney and his people. Today it is still like that at Shoprite,' he said in 1983.[4] Some of the other pillars at Pep had been positive thinking, hard work, enthusiasm and compassion – all of which were values important in Shoprite as well.

Shoprite and its people knew their market and gave their customers what they wanted, at the lowest prices. But Whitey did not always get it right immediately. Among other things, it did not prove so easy to get the gift market right. 'When we opened in Grabouw, we sold those little dogs with the bobbing heads that people used to put in the rear window area of cars, and one day a woman and her son came into the store and thought they were the prettiest and cutest things ever. They ended up buying six. As time went on, we sold thousands of them,' Whitey recounts.

'And those kaleidoscopes you could turn. Marbles and tops were also very popular. These products were called the "basic range", and they always had to be on the shelf because they sold throughout the year and not only at Christmas. They were the things the mothers would buy to keep the kids quiet. Selwyn and Barney called them *tchotchkes*, which means knick-knacks. You sell large quantities of those items, and the children want them and pester their parents for them.

'On one occasion I bought a range of toy boats and tumble dryers, but we failed to sell any. They were nice toys, and I couldn't understand why. It then dawned on us that most of the children had no association with these items – they didn't have boats, washing machines or tumble dryers at home.'

* * * *

In 1981 there was a turn of events in the bigger picture that would also have consequences for Whitey and Shoprite. After a six-year stint at the Cape Bar, Christo Wiese returned to Pep Stores early in 1981. The 40-year-old Wiese, however, had been a director of Pep from the age of 27. In November, Renier van Rooyen announced unexpectedly that he was resigning as executive chairman and that Wiese would be taking the reins from him. Tom Ball became managing director. The news came as an 'enormous shock' to the business community, wrote David Meades in *Afrikaner-Kapitalisme*.[5] Van Rooyen had only recently turned 50.

Van Rooyen also sold a large part of his stake in Pep to Wiese. Wiese already owned a substantial block of Pep shares, and this gave him an interest of 25 per cent in the group.[6] Van Rooyen finally left Pep on 28 February 1982 but remained a director until 2000.

In 1982 Wiese embarked on his 'financial engineering', as Meades calls it, and a new holding company, Pepkor, replaced Pep Stores on the Johannesburg Stock Exchange. Wiese and his team restructured the group into four divisions: clothing stores, food retail, manufacturing and property. At that stage Pepkor had five operating subsidiaries: Pep Stores and Half Price Stores with 485 outlets, Shoprite with 15 outlets, Pep Manufacturing with 12 arms, and Pep Property Investments with properties worth R15 million.[7] To entrench control, Wiese and his team set up a pyramid structure and in April 1983 they also listed Pepgro, which held a majority stake in Pepkor and in which he and his allies in turn held most of the shares.[8]

Whitey admits it was to his advantage that his friend Christo was then the chairman and largest shareholder in Pepkor. 'It benefitted my style,' says Whitey. 'I would either have done Shoprite on my own, or I would have had to get a guy like Christo. We basically agreed that he would look after the clothing side of the business, and I would take care of Shoprite. We would discuss acquisitions and strategy, but he never interfered at Shoprite.'

Whitey also observed jokingly to Ebbe Dommisse, the author of *Fortuine*, that Wiese had had more time on his hands to amass shares than he had: 'I had to do all the work, and he made all the money!' But he added that he had always had the greatest respect for his long-standing friend and chairman.

'I always say, Christo Wiese is one of the smartest guys I've ever met, but he was not a retailer. He is an excellent strategist, and we had a wonderful working relationship. He never interfered with my decisions.'

* * * *

After Grabouw, Somerset West followed in 1981, Strand and Kraaifontein in 1982, and Worcester in 1983. When the Worcester branch opened on 30 November the group already had 21 stores, all still in the Western Cape, but they were now meeting the needs of customers in a broader range of income groups than had been the case just a few years before. 'We expect to open between six and ten stores annually over the next four years,' Whitey told *The Argus*.[9]

This paper described him as one of 'the new generation of mass retailers – dynamic young men who find adventure and excitement in this highly competitive industry'. Whitey was quoted as follows: 'I enjoy the challenges and excitement of retail. It's a fast-moving industry where you meet many people and things are constantly happening. I find it fascinating. I won't be able to return to practising as an accountant.'

The store in Grabouw was opened to test how Shoprite would perform in a platteland town. 'It has gone very well with the store . . . we have overcome the problem of distribution and logistics in small rural towns.' Shoprite's philosophy was to keep all prices as low as possible. 'I believe the cost of a total month's shopping would be lower from us than from rival chains,'[10] Whitey told the paper.

At that stage Pick n Pay, with Raymond Ackerman at the helm, was one of Shoprite's biggest competitors. 'I was very motivated by Pick n

Pay, for apart from Renier van Rooyen, Raymond Ackerman was one of the only guys who could really do retail.'

Whitey watched his big rival like a hawk and examined his vision, strategy and plans in detail. When he took his first step in food retailing, he commissioned an in-depth study on Raymond Ackerman and studied his profile. And Whitey's plan – his vision and mission – was to surpass Pick n Pay in size.

At that point, however, Shoprite had certain advantages over its larger rival. It was able to make and execute decisions quickly and easily, and to employ 'guerrilla tactics'. Whitey explains: 'We were too agile for them. We did things they simply couldn't understand. For instance, Pick n Pay wants to show they're cheaper by selling HTH [swimming pool chlorine] at discount prices. Then every Shoprite manager would buy lots of HTH at the nearest Pick n Pay, and I advertise it at an even cheaper price. Most of my customers don't have swimming pools, and these aren't big ads anyway. But then people would think, wow, Shoprite is cheap, and buy other goods from me as well.

'I also knew Ackerman was reading our ads. He and his buyers would go to the supplier and ask, what's going on, is Shoprite getting it at a cheaper price? So, of course, the supplier says he didn't supply to us, but then I would say they're lying – they just don't want to admit it!'

Whitey did the same with cooking oil, which, unlike HTH, was (and still is) a key product for Shoprite's target market. 'As a retailer, you got a certain allocation of cooking oil. When there was a price hike, I would buy up all the other retailers' and wholesalers' oil – I would even rent trucks to load it up.

'Shoprite's brand is built on price, and price is a perception,' he elaborates. 'Our ads don't say, this toy car is cheaper. We would say we're the biggest buyer of toys, and then show a Chinese toy factory that ships the merchandise to us. So people would think, gosh, these guys really buy a lot, they must be cheap.

'All the retailers were very close to each other when it came to prices. Hence everything was done on perception, and we would tell stories. My promotions were called "reasons". Everything we did or advertised had to be backed up by a reason. A customer had to be able to see why we were the cheapest – we had to be able to provide an explanation.'

Whitey's strategy paid off, particularly in the smaller towns, and even in the 'larney' Graaff-Reinet. 'If Checkers in Johannesburg sold a block of margarine for 99 cents, they would press a button and a computer decided what the price was in other places – it would consider, for instance, the distance, the market, and various other factors. Then that same margarine would cost R1,04 in Graaff-Reinet.

'But that practice also had its drawbacks. In Graaff-Reinet I sold mine at 99 cents, even if I lost money. So when I drove into a town, I would take certain lines and say, these products are sold at these prices, and it would stay like that until I visited the town again. We didn't have computers.

'That was how we killed the Checkers branch there. The people would say, wow, Checkers is more expensive than Shoprite, and they come to us to buy the margarine but then end up buying sugar, rice, oil and chicken as well.'

But Shoprite was also planning to computerise. *Pep Nuus* quoted Whitey as follows: 'A start has already been made with a central computer system for the company that will link up with the main Pep computer at the head office in Kuils River and will make it possible to keep control of the total flow of inventory per item line. Once this system has been installed by the end of November this year [1981], it will be easier for Shoprite to enter the rural areas as one will then be able to communicate directly via computer with the buyers and central warehouses regarding the replacement and purchasing of stock.'[11]

Whitey and his team were bent on growing and on capturing market share, but at times his tactics made some of the board members and executives nervous. 'Sometimes the GP [gross profit] would be 16 per cent instead of 19 per cent, and then the guys would get anxious. But then I'd say, guys, did we or didn't we gain market share, and did we or didn't we make profit? I knew we couldn't build a big business unless we increased our sales volumes and captured market share.

'We decided not to take on our opposition head-on. But we couldn't do that anyway, as we didn't have the money. The strategy was to first grow strong in the Western Cape and then expand to far-flung places. We knew we couldn't take on Pick n Pay in Johannesburg, but we could thrash them in Vryburg and Hartswater.'

One of Shoprite's problems was that they struggled to obtain premises. 'When developers built shopping centres and looked for anchor tenants, Shoprite was not on their radar,' Jimmy Fouché recounts. 'They would opt for Pick n Pay or Checkers. Some of the big shopping centres didn't want a Pep either because it didn't tie in with their upmarket profile. For years Pep relied on small main street stores, and where we were unable to rent, we built a store here and there.'

The towns they selected had to be large enough to sustain a supermarket. 'The philosophy was that of filling the market from the bottom up,' Fouché continues. 'We had difficulty getting space in the shopping centres, so you would get to a town and you negotiate to obtain premises. If there was someone who could build it for you, that was wonderful, otherwise you had no choice but to develop it yourself.

'And you build a Shoprite that is based on the bottom end of the market but becomes the most important shop in the town. If you're at the bottom end of the market, and you want to put out feelers towards the high end, it's almost easier than the other way round. But your base, your continuity, remains the bottom end.'

The senior team convened on Friday afternoons to decide which towns they would visit for a recce. 'Whitey would arrive later and approve the itinerary. Before we closed a deal, Whitey first had to stand with his feet on the premises in question and look around. Every single one,' relates André van Zyl.

'We would stay over in hotels, and Whitey was often late. Then we had to hurry him up. He was also quite forgetful at times, and then it would be: 'Where are my glasses or my pen?' And the bed would have to be lifted up and couches overturned to look for it. Because his mind was occupied with other things – he would be thinking of many things simultaneously.'

In 1983 Shoprite opened a store in Hartswater in the Northern Cape – its first outlet outside the Western Cape. It happened after expansion to the rural areas had been thoroughly investigated and planned by Whitey and his team. But they soon realised you could not 'cut and paste' the design and layout of your store – especially not if you intended expanding beyond the Western Cape.

'In the Western Cape your cold rooms were considerably bigger than your freezer rooms, but in Hartswater and the Northern Cape it was the other way round,' explains Whitey. 'You don't have fresh produce every day, so you have more frozen goods. Since the people live on farms, they want more frozen goods. But then I built all my cold room facilities the wrong way round.' He quickly rectified his mistake and equipped the store with appropriate fridges and freezers. Whitey derived great pleasure from store design, and true to his management style, he was involved in the design and layout of all his stores.

Rising building costs and higher interest rates also compelled Whitey to form his own 'building team'. From then on he and Barney Rogut had weekly meetings with Dennis Gladman, group engineer for Pep Stores, and Barry Slavin from the architectural team to discuss their building programmes. In this way most of the building projects were managed centrally, and building costs were considerably curtailed. Where Shoprite did not build themselves, moderate leases were negotiated for the Shoprite supermarkets, which also meant they could reduce their rentals in new shopping centres.[12]

Whitey confirms: 'One of the things I liked most was the designing of stores and shopping centres – the architectural thinking, if I can put it like that. I devoted a lot of time to it. For 37 years I would receive the plans from the architects every Friday afternoon. Sometimes I just drew the layout plans myself and would say, for instance, if you turn these two freezers like that, you save ten square metres. Because you should trade on 50 per cent to 60 per cent of your store space.

'Later I could tell you off the top of my head how big each area of the supermarket had to be so that it would be suitable for the next fifteen years. I put lots of time into the designing of the stores.' And there were new stores aplenty. 'From the start I had set the goal of becoming the second-largest retailer in South Africa. We grew bigger and bigger. But Pick n Pay was massive, and I realised we had to do an acquisition if we were to stand a chance.'

In 1984 Shoprite bought six stores from Ackermans, which was part of the Edgars group. The latter had decided to dispose of its grocery stores as part of its strategy to return the company to profitability. The stores – in Beaufort West, Mossel Bay, Wellington, Kensington, Vasco and Parow – were all swiftly converted into Shoprites.[13] This acquisition was fairly modest. A bigger one lay just around the corner – a dress rehearsal for the two enormous acquisitions that were to propel Shoprite to the next level. But the next step would be listing on the Johannesburg Stock Exchange.

15

The north beckons

Some people travel east, while others west, while the same winds blow. It's not the gale, but the set of the sail which determines which way you go.

– Ella Wheeler Cox
(a regular quotation of Whitey's)

By 1986 South Africa was a country of apartheid and homelands, a border war, a national state of emergency, and escalating violence in the townships.[1] Besides political uncertainty, an economic recession, high inflation and unemployment added to the pressure experienced by consumers and retailers. Shoprite, however, stood on the eve of large-scale expansions, and the plan was still to expand the group nationally.

In August 1986 Pepkor announced that it was listing its retail chains Pep Stores and Ackermans on the Johannesburg Stock Exchange, and that Shoprite would follow in December.[2] 'Shoprite is indeed a very successful company that reported 30 per cent in trading profit earlier this year [1986], with a 14 per cent customer growth in established stores and serving 1,6 million customers per month,' *Pep Nuus* reported.

Whitey told *The Citizen* that since 1982, the group's turnover had grown at an annual compound rate of 41 per cent to R126 million in 1986.[3] 'Although we are currently active in the Cape only, we do plan to open stores in other parts of the country in due course,' he said. He also believed that in the five years from 1986 to 1991, the profit before tax would increase by at least 25 per cent per annum.[4]

'Unfortunately, Shoprite's profit history is not that impressive,' read an article in *The Star*. Although turnover had quadrupled from R32 million in 1982 to R126 million in 1986, the profits had not grown so spectacularly. But Shoprite's market share was increasing steadily, and that was also Whitey and his team's chief objective.

Shoprite's stores were all in the western, southern and northern regions of the Cape Province, with a customer base in the lower- and middle-income groups,[5] but in November 1986 it opened its first Orange Free State branch in Bloemfontein,[6] which brought the total number of outlets countrywide to more than thirty.

The listing, too, went off smoothly. A total of 29 550 000 shares were offered at R1 each, and the company therefore had a market capitalisation of nearly R30 million.

For the year ending February 1987, Shoprite's earnings showed a 55 per cent increase despite the difficult trading conditions. Turnover grew by 35 per cent to R170,6 million, and the operating profit by 33 per cent to R5,2 million.[7]

In the 1987 annual report – the first since the company's listing – Whitey wrote that the outlook for Shoprite's sustained growth was bright.[8] 'Shoprite has become a major force in its field in the Western Cape. The group is today the second largest – and perhaps more significantly, probably the most profitable – in the region.

'The company's highly successful policy of providing customers with a wide range of food and other consumer goods at the lowest prices in the cleanest stores will remain fundamental to our business and will continue to be a cornerstone of our future development.'[9]

He also noted that the country was changing. Urbanisation would undoubtedly result in an increase in the size and number of cities, with

PROKURASIE

Ek, die ondergetekende

RENIER VAN ROOYEN

nomineer en stel hiermee aan JAMES WELLWOOD BASSON, 'n
aandeelhouer van PEP STORES BEPERK, om gedurende my
afwesigheid of indien dit nie vir my moontlik is om
op te tree as direkteur nie, op te tree as direkteur
in my plek en om enige handeling by enige vergadering
of ander plek of instansie te doen wat ek sou kon
gedoen het as direkteur van die maatskappy PEP STORES
BEPERK en enige van sy filiale waarop ek as direkteur
dien en ek ratifiseer en bevestig enige handeling
gedoen deur gemelde JAMES WELLWOOD BASSON in navolging
van bogemelde volmag.

ALDUS gedoen en geteken te *Kuilsrivier* hierdie
29*ste* dag van OKTOBER 1974.

AS GETUIES:

1. W.J. Delport

2.

In October 1974, Renier van Rooyen gave Whitey unlimited power of attorney
to manage Pep. Whitey would cut his teeth at Pep and prepare himself for his
next major challenge: making Shoprite as big in groceries as Pep was in clothing.

Renier van Rooyen, founder of Pep Stores and Whitey's greatest mentor. Here he is standing in front of a Johannesburg branch of Papillon, a chain of fashion boutiques Pep acquired in June 1976.

What a bargain! An early Shoprite advertisement that highlights the all-important chickens.

Whitey and Barney Rogut, seasoned retailer and owner of Shoprite at the time of the acquisition. He would stay on at the company and school Whitey in the art of retail. They also became good friends.

A Chinese doctor treating Whitey for ankylosing spondylitis, 1981.

"Hello Darryl, Rob...ja, just wait, hold on a minute...OK Brian het jy Wilhelm op die cordless...right manne luister now goed - hier is die brief..."

Whirlwind Whitey in his Shoprite office, 1992.

Whitey apologising on his knees at a divisional meeting after losing a bet.

Whitey and Annalise outside a function in celebration of their 21st wedding anniversary. While Whitey focused on Shoprite, Annalise took charge of affairs at home.

Whitey always hankered after a return to farm life, and in the early 1990s he and Annalise decided to exchange the bustle of Bellville for the countryside. The house on Klein DasBosch was completed in 1993.

Whitey and Nikki on their horses at Klein DasBosch before setting off on a ride in the mountains, 1995. Standing in front are Mari, Cornell and Adrian.

Whitey and Annalise at one of the many annual functions hosted for the elderly at Klein DasBosch, 2002.

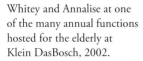

new population concentrations likely to emerge. Whitey believed that Shoprite's strategic approach to store location and market segmentation positioned the company ideally to meet these opportunities.

'We are proud of the fact that our growth has resulted in the creation of many new job opportunities. I am also delighted that, through a preferential placing, we were able to offer shares to a number of our business associates and make an allocation to the company's newly formed share incentive scheme. This scheme will enable our management and staff to participate in our future success.'

According to the 1988 annual report, staff of the company and the group held some 18 per cent of the total issued share capital of the company, both privately and through participation in the share incentive scheme.[10] Whitey, however, intended to increase employee participation in the profits of the company, as he regarded it as 'essential to motivation and the creation of individual wealth'.

The listing of a company naturally broadens the community of stakeholders, but Whitey's loyalty still lay mostly with his staff. 'Keeping the shareholders and the board happy was important to me, of course, but when it came to doing business, my primary focus was the people within the company. And that helped us a lot, because people were loyal and did so much more.

'I have always been a great believer in letting staff share in the profits of a company through shareholding. In the early years we gave our people – from receiving managers upwards – shares. Because when you go home, you want to be able to say: I'm a shareholder in Shoprite. And employees are proud of that, and consequently take more ownership. So when you notice something that is being done incorrectly, you say: don't do that, it's *my* money that you are losing. The pride of ownership is vital for successful businesses.'

During the 1980s Whitey's management style also began to take shape – and in his view, you can't be oversensitive if you want to be successful.[11] 'I like riling people up when the situation warrants it,' he admits. 'I get the truth out of them, and I get it fast.'[12]

Whitey learnt this 'style' from the managing director of a company called General Shopping, a Dr Alexander Siebin. General Shopping was a big investor in retail in South Africa and held shares in Pep Stores, among others. In fact, it was while Whitey was still at Pep Stores that he had crossed paths with Siebin.

'Siebin, a Swiss gentleman, came to look at our stores, and Tom Ball, a mild-mannered man, was very dejected that evening because Siebin had grilled him about his inventory. We were having dinner at Renier's house, together with Siebin. By then I was fed up with him because he was verging on arrogance. Our wives were also at the dinner, and at a point he again started asking such semi-aggressive questions. So, I became annoyed and told him: I don't work for you, I'm not your child, and when you ask me questions and you insinuate that I might be giving you the wrong answers, I want to have nothing to do with you. Go put your questions to some other sucker, but not to me.'

Siebin then invited Whitey to have breakfast with him the following morning. 'I apologised for the night before, since Renier was unhappy because I had given one of his biggest shareholders an earful. Siebin explained that his tough questions didn't imply that he didn't like us, he merely wanted to see whether we could handle the pressure. He hadn't meant anything by it, that was just his style. And then he said he felt very comfortable with his shareholding – his intention had only been to test us a bit.'

Siebin subsequently also arranged a number of overseas trips for Whitey so that he could seek information from other companies in developed countries. 'I learnt quite a lot. From the Swiss I learnt lessons about financial discipline and about marketing. For example, when you run an ad, you monitor what the impact is on sales. In South Africa, the guys would just carry on regardless – all that counts is your profit. In Switzerland everything would be measured, including the success of your marketing strategy. When you cut your prices, how much profit are you giving away and how many extra sales are you getting?

'I was a hard taskmaster at Shoprite, but I always put my people's needs first. And I was very fair. I don't think there is one person who can say that I wasn't fair. People also knew exactly where they stood with me.'

One of these people was Carel Goosen, who in 1987 also came over from Pep to join Shoprite. By that time Goosen, a chartered accountant like Whitey, had been working as an accountant at Pepkor for several years. Goosen recounts how he ended up at Shoprite: 'Jan le Roux was the financial director at that stage. When Whitey asked difficult questions at board meetings, Jan always used to say, let's ask Carel. Rumour has it that at a point Whitey asked Jan: "So why doesn't Carel attend the meetings then, and you stay outside?" Whitey decided later that he wanted me at Shoprite and so I moved there.' Goosen would work at the group for almost 30 years and become Whitey's right-hand man.

Goosen also describes the culture that was established at Shoprite. 'The company was successful, and we felt we were sharing in the success. When you did something, and you saw the results, you were motivated to achieve even better results and help the business grow further.

'Whitey is a phenomenal manager. Apart from the fact that he's very smart, he is a true entrepreneur, despite having been trained as an accountant. He doesn't have that conservative accountant mindset that I have, for instance. He could think on his feet and spot opportunities that not everyone was able to recognise.

'And we remained humble because the market never saw Shoprite as a glamorous investment. We started Shoprite for the bottom end of the market – everyone was always more excited about Pick n Pay and Woolworths, who targeted the top end. It was supposedly better to serve the aunties in high heels than the general worker, you know,' recounts Goosen.

'We always fought from that corner, always from below, and that, too, motivated us. And Whitey created that environment. He didn't make many mistakes, and it was nice working in an environment like that. He took good care of us financially as well. So, we really wanted to make our mark.'

* * * *

Shoprite wanted to make its mark in the whole of South Africa. Whitey and his team did in-depth research on how and where Shoprite should expand. According to retail strategist Doug Parker, who had done some work for Pep and had met Whitey there, the company did not follow a 'scattergun approach'. 'It didn't make sense to open stores one by one in Durban, Johannesburg and Vereeniging – that would create all kinds of logistical problems, and the management would be stretched thin. Whitey wanted to focus on a specific area and grow the business there before expanding to the next one.

'We analysed our rivals – where they were active, their market share, and so on – and the decision was that the greatest potential lay in the then Transvaal province.' In 1988 a branch was opened in Pietersburg, followed by one in Tzaneen.

'This says a lot about Whitey,' says Parker. 'He is bold but not reckless, and he doesn't make rash decisions. Once he had decided on something, he would first work it out carefully, do his homework, get his ducks in a row, and then go ahead.'

132

Without much fanfare, Shoprite expanded further to the rest of South Africa. 'Because Shoprite has no doubt whatsoever about its future and its position in the food retailing business in South Africa,' *Pep Nuus* wrote.[13] Whitey's next big acquisition, however, was to give him the necessary foothold in the Transvaal he had been looking for.

PART FOUR

THE ACQUISITION YEARS

16

A grand affair

I wasn't happy to run thirty or fifty stores.
My idea was to be as big in foodstuffs as
Pep Stores was in clothing.

– Whitey Basson[1]

In the early 1980s Whitey approached Grand Bazaars with an offer to acquire the company. This national retailer owned a number of stores in the Transvaal, which would give Shoprite's expansion a boost. Whitey still thought Shoprite was too small. 'We couldn't reach the size I wanted,' he states today. Shoprite also sought to augment its growth through acquisitions because it was (and still is) more difficult for smaller and lesser-known retailers to secure good locations for their stores. The owners of these good premises and centres mostly preferred doing business with the big, established chains.[2] Whitey saw the acquisition of Grand Bazaars as a way to start solving this problem.

'As a listed company, we knew we had to grow by at least 20 per cent per annum to attract attention,' recounts Carel Goosen, who was Shoprite's financial director at the time. 'And we knew if we only kept opening new branches, it would take us for ever to compete with Pick n Pay, Checkers and OK Bazaars. Without acquisitions we wouldn't be an opponent to be reckoned with. We adopted that as a strategy and started with Grand Bazaars.'

Whitey initially had his doubts about Grand Bazaars and its chief executive (CEO), Manual Sachar: 'One day I asked Manual to show me his storeroom. Between his office and his storeroom there was a specific route – one had to go in and out through doors, and in between buildings – and it turned out that he didn't know the route. Then I knew: the man never visits his storerooms, and he doesn't know what is going on in his business.'

This was of course contrary to Whitey's approach. 'At that stage my office and our storeroom was above the store in Lansdowne. On my arrival at the office in the mornings, I usually went up the stairs, walked into the storeroom, checked which orders were outstanding, and also chatted to the managers and the other people on the floor.' Moreover, Grand Bazaars was in the red, and Whitey wondered whether he would be able to turn the company around. 'I would always look at the weaknesses of the guys from whom we wanted to take over and ask myself: what are my chances of doing better?'

Whitey believed he could pull it off, but personalities proved to be the factor that complicated the deal and ultimately sank it. Sachar's conditions were the last straw. 'Sachar was a strong personality, and from the outset he tried to determine the agenda of the takeover. He said, for instance, that we had to work on Sundays because he didn't work on Saturdays. So I said in turn, I don't work on Sundays. And there were all kinds of conditions, such as safeguarding the positions of a brother, a brother-in-law, and other friends and family.'

Shoprite decided nonetheless to go ahead with the deal. 'Everything was on track, but then Manual came to us and demanded that he stay on as chairman of the new combined Shoprite and Grand Bazaars group.' To Whitey, this was not a big sticking point at first. 'We can make you super chairman, or whatever you want to be called,' he said. But the idea did not find favour with Barney Rogut. During Rogut's years at Grand Bazaars, there had been no love lost between him and Sachar. As mentioned earlier, it was a falling-out with the very same

Sachar years before that had caused Rogut to walk away from Grand Bazaars, whereafter he had started Shoprite.

'Barney said in that case he would rather resign because he didn't see his way clear to working with Manual again. Christo, too, was not happy with the proposal. I told Manual I'm not going to have Barney resign, and that it was an unreasonable request. The chairmanship was a crisis. And so we cancelled the deal a few hours before the cocktail party where it was supposed to have been celebrated.'

Not long afterwards, Carlos dos Santos from Metro Cash & Carry purchased Grand Bazaars and made it part of Score. According to Whitey, he soon realised that Dos Santos, who was more of a wholesaler, wouldn't make headway with the business. 'A few years later I walked around in one of his stores in Port Elizabeth and realised he was in trouble. Then I phoned him and said, sell the business to me because you're making a mess of it – you're a wholesaler and not a retailer.' They talked and soon struck a deal, as Score was indeed unable to turn Grand Bazaars around.

In August 1990 Shoprite bought Grand Bazaars (which had meanwhile been renamed Grand Supermarkets), which then comprised 27 stores, from Score for R18,6 million. 'And I think we bought the business for less than I would have paid Manual originally – but definitely for less than what Dos Santos had paid for it,' Whitey adds. He closed some of the stores and converted the rest into Shoprites. Suddenly Shoprite had more than 70 stores and had become a national chain overnight.

Another consequence of the acquisition of Grand Bazaars was that journalists, mainly the financial press, started taking a greater interest in Whitey. 'Wellwood', as they still mostly called him, was at that stage rather media shy. An article in the *Financial Mail* based on an interview in Whitey's 'office with no frills' shed light on his 'no-nonsense style':

Wellwood Basson says he won't go Hollywood. As MD of Shoprite Holdings, he might be expected to show his face in advertisements like some other supermarket impresarios. But that's not his style.

He says he's essentially a shopkeeper and prefers to focus on his primary goal – a profitable, well-run business. Not even a turnover now nudging R1bn from 75 supermarkets following his takeover of Grand Bazaars will tempt him into the spotlight.

He wants to avoid an interview, citing all the time demanded by the restructuring following the takeover. Then he doesn't want his photo taken: he isn't wearing a tie and he needs a haircut. But he finally relents, dons a Shoprite tie (what else?) and chats while the camera clicks.[3]

With regard to the start of Shoprite, he joked (a joke he would often repeat): 'We had a board meeting [at Pep] and it was decided that because I knew the difference between peas and baked beans, I would manage the food division.'

He said there was no 'magic formula' for success. Shoprite simply filled a gap in the market that was being neglected while the other players were 'busy chasing rainbows' and ignoring the need for good, basic marketing.

The article also provided a rare glimpse into his personal life. 'He used to play golf and is a keen fisherman [mainly at Langebaan], but the business bites into more and more of his free time,' the *Financial Mail* wrote. What he enjoyed most was relaxing around a braai fire with his family and friends, holding a glass of his favourite wine. 'His youthful looks belie his age [44], but he denies that it's an indication that running Shoprite is good for the health. "It's all in the genes," Whitey says.'

Following the acquisition of Grand Bazaars, Whitey's expansion plans were beginning to take shape, and he stuck to his goal of offering customers the lowest prices and the best value for their money. In 1988, a survey by the South African Consumer Council showed that a trolley of food cost R254,46 at Shoprite, followed by OK Bazaars (R258,69), Pick n Pay (R260,49), Checkers (R265,10) and Spar (R281,89). According to the survey, Shoprite was indeed South Africa's cheapest supermarket.[4]

17

Checkers goes downhill – and rises again

Why should we want to take over other people's problems, after all?
— Raymond Ackerman on the possibility of
purchasing the struggling Checkers.[1]

With Whitey at the helm, Shoprite was going from strength to strength. Checkers, on the other hand, was moving in the opposite direction. In March 1991 the press reported: having been ailing for years, Checkers was for sale. It still had a strong brand and was one of the three largest retailers in the country, along with OK Bazaars and Pick n Pay. The group, with Sergio Martinengo as managing director, comprised 168 stores across South Africa and had a turnover of R3,5 billion.[2] But it was suffering substantial losses.

This was the kind of challenge Whitey relished. He knew, too, that a further acquisition, after the recent purchase of Grand Bazaars, would bring him another step closer to the size he had always aspired to. But turning a supertanker like Checkers around was a daunting task. And besides, Whitey and his team were still engaged in the process of integrating Grand Bazaars into Shoprite. In its 35-year history, Checkers had seldom been profitable. Every few years there was a different person at the helm. A financial magazine described the company as a 'notorious retailers' graveyard'.[3]

Raymond Ackerman later wrote in his autobiography that when Checkers finally went broke, Pick n Pay weighed up the situation but decided against buying it. 'When . . . Whitey Basson took on the Shoprite challenge I admired their courage and respected their ambitions, but I remained well pleased that the challenge of Checkers was theirs and not mine.' And the challenge was indeed enormous. Checkers' losses almost equalled Shoprite's total turnover.[4]

* * * *

Checkers had a long history that was entwined with the development of supermarkets in South Africa. In 1927 – the same year in which OK Bazaars was founded – Harry Herber and his half-brother Somah opened a retailer they would later call Greatermans. In 1951 OK Bazaars opened a food division in its flagship store in Eloff Street, Johannesburg – the beginning of the 'supermarket' in South Africa. Herber then also opened a supermarket in one of his stores in Springs, where Raymond Ackerman worked as an assistant manager.

In 1954, following the death of his father, the 31-year-old Norman Herber took over the reins at Greatermans. He travelled to America to study retailing, where he got the idea for a food retailing chain. New York's yellow Checker taxicabs with their black-and-white chequered pattern served as inspiration for the name and colours of the envisaged new chain.[5] In 1955 Greatermans opened its first Checkers store, with yellow and black as the corporate colours.

By the mid-1960s Checkers was a national institution, with Ackerman leading its expansion as managing director. But after a heated disagreement he was unceremoniously fired by Norman Herber, a step many believed to have been the start of Checkers' woes. According to Ackerman, Marinus Daling, executive chairman of the insurance giant Sanlam, subsequently described this dismissal as the single greatest error in South African business history. A year after Ackerman's dismissal, he bought a few stores in Cape Town that were trading under the name Pick n Pay from the founder, Jack Goldin.[6]

By the time Whitey visited Daling one Sunday afternoon in the early 1990s, Pick n Pay was the market leader and Checkers a shadow of its former self. Around the braai fire, Whitey asked his friend Daling 'to get things in place so that we can do a deal'. Daling was at that stage also CEO of Sankorp, an investment arm of Sanlam. Sankorp controlled Tradegro, which in turn owned Checkers. Daling then decided to ask Whitey to take over the reins at Checkers and try to turn it around.

The financial media speculated about Checkers' fate, as well as who would be the best appointment to steer Checkers in a different direction. 'The easiest move would be to lure back Clive Weil [former MD of Checkers] . . . Even better, Shoprite's Basson would be worth a premium,' a report in the *Financial Mail* read.[7] Weil had been one of ten managing directors in ten years at Checkers and had become known for his 'trolley-for-trolley' TV adverts.

'So they sent a headhunter,' Whitey recounts, 'and offered me the world's money and shares. But I let them know: boys, this isn't a job for one man, you need a team to turn this thing around. And I'd rather commit suicide on the beach than in my office. I then proposed that Sankorp sell Checkers to us at a fair price and hold shares in the joint venture. Christo and his team would sort out the structure, with all kinds of shareholdings, and I would focus on the business. So Daling said, okay, let's sit around a table, and we began negotiating and came to an agreement. We finalised it quickly and merged the two groups.'[8]

Whitey makes the process sound simpler than it actually was. A complicated deal was struck which saw Shoprite reversed into Checkers' holding company. In terms of the deal, Shoprite became the owner of what would eventually be known as Shoprite Checkers.[9]

* * * *

One of the reasons why Whitey and Pepkor decided to take over Checkers regardless of its problems was the good price. Checkers had been in the market for so long, and the challenge was so formidable, that no one else was interested. Shoprite paid only about a quarter of the price they would have paid a year earlier.[10] In September of the previous year, Pepkor had been involved in negotiations whereby Pepkor would have bought Tradehold (the holding company of Checkers owner Tradegro), but that deal had fallen through.

But this time things fell into place and Whitey and co. knew it was a golden opportunity. Checkers would give Shoprite a large footprint in the white suburbs and increase the size of the company very quickly. At that stage it would have cost about R1 billion to establish a chain of Checkers' size. It had taken Shoprite more than ten years to grow to more than 70 stores. 'With the acquisition of Checkers, Pepkor bought 30 years in time, as it were,' wrote *Finansies & Tegniek*.

At the same time, no supermarket group of that size in South Africa had ever really succeeded. Shoprite stood at just over 70 stores and was still relatively small. Pick n Pay stood at 120 stores (including 14 hypermarkets) and was sailing on. But the two giants in the market were struggling. Checkers stood at 170, and OK Bazaars, which had also been ailing for years, at just over 200. For the year ending February 1991, Shoprite's sales stood at about R732 million – peanuts compared to Checkers' turnover of about R3,5 billion.[11]

* * * *

Just before the takeover, Whitey and his senior management team visited all the Checkers branches in Port Elizabeth one Saturday. Gerhard

Fritz was the general manager of Checkers Greenacres, which at that stage was achieving the biggest turnover in the entire Checkers group. 'When Whitey walks into a room, everyone can see immediately he's the boss,' recounts Fritz. 'He's larger than life – once you've met him or talked to him, you'll never forget him again.

'Whitey walked through the whole store and pointed out mistakes. Barney Rogut was with him, and between the two of them they more or less pulled my store apart. Then we walked to the OK, and there too I had to hear how wrong and bad the OK was.' At that point the acquisition of Checkers had not yet been completed, and Fritz failed to understand 'how the guys could be so outspoken about a business that didn't even belong to them'.

Whitey invited Fritz to lunch, but his pride had been hurt and he declined the invitation. 'Later that afternoon, someone came to the store with Whitey Basson's phone number on a piece of paper and a message that I should phone him at seven o'clock that evening.' Whitey then told Fritz that he wanted him at Shoprite, 'but he also told me I shouldn't be so touchy'.

Today, 30 years later, Fritz is still at Shoprite and the chief operating officer of their non-RSA outlets. Over three decades he has learnt that Whitey will make no bones about telling you that you are wrong, and how things are really supposed to work. 'But everyone knew where they stood with him. Sometimes he would be too forthright. But when you proposed something, you knew exactly what he thought of it, and if he considered it a bad idea, he would tell you so bluntly. After a bruising session like that he would always call to tell you he's not angry with you and that he actually likes you, but you just need to fix what is wrong, and then we move on.

'It was because he was passionate about his company and was constantly looking for new ways of improving things,' Fritz adds. 'As leader he was steadfast and totally focused on making Shoprite the biggest retailer. And the thought of leaving never even crossed your mind because you had a fantastic job, with many possibilities and huge responsibilities, and you were generously compensated for it.'

* * * *

While the experience Whitey had gained through previous acquisitions came in handy, the takeover was 'of course a big training school for us, because in the case of Checkers the losses almost exceeded the entire profits of the rest of the group', he told the author Theo Vorster.[12] On 30 October 1992 Whitey appeared on the cover of *Finansies & Tegniek* where he was shown standing in Shoprite's warehouse. The cover line read: 'Hoe Whitey Basson Checkers regruk' (How Whitey Basson is turning Checkers around).

One of the first things he did was to change the internal culture. He believed that every cent they could save at Shoprite had to be passed on to the customer. 'Barney always reminded us that in our industry there are only two cents' profit in every rand. If you waste those two cents, you suffer a loss,' Whitey told Die Burger.[13]

At Shoprite, therefore, frugality was the order of the day. At Checkers, the opposite was true. On the first day he walked into the Checkers head office in Johannesburg at 220 Commissioner Street, Whitey was struck by the extravagance. And his turnaround started that very same day. Later he recounted during a radio interview: 'And its marble floors, and the top management are sitting on a floor of their own, and I see everything that is contrary to what Shoprite stands for. That afternoon I saw a guy I knew in the corridor, and I invited him for lunch, but he said thanks but no thanks – here you are fired straight off if you're not on the right level and you go to eat in managements' dining room.

'So we ate there that afternoon, and I felt like someone in those movies where you are dining with Cleopatra and people serve you grapes and pour your wine, and how would you like your steak, the waiters with the white gloves ask. And all I'm thinking is – how much does all of this cost? Because it's larney, it's like the Mount Nelson, and no one else is allowed to come there, only the top management.

'I knew then that this was not the type of culture I wanted. It just didn't fit in with a supermarket that wanted to offer the lowest prices. So I said: you guys have probably heard of the last supper, well, this was the last lunch, and this afternoon I'm locking the dining room. And give the food that's left to the poor, because from tomorrow we're eating our own sandwiches.' They would no longer waste Shoprite's money. From then on lunch at Checkers meant 'that at five o'clock you realise you've missed your lunch altogether'.[14]

The other problem was that Checkers was not managed by people on the shop floors but by management in their fancy offices. Whitey's mantra had always been the opposite. 'We had bought a business with just a name – there was no fire or drive or energy. It was run by people in boardrooms.'[15] Changing the company culture was one of the first steps in turning Checkers around. Although Whitey and his team were ready to take Checkers over, it was still 'nerve-racking because if you're losing that kind of money per day, you have to work very fast and very hard. But it wasn't as if we were scared of doing it, or that we didn't believe we were capable of turning it around'.[16]

18

The retail wizard

Trust everyone – but brand your cattle.
— Whitey to a colleague.[1]

Some were initially sceptical about the acquisition, as previous attempts to revive Checkers had all failed. The internal culture was but one of numerous problems. For a long time, Checkers had not been run by 'real' shopkeepers, and with Whitey and his team at the helm, remedying this defect was the first step in the right direction. In some circles there was also scepticism about Whitey, for in the view of analysts he had not yet proved himself as 'an entrepreneur of a large retail chain'.[2]

Whitey had to get cracking at once to put the business on a different trajectory and to prove his critics wrong. *The Financial Mail* wrote that Shoprite's plan to 'revive' Checkers would have to be quite radical.[3] According to Whitey, it was simple: 'I turned Checkers around by running it like a business. I walked in and made sure everything was done right. Show me your books, and how much time are you guys spending on administration and how much time on the floor? The culture was changed, stores were cleaned, and dead wood was cut out,' he recounts. To save costs, Checkers' head office was moved from Johannesburg to Parow. The four key pillars of the company – marketing, properties, financial administration and personnel administration – were now controlled by Whitey and his Cape Town team.

During a branch visit in Bloemfontein, Whitey also soon realised that the bookkeeping was nothing to write home about. 'Every branch had an accountant, which was totally unnecessary. But in Bloemfontein the accountant had a whole ledger that just kept getting thicker and thicker every month. So I asked the guy, but how are you working with this stuff? It's like the bookkeeping that is taught to a child in standard two.

'So Callie Goosen and I looked at all the existing financial reports, covered four of five tables with stacks of all kinds of reports, and threw about 70 per cent of them away. And no one came back to us and asked, where is my important report. I designed new management reports – much simpler and easier to understand. Within six months there was only a single four-page report on the financial position of every store, containing only the most important statistics such as sales per customer and inventory turnover – something that didn't exist before. Suddenly the branch managers were part of the business – they knew exactly what was going on and what they needed to work on.'

He also expected his managers to be shopkeepers in the true sense of the word and not to manage their stores from an office. Morale was low at Checkers, and an incentive scheme was introduced. 'It's the old principle of profit sharing – people work harder if they stand to gain something from it. I didn't think it up – that's just how it is, and how human nature works,' says Whitey.

The new group had 240 branches that were divided into six regions: two regions each in the Transvaal and the Cape Province, and one each in the Free State and Natal. Whitey appointed a general manager for each region with a chartered accountant as right-hand man, as well as a head of purchasing and marketing. 'And then I would fly around once a month and visit each division.'

The staff complement had to be reduced. To Whitey, this was not an easy exercise because people are his passion. He wanted to work alongside his people and believed this was where the power of a successful business lay. 'It was painful to realise that we had to get rid of some staff – by way of early retirement, or transfers. It's terribly hard to choose between, say, a thousand people who may lose their jobs and 17 000 or so to whom you can give a better future,' Whitey recounted in an interview after the takeover.[4] 'But for those 17 000 employees you were restoring their human dignity – by *not* working for a business where others constantly impress on them that they are actually in a bad way, *not* having to wonder whether they would still be there next year . . .'

Today, Whitey wonders whether they may perhaps have acted over-hastily. 'We had to get rid of the weaker people and relieve people of duties that were meaningless, more or less overnight. I may have done it too quickly, and we lost a few good people as a result of my cowboy style. But there were thousands of superfluous employees.' On completion of the process, Checkers and Shoprite combined had about 19 000 employees, compared to the 22 000 Checkers alone had in their employ at the time of the takeover.[5]

* * * *

One of those who did not count among the 'weaker people' was Cobus Zwennis. As regional manager at the ailing Checkers, he crossed paths with Whitey at the time of the takeover. 'In his brutally frank but motivating way, Whitey informed us of what was happening and what he expected of us,' Zwennis recounts. 'What impressed me most was his in-depth knowledge of our doings with regard to our achievements in Checkers. I walked out of there and told my colleagues: "With a man like that at the helm we're going to reach great heights." It was exhilarating getting up every morning knowing you were now working for a dynamic and successful retail group with abundant opportunities for promotion, provided you did your part.

'Mr Basson's puckish sense of humour was always something worth witnessing. He also had the ability to concentrate on two things simultaneously, which made it quite nerve-racking for the person leading a meeting. For instance, during meetings he would be concentrating intently on a memorandum or figures in front of him and then suddenly ask you a question that had you jumping around like a cat on hot bricks. I quickly learnt: know your facts 100 per cent!'

* * * *

Lease agreements were another headache at Checkers, but in reality, yet another golden opportunity to get the company into shape. 'My biggest worry was, how do I get rid of Checkers' bad premises?' says Whitey today. They were not only bad because of unfavourable lease agreements but also as a result of poor locations, design and layout. Space utilisation was not optimal – the sales per square metre were low – and Whitey requested drawings for every building and store with the underutilised spaces indicated in red.

'It was shocking to behold, and a major reason why they were performing so poorly. Turning this around was a huge process, and I devoted much attention to it. They had also entered into bad lease agreements – the rent is three times too high, the poor branch manager can't make a profit, so he never gets a bonus either.'

These bad agreements had their origins in the early 1980s, when Checkers had expanded rapidly. In an attempt to improve its cash flow, the company had sold its interests in new properties through leaseback transactions, whereby it leased the properties back from the purchaser. Clauses in the lease agreements forced it to keep the stores open. Checkers was therefore obliged to pay rent and remain open, in certain cases for 20 years, even if the stores in question were not profitable and it would have been better to close them.[6]

Whitey and his team renegotiated dozens of these agreements. 'I walked in one morning and said that no branch would pay more than two per cent of its turnover on rent, and the rest we'd pay from head office. Store managers immediately responded positively and picked up courage again. Besides, it meant that we lost fewer of our managers to the competition.'

Whitey and his team were also faced with a massive decision: do they create a new brand for the whole group, do they keep either the Checkers or the Shoprite brand, or do they retain both? Whitey enlisted the help of retail strategist Doug Parker, who specialised inter alia in 'strategic market positioning'. Parker had done work for Pep before, and had met Whitey then. 'My first impression of Whitey was rather a strange one,' he recounts. 'I was doing a big presentation to Pepkor's senior management, and it included a five-year plan. Right at the end I added something extra – by then Pep was well established and represented nationally, and there were not many possibilities for new locations.'

So, he proposed that Pep start a new chain with children's clothing for more affluent consumers. Parker knew of Whitey at that stage, but had never met him in person. 'I was explaining the idea when a fair-haired man walked in and sat down. After about five minutes, he stood up and said: "This is a load of crap," and walked out again. I wanted to know who he was. "Don't worry", someone said. "It's Whitey Basson, and that is just what he's like."'

Parker did not hear from Whitey until, some months later, Whitey asked him to come and see him at his office. 'Naturally, I was quite surprised and wondered what the meeting would be about. Whitey was under pressure to expand Shoprite, and they had three possible premises in mind. He wanted me to evaluate them thoroughly because he couldn't afford to make a mistake so soon after the takeover.'

Parker and his team analysed the premises, estimating among other things how many 'feet' would come through the doors and what turn-overs one could expect. 'Our research proved to be spot-on, and the stores were successful,' he says. 'Whitey and I became good friends, and over the next 30 years we did most of Shoprite's research for new store development. From the outset Whitey understood the value of research and once he saw how credible it could be, he strongly relied on it.'

Accordingly, thorough research was also done regarding the two brands. 'The Checkers brand was simply too good to be abandoned,' Parker relates, 'and Shoprite was an up-and-coming brand with good momentum.' Hence the question was how they should best exploit both brands. In the end they decided to retain the separate brands for the stores but to advertise them together. While Shoprite focused on the middle- to lower-income market, Checkers targeted the middle- to high-income market. Whitey adds: 'I felt we needed several more brands because of the disparities among our customers, who ranged from rich to poor. Thus, we reduced Usave's prices to even below those of Shoprite, and offered more limited product ranges in smaller markets in other ways as well. But all of this had to be done at the right time.'

* * * *

Whitey knew his customers and these market segments, and quickly worked out where he should convert a Checkers into a Shoprite. In the first year, nineteen Checkers branches were rebranded as Shoprites and their sales rose immediately.[7] He and his management team also intended to position more of the Checkers stores in the broader middle market by converting them into Shoprites.[8]

Although the stores themselves retained their names, they advertised jointly as the somewhat clumsy 'Shoprite Checkers'. According to Whitey, they decided on this because the group couldn't sustain two separate advertising budgets. Nevertheless, the problem of size was solved through the acquisition of Checkers. 'Checkers was a good takeover for us in the sense that it gave us the size – prior to that we didn't have scalability,' he explains.

The new size provided another benefit. A large part of the success or failure of a supermarket group depends on its inventory management, and how quickly it can pay its creditors. The speed with which it sold its products was in the hands of the company, but because of its size Shoprite Checkers could negotiate more favourable discounts and credit terms with its suppliers. If the products could move off the shelves within 30 days, on average, and the company could maintain or improve its average payment term, Shoprite Checkers ought to do well.

Moreover, they now received offers for prime positions in shopping centres that would previously rather have been earmarked for Pick n Pay. 'When we added Checkers, we had sufficient turnover to really take on the rest of the market,' Whitey states. 'For the first time we were invited into major shopping centres. Previously, it would only be Checkers, Pick n Pay or OK. We never got the chance to go into Kenilworth Centre or any other profitable shopping centres. The result was that we were not close enough to throw a punch.'

* * * *

In a remarkable turnaround, the new company was profitable again after only nine months. Thousands of jobs had been saved. 'We worked our butts off and were never at home – we were always on our way to somewhere,' Carel Goosen relates. 'We would fly up to Johannesburg on Tuesdays to do Checkers work and fly back on Thursdays, and did Shoprite work on Fridays, Mondays and over weekends.'

Their Herculean efforts paid off. In the 1993 financial year, a year of 'extremely difficult trading conditions', the group made an operating profit of R38,9 million, against a loss of R24,5 million the year before, and its turnover grew by 14 per cent to R5,3 billion. This was due to streamlined operations, effective cost management, enhanced discipline, and an aggressive focus on the lowest prices.[9] The group now operated 235 stores countrywide, and their market share was close on one-third of the supermarket industry. All of a sudden Whitey was boxing in the heavyweight category.

It was 'an influential position which we will use single-mindedly to benefit our customers whose spending power propels our business. Our business will continue to be driven by the fulfilment of the needs of these customers by providing them with the lowest prices in the cleanest stores,' Whitey wrote in the 1993 annual report of the company, which was temporarily known as Tradegro.

He told *Rapport* why he enjoyed visiting the stores personally. 'Once a month I talk to the workers on my farm at Porterville. We sit down under a tree and we *talk* . . . The same with the fishermen at Langebaan. They possess great wisdom. They have plenty of time to think while they sit there fishing . . . I like all kinds of people. That's why I try to visit the stores myself as much as possible. There I hear the truth – what is really happening on the shop floors.'[10] Few chief executives showed such interest in their staff, from cashiers to senior managers. At the top of every page in Whitey's diary were the names and phone numbers of employees whose birthday fell on that day. He would call them personally to congratulate them.

At the time of the takeover, Sergio Martinengo was managing director of Checkers. When they asked him to stay on, but under Whitey as

MD, he had no qualms about saying yes. 'Why? Because I had got to know this urbane young man who exuded an air of confidence and focus. He told things as they were, never beating about the bush, and at the same time always being the perfect gentleman.'[11]

Today, Whitey says: 'Sergio assisted us enormously. I asked him right at the start to help keep the staff members calm and get them on board for a merger between Shoprite and Checkers, and therefore also to ensure that we didn't lose good people. Unfortunately, we did lose a number of good people who didn't give us a chance, but Sergio was prepared to do so. He and I are still very good friends today.'

* * * *

Whitey also realised that as CEO of one of the country's largest retail groups, he would now be more in the limelight and therefore had to change his attitude towards the media. 'I'd always tried to maintain a low media profile,' he explains. 'But when we bought Checkers, it was said that in order to have a successful business in food retail, people needed to know they could trust the company and those behind it – it's almost like the brand of a big bank.'

There was quite a debate about what name he should use. Up to that stage he had mostly been referred to as Wellwood, in Shoprite's own reports and media statements and thus in the media too. 'Then I said, I'm Whitey. Some people feared it might be perceived as having a racial connotation. But it went down well because I said it's not a name that intimidates you – it's your pal Whitey.'

Accordingly, *Rapport* interviewed 'Checkers' Whitey Basson' and asked what changes regular customers of Checkers could expect following the takeover. 'The lowest prices,' he replied. 'We're going to introduce Shoprite's low prices in Checkers. Furthermore, hygiene has to be of the highest quality and the perishable products fresh. But we *will* be the cheapest.'

Once again, he used the boxing analogy. He was asked about stress and burnout. 'It depends on what kind of pressure you put on yourself,' he replied. 'We have an informal management style. We still laugh during board meetings. We don't use all kinds of highfalutin jargon. We don't waste time on unnecessary rubbish. And the longer you've boxed in the backstreets, the longer you can carry on boxing. I've boxed in the backstreets for a long time – figuratively speaking. No, actually this job is the only one I know . . .'[12]

19

Exodus to Stellenbosch

I grew up on a farm and need space around me so I can breathe, walk and think. My farm in Stellenbosch is essential in recharging my batteries. It's incredible how many ideas come to me as I walk to the horses or inspect the vines.

– Whitey Basson[1]

Whitey may not have been feeling the pressure, but the bustle of the city bothered him. Since his days as an auditing clerk, he had been a city dweller and he hankered after farm life. According to Annalise, Whitey felt the city was 'suffocating' him. The family regularly spent weekends at DasBosch, the family farm outside Porterville. But Whitey had been looking for his own place on the outskirts of Stellenbosch for some time. Stellenbosch was the town where he had been a student, where he wanted his children to attend school and hopefully later go to university as well. He wanted to keep horses and perhaps dabble in some winemaking with a few hectares of vines.

And then, a few kilometres outside the town, past the suburb of Paradyskloof on the banks of the Blaauwklippen River, he found the ideal place. 'I can still remember the night I realised I was unable to unwind in Welgemoed. That's why I bought this farm – so that I could close my gate and relax,' Whitey told a reporter in his study at Klein DasBosch.[2]

The farm was called 'Step Aside' but Whitey renamed it Klein DasBosch.

Another reason for their move was that Whitey and Annalise wanted to have their children close to them if they should decide to go to university. Their elder daughter, Nikki, would soon become a student at Maties, and their elder son, Adrian, was already a pupil at Paul Roos Gymnasium. The two laatlammetjies, Mari and Cornell, would be enrolled at Laerskool Eikestad before continuing their high-school careers at Bloemhof and Paul Roos respectively.

* * * *

Annalise finally got the opportunity to realise her dream of designing a new house with an architect. Once the building was completed, the family moved from Welgemoed to Stellenbosch. It is a modern house – spacious, but simple – next to a dam with ducks, a paddock and stables, situated among vineyards and surrounded by trees and mountains. The house is divided into three sections, each of which can be closed off with glass doors. The front section is for formal functions. In the middle section, where the kitchen is also located, they entertain close friends and spend time together as a family. The third section is private, with bedrooms and bathrooms for the family members. The house is designed in such a way that if Whitey wanted to go to bed while people were still partying, he could do so.

In 1997 Whitey talked to the magazine *Sarie* about his own involvement in the design of the house. 'In the first number of years at Shoprite I visualised many stores and saw them coming into being, but in recent years my position has become more management-oriented, with the result that I can't always take part in the creative process. It was nice to satisfy that creative hankering with our own place. I like an open lifestyle, an outdoor orientation.'[3]

When it comes to design, says Annalise, Whitey has only two words:

'yes or no, and it's usually no!' He adds in mitigation: 'I've been influenced by magnetic fields since childhood. The foundations had already been poured when I realised I'd never be able to come to rest. So I had the entire house turned more towards the mountain by about three metres.'

According to the architect, Louis Steyn, he and Whitey were often at odds. Steyn was inspired by the Bauhaus style of architecture – simplified, rational and functional design, and a geometric and abstract style without any sentiment or nods to historical precedent.[4]

A word to the wise is enough, and Steyn says that while Whitey was one of his most difficult clients, he was the quickest at grasping his ideas and concepts. 'He definitely had a sense of design.' Steyn and his company would eventually also design stores and centres for Shoprite, and today Steyn considers Whitey and Annalise good family friends.

Regarding Klein DasBosch, Annalise related in an interview with *Die Burger*: 'There was nothing here in the beginning. We struggled like mad to get everything to what it looks like today. But it was delightful to see all of it taking shape.' Most people know Whitey as a hard-boiled businessman, but as a husband and father he is the complete opposite, and as a result of the move to Stellenbosch he could see his children more often.[5]

Today, Annalise says the house was always filled with students and the younger children's friends. 'Those were good times because Whitey enjoyed the young people a lot. He enjoyed giving advice and seeing how they developed. Our home was also always "open for business". There was seldom silence, but it was tremendously stimulating. Here people argued, fought, negotiated and planned from early morning till late at night.' Whitey jokes: 'We always made sure we were stocked up with food and wine, so they would drop in regularly with their pals.'

While Whitey was at least now sometimes surrounded by the

tranquillity of the farm, life at the helm of a big supermarket group was anything but tranquil. In 2010 he related: 'I go to sleep every night with a notebook next to my bed – nowadays with a tape recorder. Among other things, after every function or meeting I try to keep a record of anything someone said that can help the business to perform better. Because you have to stay ahead.'[6]

At night he did 'routine work' he had not got around to in the course of the day. 'I can never fall asleep unless I know everything I needed to do has been completed. And I wake up at night and don't go back to sleep again. Much of my thinking is done at night when I'm supposed to be sleeping. If something bothers me, I write it down or put it on tape – what do I have to do urgently tomorrow morning? Then I would get up the next morning with clearer vision. My dad always used to say, you don't make big decisions at night, you wait until the next morning. And that's what I did as well – I would first become calm in the shower, and plan the day in my head. I shower until the geyser is empty and then tackle the day.'

He also learnt a form of meditation from Renier van Rooyen that helped him fall asleep. 'Renier had a record, and later a tape, and I had it copied onto a CD. It's just a metronome and a calm voice that tells you to raise your feet, breathe in and breathe out, and relax. And in that way, I could hypnotise myself. We would be invited to parties and Annalise would say, gosh, you look so tired. There would often be a couch with the curtains and windows directly behind it, so I would take a nap behind the couch among the curtains for about an hour or two. When people asked where I was, Annalise would say, he's probably outside in the garden, chatting to someone. Meanwhile I'm fast asleep behind the couch!'

* * * *

An issue that did give Whitey sleepless nights, however, was labour relations. In 1993 the South African Commercial, Catering and Allied Workers' Union (Saccawu) and some 10 000 Shoprite Checkers employees embarked on a strike that lasted five weeks. During the takeover of Checkers Whitey realised that the trade union's recognition agreement, which dated from the early 1980s, included several outmoded practices, and he wanted to negotiate a new agreement. 'I tore up the Checkers wage agreement – I told them, I don't keep to agreements that are one-sided.'

For instance, short and minor disruptive strikes were a regular occurrence because the company couldn't dismiss workers if they went on strike for less than five hours. Workers were also allowed to appeal against disciplinary steps up to three times, which took up a great deal of the managers' time.[7] Saccawu missed the deadline for negotiating the new recognition agreement with Shoprite and was very unhappy when it lapsed. 'So they wanted to strike. And I said, strike if you want to. But you need to understand that it will be cheaper for me to close certain stores than to keep them open.'

The strike went ahead. 'And I closed stores and only paid the rent. In Port Elizabeth in particular they made me very angry. When the strike was nearing its end, I kept the store closed and said: *I* am still on strike. I'm not going to open now, this is my time to strike because I have a business to turn around. And if you don't understand that, you're going to lose your jobs because then I can keep the shops closed permanently.'

Finally, Whitey and the trade unions arrived at an agreement. Although a large part of the old recognition agreement was reinstated, certain provisions that would have made it more difficult to do business were changed into more practical arrangements.[8]

Whitey knew full well that in the long run they would have to cooperate better, for the good of the company and its employees. 'We sat around a table and said, we can't hurt each other like that – we must make and agree on compromises that help the employees, the customers and the shareholders. And we had to make a plan to get our trade unions on board. Many of the strikes were politically motivated, and we wanted to get the trade unions to understand our world better.'

Consequently, they arranged that the company would send a certain number of shop stewards to other countries annually so they could learn from other trade unions, gain insight into how labour relations were managed and how the retail sector operated. 'They could choose where they wanted to go, for a few weeks at a time, not just to have a holiday but also to meet trade union leaders in those countries, to look at how they did things and to see what viable solutions there were. Because we can't always argue about political situations, clash constantly, and push a socialist world view against a company that wants to move ahead and create jobs.

'The mere fact that they were able to rub shoulders with people from other cultures – like in the United States – held great advantages. You can say what you like, but the United States is in many respects more advanced than the rest of the world. So our people not only gained trade union ideas but also saw how retail worked in other countries, and that was very important. One year they chose Cuba, and on their return they said they didn't want to go there again because it's not a nice place!' Whitey says with a laugh.

* * * *

Klein DasBosch would also become the venue for legendary parties and functions – for colleagues, employees and suppliers. Annalise realised that Whitey was married to Shoprite and its people, so they had to become part of her family too.[9] When Whitey started at Pep Stores, everyone had been like one big family, and this was again the case at Shoprite, she recounts. 'Just after we had settled into our home, we started organising informal functions every year just before Christmas so that members of the top management could socialise around the pool with nice food, wine and music.

'These get-togethers gradually evolved into bigger functions with more guests, food, wine and music. Beautiful performances were presented by well-known South African artists. That was how we became good friends with many of our talented South African performing artists. They performed regularly at Shoprite promotions as well, and it was also Whitey's aim to offer young artists new opportunities.'

At one stage four Christmas functions for up to 200 guests each were organised in their front garden in the space of one week. These would later become two events, with up to 800 guests per night. One function was for Shoprite staff and the other for suppliers, with prizes in different categories awarded on each night. Staff flew to Cape Town from across Africa to attend the functions.

Parties were also held for the elderly. The parties for senior citizens were at first modest gatherings, with just umbrellas on the lawn and snacks and drinks for about 150 people. As the parties grew, Whitey offered that Shoprite would sponsor the functions. Annalise relates: 'It later became a big event. The people were transported in buses to Klein DasBosch and driven to the tent in golf carts. They were treated to tea and cake, as well as a delicious lunch. Artists performed voluntarily, and we also got soapie stars to attend the event so that the elderly guests could take photos of themselves with the celebrities.'

20

Whirlwind Whitey

The heights by great men reached and kept were not attained
by sudden flight. But they, while their competition slept, were
toiling upward in the night.

– A quote by Henry Wadsworth Longfellow
that Whitey's mother Maude instilled in him.[1]

After the transition to democracy in 1994, Whitey and his team maintained their single-minded focus on the mass market, which held significant growth potential. With 20 million shoppers visiting its outlets monthly, Shoprite Checkers was now one of the country's largest food retailers.[2] With the economy just emerging from a six-year recession, the group's growing success was a remarkable feat – particularly considering that only a few years before the survival of Checkers had been under serious threat and the jobs of about 20 000 staff had been at risk.

Poverty and unemployment, however, were still a major concern. Whitey highlighted this challenge in the 1995 annual report: '. . . the country now faces the huge task of overcoming massive unemployment and poverty. If the Government's policy of reconstruction and development is to succeed, it must focus on a high and sustained growth of the economy. Economic efficiency must be based on sound macro-economic policies, reinforced by cooperation between government, labour and business.'

But he stated that they were 'optimistic, not only about South Africa, but also about the African continent, which is awakening as a force in the world economy, in which we intend to play an active part' – the first indication of the company's plans to expand into Africa.

A nationwide survey for March 1994 conducted by the Housewives League of South Africa showed that Shoprite Checkers was fulfilling its mission of offering its customers the lowest prices. A basket of 43 basic unbranded items cost R193,47 at Shoprite, which was less than at OK, Pick n Pay and Spar.[3]

* * * *

By 1996 the group's profit margins had improved considerably, and Whitey could sleep more peacefully. One of the targets they had set at the time of acquiring Checkers was to achieve an operating margin of 2 per cent – the industry norm of the food retail sector – by 1996. The operating margin is how much profit a business makes on a rand of sales after paying its costs (excluding interest and tax). Competition in the sector was among the fiercest in the world. In other parts of the world – including the United States – the margins were 4–5 per cent.

Shoprite showed that the successful supermarket groups were those that were 'penny-wise' and met customer needs.[4] Whitey attributed their performance to their combatting of losses due to shrinkage (theft, actually) and the fact that costs had risen by less than the turnover.[5] In his chairman's report in the 1996 annual report, Christo Wiese ascribed the group's success to a sense of purpose, a will to win, and the entrepreneurial spirit that management 'have blended with the professional manner in which they conduct business'.[6]

The will to win meant that Whitey and his team did not rest on their laurels. Shoprite extended its reach considerably with the takeover of Sentra, a central buying organisation for 550 independent supermarkets. The acquisition allowed Shoprite to expand into franchising and to compete in smaller markets where the focus was on convenience.[7] In the past this had been mainly Spar's territory, with no noteworthy competition. Shoprite was now in a position to take Spar on in towns and in rural areas where a Shoprite outlet wouldn't necessarily have succeeded,[8] and it also had much greater buying power.

The purchase price of R21 million for the total business included the brand names Sentra Red Band, Sentra Blue Band, Megasave and Value Stores.[9] The plan was that Sentra would continue operating under its existing management, who would be supported by the Shoprite corporate division. Shoprite also acquired the remaining interest in Freshmark, which supplied the group's stores with fresh fruit and vegetables. The majority interest in Freshmark had already been acquired along with Checkers. As a counter to George Hadjidakis's successful 7-Eleven chain of convenience stores, which already boasted more than 100 outlets,[10] Shoprite launched a new chain of smaller, extended-hours stores called 8 Till Late.

Whitey always kept a close watch on his rivals. 'I want to know what my rivals are doing and how they think,' he told *Die Burger* in August 1997. 'My senior managers must visit a competitor's store on a weekly basis and report on one good aspect. I believe everyone can learn from their competitors. Renier van Rooyen always used to say it's better to fight against the smart guys because the third-team players only hurt you and cost you money on top of that.'[11]

* * * *

Shoprite also entered the fast-food market with its first fried-chicken restaurant, Hungry Lion. The first restaurant was in Stellenbosch, but it gradually became a chain. Whitey had already considered expanding into this sector at an earlier stage. The acquisition of Checkers included a factory that produced potato chips, and Whitey himself once visited Chicago to discuss 'fast-food outlets across Africa' with McDonald's.

Expectations were created. Shoprite Checkers conducted research on where it could source the special kind of potatoes for McDonald's chips. Representatives of the American fast-food giant visited South Africa and were given a tour of Shoprite Checkers premises. 'We were kept hanging the whole time, and the next thing we knew, McDonald's opened its first franchise in South Africa,' Whitey recounted.[12] Talks with Burger King had fizzled out as well.

This snub served as a further incentive for Whitey. 'According to the students, McDonald's sells the best milkshake in Stellenbosch. So, I instructed my team to sell a tastier milkshake at ten cents less within one week,' he related when Hungry Lion was launched. The profit margins on fast food were considerably higher than those on groceries, which was of course attractive to Shoprite. The group was already buying vast quantities of chicken and, given its bargaining power, it would also be able to sell fried chicken at a lower price.[13]

* * * *

While Whitey was endeavouring to diversify locally in a saturated market for supermarkets, the cover of the group's 1996 annual report gave an idea of its new focus: it featured a drawing in green of the African continent. In Zambia, Shoprite had bought six shops from the country's state-owned National Home Stores chain for R10 million. The supermarket in Lusaka would begin operating in October 1996, and the others in December. Shoprite Checkers was also developing a shopping centre worth R28 million in Maputo. It was the first of its kind in Mozambique, South Africa's neighbour.

Whitey told the *Financial Mail* he was 'totally comfortable' with expansion to the rest of Africa. Although Africa's buying power was considerably less than that of South Africa, and it would only be able to sustain one chain-store group, the group with first-mover advantage would 'enjoy many good years of trading'.[14]

In 1997 Shoprite ventured into financial services as well. Its customers could now buy insurance with their chicken, milk and bread. Furthermore, the company announced it would sell uniquely structured funeral policies. The Old Mutual Group Schemes and the HT Group, which included Goodall & Williams, underwrote the product and were also partners in the venture. This unusual step saved customers not only time but money too – the policies were up to 40 per cent cheaper than 'conventional' policies with similar cover. This was possible because Shoprite cut out the middleman and utilised its existing systems.

Whenever people told Whitey, 'There's a gap in the market,' he would ask them: 'Is there a market in the gap?' Here, there were both a gap and a market. 'About 20 million customers visit our points of sale every month, and the policies become much more accessible. Applicants don't even need to have a bank account,' Whitey explained.[15] This initiative demonstrated once again how Whitey focused on his customers' needs and made decisions that were best for his business. In this case, he was now selling Old Mutual policies despite the fact that their insurance rival Sanlam was the second-largest shareholder in Pepkor – Shoprite's major shareholder.

'We have a responsibility to our shareholders but also an obligation to our customers,' he told *Die Burger*. 'Putting business profit of R250 million into question because your shareholders have certain interests is not acceptable to the customers.'[16] Shoprite was opening stores left, right and centre. Whitey regularly visited all the branches in South Africa, explored opportunities in the rest of Africa, and held meeting upon meeting.

* * * *

A magazine described his whirlwind schedule as follows: 'Just recently, his working week started on a public-holiday Monday in Maputo. The next morning, he travelled to Zimbabwe, that same afternoon to the border of Zaire, and on Wednesday he returned to Cape Town before heading off again on Sunday, this time to Botswana. The following Tuesday he paid a short visit to Bloemfontein, spent two days in Johannesburg, and quickly dropped in at Durban and Port Elizabeth before returning to Cape Town on the Friday.'

At times Annalise would take clean clothes to the airport, and occasionally Whitey's loyal personal assistant, Anita van Rensburg, would do the same with medication or documents that had to be signed.[17] Trying to eat healthily was not always possible 'because I have such a rushed life and eat out constantly', Whitey told a Sunday paper. 'When I have a week of eating my wife's carefully planned meals at home, I usually shed a kilo or two without effort.'

Whitey told the glossy magazine *De Kat* the only way for him to stay fit was by doing something he really enjoyed. He liked horse riding and also enjoyed playing golf. Because of growing pressure and little time at his disposal for anything other than Shoprite, however, he was playing increasingly less golf. He reckoned he played reasonably well – although he never reached a single-digit handicap, he did once score a hole in one in Parow. On the wall of his office hung a photo of himself and Gary Player on which Player had written: 'Aan Whitey. U spel was uitstekend'.

There were also photos of Whitey with the legendary Jack Nicklaus. On this particular day, Whitey's Porsche was giving him trouble and while he was struggling to get the engine going, Nicklaus walked past. Naturally, Whitey did not hesitate to ask the 'Golden Bear' to help by giving him a push. 'Just then Wiese and the rest came past and couldn't let the opportunity pass to photograph the scene – Nicklaus pushing my car – and then of course joking about the fact that my car needed a push!' Whitey said with a laugh.

Walking was something he usually tried to make time for, and he was particularly fond of walking in the mountains. 'In surroundings that are as scenic as Stellenbosch you can at least think up bright ideas while you're sweating.'[18]

* * * *

Notwithstanding his work pressure, he was a devoted and enthusiastic father and did his best not to neglect his family. They always had 'first claim on my time whenever they needed me', he told *Die Burger* in 1997.[19] But he would like to spend even more time with his four children, he said.

In the same year, *Rooi Rose* magazine wrote as follows about Whitey and his family in an article titled 'Afspraak met Pa' (Appointment with Dad):[20]

What he would love to do is to drag them along to the golf course, but as yet only the boys share their dad's passion for the game.

Horse riding provides opportunities for many special family moments, particularly between Nikki (23) and her dad, because they make sure that the four horses on the farm are exercised regularly. Mari (16) is mad about hockey and wishes Whitey could attend more of her matches and watch her play – on top of that, he struggles to understand the rules.

Adrian (21) enjoys nothing more than picking his dad's brain about business. He is following in Whitey's footsteps and studying BCom. The youngest, Cornell (14), has a secret plan to persuade his dad to sail with him around the world. The Bassons all like skiing because Whitey considers it one of the best ways to escape from city noise and telephones. It is something they can do together as a family, although the children complain that their dad moves too slowly down the slopes.

They would also regularly go camping at Keurboomstrand, but Whitey worked even while he was on holiday. His sister Juel recounts that Dali Tambo did a television interview with Whitey in the 1990s. In the end the whole family was gathered around the dining table, and Tambo asked Cornell: 'So what are all the things you do when the family goes on holiday?' Cornell replied: 'We drive to all the Shoprite branches in the vicinity to make sure everything is in order!'

Nikki, Whitey's elder daughter, tells a similar story – road-trip holidays were invariably interrupted by unscheduled branch visits. 'He would tell us he's just dashing in quickly to see if everything is all right. But "quickly" was always an hour or more, because after the walk-through everyone would first come up to him to shake hands and chat. We also never knew what mood he would return in afterwards.' The only thing his children can't ask of him is to retire, Whitey said. 'How can I stop doing what I enjoy most of all in my life?'[21]

Towards the end of 1997, Whitey won the *Die Burger*/Cape Town Business Chamber Business Leader of the Year Award. He was in august company – the first recipient of the award had been Johann Rupert (1990), followed by Christo Wiese (1991), Ton Vosloo (1992) and Raymond Ackerman (1994).[22] Whitey was described as 'a people person', and it was also obvious that he was an optimist.

'I want to share my life with ordinary people and enthusiastic people and not with those who always see the negative side,' he was quoted in a report on the award in *Die Burger*.[23] 'Positive thinking was Renier's driving force, for instance, he would never wait until a store had a roof before determining the opening date. To this day, thanks to positive thinking, Shoprite has never had rain on an opening day.'[24] According to Whitey, his biggest passion in life was opening successful stores through teamwork. He also emphasised that the success of a company did not depend on a single individual. 'It is important to him to acknowledge that excellent companies are run by excellent people in excellent teams,' *Die Burger* wrote.[25]

Whitey received a congratulatory letter from Bernhard Andrag, a business acquaintance, who said that he 'more than deserved' the award. Andrag continued: 'What prompted me in particular to write this letter was a minor incident you may perhaps no longer recall. Years ago, I phoned you about collapsible plastic shopping baskets my godson wanted to import. You referred me to one of your staff members, and what impressed me enormously was that you phoned me a few months later to inquire about the outcome of the matter. Success goes to so many people's heads to the extent that they forget the small things and the value of being human as well as remaining humble. You have not fallen into that trap . . .'[26]

At the gala dinner that was attended by some 400 guests, Christo Wiese also delivered a speech. 'The world does not put up with that which is mediocre,' he said. 'It insists on the very best. If we want to compete at an international level, that is what we will have to deliver. We therefore need more people like Whitey Basson. People who have set their sights high, people who are inventive and enterprising and always aim for the highest standards.'

Wiese also touched on the group's optimism about Africa's economic potential. The hurdles, which included sanctions, had been removed, and 'we now have the chance to fully become part of our continent'. He pointed out, however, that a country's economic system (the free-market approach rather than a socialist order of some kind) and the quality of its leadership were crucial determinants of its prosperity.[27] Still, in South Africa, an opportunity presented itself that few people felt equal to, but which Whitey seized with both hands. It would make him a business legend.

21

The R1 transaction

In the late 1980s Whitey and a few colleagues visited the head office of OK Bazaars in the Johannesburg city centre. OK was still the second-largest retailer in South Africa after Pick n Pay, but it was slowly sinking. The executive offices were 'incredibly opulent', with wood-panelled walls, thick carpets, big desks and chairs, and expensive artworks. According to Gert Blij, Shoprite's information systems manager, he would never forget Whitey's words to him: 'These guys are no retailers, and that is good. All it means is that we will buy them even more cheaply in the end.'[1]

Shortly afterwards, on his way home after a visit to Zambia, Whitey went to see Meyer Kahn, the legendary chairman of SAB, in his head office in Parktown, Johannesburg. Here it was the same story – big and opulent offices – and as usual Whitey's thoughts turned to how he could save SAB money. SAB, which had long owned a majority stake in OK Bazaars, was a strong and healthy company and had tried throughout to support OK. But things had kept going wrong for the once mighty OK Bazaars, and Kahn indicated to Whitey that he was welcome to take it over. Whitey cannot recall the exact amount that was proposed, but it was in the region of R250 million or R350 million. 'But no due diligence,' Kahn said. Whitey retorted: 'Mr Kahn, even a horse thief is allowed to look at the teeth of a horse before he steals it!'[2]

It would be years before Whitey would check the teeth of this horse and ride off on it, but he waited patiently. 'We knew OK would come on the market cheaply sooner or later,' he recounted. And he had reason to know, for he had had his eye on the troubled group for a considerable time.

'I used to stalk our rivals, visiting their stores and observing how they conducted business. Around 1993 or so I arrived in a smallish town, in a disadvantaged area with people who didn't have much money. And there was a beautiful OK, with a fish section, and they were selling fresh oysters. No one around there knew what an oyster was, and they couldn't afford it in any case. OK had just not thought properly.' One of OK's problems was that it had lost its focus and no longer understood its target market. 'So it wasn't as if one afternoon it was suddenly Christmas and we bought OK. There was a lead-up of quite a number of years during which I had watched them closely.'[3]

* * * *

OK Bazaars had a long and proud history – it was started by Michael Miller and Sam Cohen in Johannesburg in 1927[4] and listed on the Johannesburg Stock Exchange in 1929. The brand expanded rapidly across South Africa and became a household name.[5] Shoppers flocked to the stores, which were mostly centrally located in cities and bigger towns, for a wide variety of goods, from fresh produce to clothing and furniture. But the retail giant gradually lost direction, and by the mid-1990s OK was on its last legs.

Many erroneous decisions had been made over the years, but in the view of some analysts the real trouble began when SAB acquired a controlling stake of 69 per cent in OK Bazaars in 1973, in what was then the largest retail transaction in South African business history. At the time OK was run by Kahn, but in the mid-1980s he was transferred to SAB's head office and Gordon Hood, an architect, took over from him as managing director. The group started struggling under Hood.

In 1993 he was replaced by Mervyn Serebro, but this did not make much of a difference.

OK was in some respects a victim of its own past. The group had traditionally built flagship stores in the central business districts (CBDs) of South African cities and towns. In September 1973, only three months after the SAB transaction, South Africa's first suburban shopping mall opened in Sandton, and the face of retailing in the country began to change. In the years that followed, shopping malls 'exploded' across South Africa and shoppers amended their buying habits.

John Stretch, a business consultant and commentator, put it like this: 'Retailers responded by cancelling their CBD leases, moving from the high streets to the malls, and revamping their business models. New retail offerings emerged with focused product ranges, specialising in groceries, or clothing, toiletries or furniture. Profits of the old-style retailers in the centre of town dwindled. Many traditional high-end department stores closed and the country's central business districts began to decline.

'But OK Bazaars did not move to the malls. It remained a high street general dealer, offering a range of groceries, clothing, furniture and home appliances. For nearly twenty years, in spite of declining turnover and falling profits, OK management carried on running their stores in the country's declining CBDs. OK's 1992 annual report blamed a 27% drop in earnings on the "current recession, escalating unemployment, and continued socio-political unrest" – in a year in which competitor earnings grew.'[6]

* * * *

In 1993, after another annual loss of R45 million, SAB did not have many options. It either had to close OK's doors, which would cost thousands of people their jobs, or delist the company and try to turn it around. It went for the second option. But not everyone had what it took to make the business profitable. SAB pumped in an additional sum of about R1 billion, but this proved to be largely in vain. OK continued to make huge losses, which SAB had to absorb. Despite occasional slight improvements in its performance, the situation remained fairly dismal. In the 1997 financial year, OK again suffered a loss of more than R70 million.[7] SAB finally lost heart and decided to rid themselves of OK.[8]

Buyers were not queuing up to acquire OK. There were rumours that Walmart was interested, but they turned out to be unfounded. No one felt up to dealing with the OK's bad locations, exorbitant wage bill, antiquated systems and unacceptable shrinkage losses.

Inventory turnover – the rate at which goods are sold and replaced – was low. To discount retailers, this figure is crucial. The longer goods remain on the shelves, the more they cost the company. Just before the delisting, the operating margins had dropped to a mere 0,3 per cent. The balance sheet was weak, and liabilities amounted to more than double the capital.

OK's problems were therefore legion, but ultimately simple. Isaac Fataar, who had spent his first salary cheque at the OK in 1929 and was a regular customer of the OK branch in Cape Town's Adderley Street, told a newspaper: 'It was a place of pride but then it got expensive.'[9]

Only Whitey and his team would have the gumption to take on this challenge. The risk was massive. Raymond Ackerman's wife Wendy apparently told Christo Wiese one evening that Ackerman had considered buying OK but decided he wouldn't touch it with a bargepole. According to Whitey, that was the biggest mistake Ackerman ever made – 'because they ended up not having a brand with which they could compete against Shoprite. If they had bought OK, they could've destroyed us.'

Having studied the company for years, Whitey and his team knew that at some point it would come on the market cheaply. With OK, Shoprite Checkers could extend its infrastructure and serve larger parts of the market with lower prices. By 1997 the OK Bazaars group comprised 139 OK department stores, 18 Hyperamas, 21 House & Homes, and 147 furniture outlets, which were usually part of an OK department store. But the OK's losses could cost Shoprite dearly and might even cause the whole group to sink along with it.

One afternoon, Whitey and Christo Wiese discussed the transaction. Together they weighed up the pros and cons and reflected on the risks. Then Wiese said: 'Let's look at the downside. If someone else does the deal, you're giving him 160 stores in opposition to you, with one of the best brands in the world, and suppose he manages to turn the business around – what will that cost you?'[10]

Whitey weighed the risks against each other and realised he couldn't let the opportunity slip through his fingers. Early in 1997 rumours started circulating that Shoprite and SAB were talking. It was said that OK's senior management and other staff were nervous and uncertain about the future, and that a heavy atmosphere reigned at the OK head office. The story goes that Kahn called the OK's senior management together in a boardroom one afternoon. He was seated at the head of a long table, a beer in one hand and a cigarette in the other, with one foot resting on a chair. He was aware of the rumours, he said. 'But as long as I have a hole in my arse, Whitey Basson will not get his hands on OK Bazaars,' was the crude language reportedly used by Kahn.[11]

Commentators and analysts were voluble on the subject. Some were sceptical about whether OK could be saved at all: 'Assuming Shoprite does SAB a favour and takes over the struggling OK Bazaars, can it pull enough rabbits from a hat to turn it around? The latest figure was losses of almost R74 million for the 1997 financial year. Why does Shoprite think it can salvage this situation?' one analyst asked. Some thought there was a chance, provided the challenge was taken up by someone like Whitey. After all, he had done it before. But the OK was in much worse shape than Checkers had been.

Whitey's retailing skills were rated highly, however, and Shoprite's share price provisionally shot up to R9,60. The market believed OK would give Shoprite's local market share a boost and a greater variety of goods would improve its margins. There was little doubt that OK would benefit from becoming part of the Shoprite stable. But could the same be said for Shoprite?[12] Analysts expected that Whitey, a canny dealmaker, would pay as little as possible for OK, and a price of about R300 million was mentioned.

But the market underestimated the problems at OK, as well as the negotiating ability of Whitey and his team. They spent hours meticulously preparing themselves: 'OK didn't just fall into our lap,' Whitey later told journalist and author Tim Cohen. 'We knew they couldn't get themselves out of trouble. But if we could do a good deal and could afford to remove a few hundred million rands' losses from the system, it would give us a presence across the entire spectrum of the country's population curve.'[13]

Captain Jack Basson and General Jan Smuts were once travelling through the Free State when Smuts suddenly stopped the car. He pointed to a koppie, outlined a scenario of British troops at the top surrounded by Boer warriors below, and asked Jack how he would conquer the koppie if he were a Boer general. Jack started setting out an entire battle plan, with so many horses here and so many rifles there, but Smuts interrupted him halfway. 'No,' he said, 'you first send up your scouts to conduct reconnaissance, because you may think there are 50 British soldiers at the top of the koppie but perhaps there are 250, and then you lose the battle.' The lesson was: you never enter into combat unless you know exactly what you are letting yourself in for. It was one Whitey never forgot.

* * * *

By the time SAB wanted to dispose of the albatross around its neck, Whitey and his team knew exactly what they were letting themselves in for and were as combat-ready as could be. They negotiated for months. Once the process was nearing the end, Whitey kept himself at a distance and instructed Carel Goosen, Shoprite's financial director, to close the deal.

'I was in Durban, along with my secretary and Brian Weyers, the marketing director,' Whitey recounts. 'We were staying at the Umhlanga Hotel. I said, I can't sit so close to the fire because the detail clouds your judgement. So I specifically didn't sit at the table for the last few days. I was kept informed, of course – Callie spoke to me every two hours. But he told me at one point that if I don't leave him alone, he'd resign!'

All negotiations sometimes become difficult, which is when you can get stuck. 'You then need someone who is at a slight remove, as Whitey was in Durban, and who can tell you: listen, this is what we have to get to, and it gives you that extra courage and motivation,' says Goosen. 'It's a vital role. We weren't necessarily tough negotiators, but we were honest and the people with whom we negotiated knew that.' Moreover, the Shoprite team were always very well prepared. 'We did our homework thoroughly and always tried to be better prepared than the opposition. But it was a team effort. Whitey, myself and other colleagues such as André van Zyl worked in tandem to close negotiations.'

Whitey was the 'impact player', says Goosen. 'I couldn't negotiate without him, and I don't think he could do it without me either – when it came to the detail of the calculations, the administrative side, the nuts and bolts. And André was the legal expert. Each man had his strengths and brought them to the table.'

Goosen was also the one who signed the famous R1 cheque, with a Montblanc pen Whitey had given him as a gift. Before Whitey had left on an overseas trip, Goosen had asked him to bring him a Montblanc pen, an item that was not freely available in South Africa at the time. On his return, Whitey had summoned Goosen and showed off his own Montblanc. Alas, no pen for Goosen. 'I was pissed off,' recounts Goosen. 'But when I walked out, he gave me the pen!'

With regard to the OK deal, Whitey remarks: 'The negotiations were complicated, but the deal worked out very well for everyone. They got rid of a liability they couldn't run properly, and we made profits quickly.' Whitey and his team knew the opportunities existed, and they paid as little as possible – the first two steps of a successful takeover. With the paperwork behind them, the hard work lay ahead. The 'bargain' buy increased Shoprite's size considerably, but once again everything had been put at stake.

22

Everything is OK again

OK is like a man with a Ferrari who cannot get it serviced.
— Whitey Basson[1]

On Tuesday 4 November 1997, newspaper posters trumpeted from nearly every lamppost: 'Shoprite buys OK for one rand.' The legendary deal suddenly made the Shoprite Checkers Group much larger, and the token price of R1 for a group with some 150 stores and sales in excess of R6 billion caused a stir. At that point, however, OK Bazaars was losing about R1 million a day and more than 30 000 jobs were in jeopardy.

Analysts opined that Shoprite had done SAB a 'hell of a favour'. SAB had thrown bags of money at OK but 'simply didn't have what it takes to make OK work', *Finance Week* wrote. The feeling in the market was that if anyone could pull it off, it was Whitey.[2] 'All eyes are on Basson and his team to see whether they can perform another miracle,' wrote *Sake-Beeld*.[3] Another commentator cautioned: 'Just because he [Whitey] has pulled it off twice before doesn't necessarily mean he'll be able to get a handle on the management problems that have beset OK for the past decade.'[4] Whitey himself was fully confident. 'We were reasonably schooled in closing down businesses and opening up the next day with a different face,' he told Tim Cohen.[5]

Today Whitey does not think he assumed greater risks than other people, and his risks were always calculated. 'I never say no to anything before I have the facts at my disposal and can make a logical decision. When I worked through OK's figures, I could tell you within a few days what was wrong with the company. The other step was to ask: can I afford to take on this loss-making company, and – as Christo and I had discussed earlier – what would be my downside?' he recounts.

It was another lesson his dad had taught him: you always need an escape plan in case things go badly wrong. Whitey mitigated the risk by initially still running OK as a separate company. The two businesses were integrated operationally, but the books were kept separate. 'So if I saw that OK was going to sink Shoprite, I could dump it – liquidate. I would lose a lot of money, but I wouldn't lose my own business.'

* * * *

Whitey quickly set to work with his 'no-nonsense' style. Decisions had to be made fast. *Business Report* wrote that in his first week at the helm, Whitey was clearly in control and doing more to change things than SAB had done in the past ten years.[6] Tradition has it that OK's co-founder Sam Cohen always carried a handkerchief in his pocket with the letters 'ycdbsoya' embroidered on it. These letters represented his business philosophy: 'You can't do business sitting on your arse.' Whitey was cut from the same cloth.

'OK's daily losses exceeded our profits,' he stated. 'So if we couldn't turn it around fairly quickly, we would be in big trouble. And we had staked all our money. It was a race against time. When you're losing a million rand every day, you work very hard and put in very long hours.' But Whitey and his team were not scared of hard work and long hours, and he believed they knew exactly what they had to do: focus on the most pressing problems and solve them as fast as possible. 'As was the case with Checkers, I never doubted that we could turn OK around,' he confirms today. 'They had good stores, but they were just badly managed.'

The OK brand was renowned. 'We bought not only a chain but a piece of history. The OK was part of my own childhood years and those of thousands of other South Africans.' He recalls their annual pre-Christmas family trips to the OK department store in Adderley Street. Such a visit lasted the whole day, and Whitey and his brother and sister would spend hours riding the escalators and marvel at the dancing Father Christmases in the shop windows. Then there was the lunch-time treat, when they would go to the restaurant on the second floor to enjoy a pie with thick brown gravy. 'The OK was a family store, a one-stop shopping experience even before it came into fashion.' But there was no room for nostalgia – times had changed.

According to Jannie Holtzhausen, a senior colleague of Whitey's at the time of the takeover and who later became Shoprite's head of Operations: North Africa, OK was not only in financial trouble but also directionless. 'At Shoprite, everyone knew what they were doing. Whitey always impressed on us that we sold chickens and baked beans. All the other functions were support functions. It was not like that at OK, and Whitey quickly brought in that focus.'

Carel Goosen adds: 'If we couldn't get OK to work, it would have been the end of us. Naturally, it was an enormous challenge to buy such a struggling company and turn it around before it swallows you. With Checkers and OK you saw why Whitey was worth his weight in gold. Both of them were bigger than us, and had we failed to turn them around, they would've sunk us. Whitey took the lead and made sure everyone knew what they had to do. And he never hung back – he walked out front.'

In November 1997 a smiling Whitey featured on the cover of *Finansies & Tegniek* alongside Christo Wiese, with the cover line: 'How Basson wants to turn OK around.' He and his team soon discovered that OK's three major resources – stores, merchandise and people –

were badly managed and underutilised.[7] Later he told the *Financial Mail* that the first step was once again to establish the right culture. As in the case of Checkers, there was no respect, regard or cooperation between management, the employees and other stakeholders.[8] That was not how things were done at Shoprite.

* * * *

Julia Simons, manager of the department for wall-to-wall carpets at OK Furniture in Parow, remembers the first meeting with Shoprite in charge. 'I was amazed at Mr Basson's humanity and how he set our minds at ease by assuring us that we were now part of the Shoprite family,' Julia recounts. She eventually retired after 42 years with the group. Other drastic steps, too, had to be taken immediately. All of OK's assets, including the employees, were analysed bluntly and dispassionately, but in an 'amicable' way.[9]

Whatever did not work had to go, and you had to make profit on your sales. For OK, this was a culture shock. But although Shoprite did not fire people lightly, Whitey intended to act 'autocratically' if necessary – he would give staff at OK branches three months to prove whether they were worth their salt.[10] OK also had outdated and poor IT systems, exorbitant and antiquated cost structures, and too many stores with poor locations in declining CBDs where too few customers came through the doors.

The head office was scaled down, and Shoprite took control of the buying, stock control, accounting and administrative functions from the Brackenfell offices. OK was also integrated into Shoprite's IT systems. 'There were none [at OK] and we were flying blind,' Whitey told the *Financial Mail*. Poor internal controls were another headache.

The biggest problem was the premises. Steps were taken to optimise the use of floor space and to sublet redundant spaces. Many stores were too big, and the spaces were poorly utilised. Some of the stores were so big that 'you could land a f****** Boeing in them', Whitey recounted. If a retailer wants to make profit, it has to make efficient use of its floor space. 'I can get everything else right but if the correct trading density isn't achieved, the business is gone,' Whitey told the *Financial Mail*.[11]

Holtzhausen adds: 'Changing the stores, scaling some down and closing others, was a huge challenge. It took hours of negotiations to amend the lease agreements. When we got stuck, Whitey would jump in and use his knowledge and contacts to do what was in the best interest of all. But this step was absolutely essential.'[12]

It was decided to advertise OK together with Shoprite in the short term as well. OK was at that stage the only major retailer that ran its own advertising department instead of using an agency. This department employed more than a hundred people, compared to the six at Shoprite. The resultant saving amounted to R100 million per year. Following the acquisition, Whitey was also able to serve a broader spectrum of the population. He and his team put all the existing brands in a 'pot' and looked at which stores worked where. Accordingly, stores were closed or rebranded to become appropriate for their location and their customers.

As usual, Whitey moved fast. Holtzhausen relates that no time was wasted on 'philosophising' about where the OK stores should fit in, because the new owners knew what worked and repeated the recipes of Shoprite and Checkers. 'By this time Shoprite was a master at integrating stores and businesses into the Shoprite culture,' he says. 'That knowledge and experience, and customers' trust in the Shoprite stable, were very important. And one of Whitey's mottoes was: do what works now, and you have the rest of your life to make minor adjustments.'

Most of the OK stores were converted into Checkers or Shoprite stores, and others were closed. The remaining outlets were operated as OK franchises. They carried the OK brand and were supplied with merchandise by Shoprite, but were managed by third parties. The plan was also to convert Sentra stores into the better-known OK brand, which would improve profits. Existing OK stores would not compete directly with Shoprite, which was still the group's main brand.

Given OK's renown, some analysts were surprised that the Shoprite brand was still being used for the lower market segment and thought it was merely a matter of pride for Shoprite. But Whitey told *Business Report* that OK had not been competitive for years, and Shoprite's image in terms of low prices was much better.[13] Checkers was being repositioned to challenge Pick n Pay. Hyperama would also take over some OK stores that were too large for the Shoprite formula.[14] Once the head office problems and the locations were sorted out, it would be a matter of applying sound business principles and doing the basics right – pushing up sales, improving stock turnover, and increasing productivity, which were all of course interconnected.[15]

As in the case of the Checkers takeover, every OK branch got a 'buddy' in the shape of a senior member of Shoprite's management who was familiar with the group's practices and could take the lead in a crisis.[16] In Whitey's view, OK's staff were excited about the takeover. 'They feel comfortable with us and know we are just retailers who don't wear ties. However, the success or failure of the deal and their own future are in their own hands. If they work hard to increase the turnover, we can employ more people,'[17] he said to *Sake-Beeld*.

* * * *

For OK's employees, it came as a huge shock when they heard the group had been sold. 'But I realised at once that this company knew what retail was and had a leader who understood how retail worked,' recounts Martin Joubert, who worked for OK at the time. 'Everyone who was prepared to work got an opportunity to grow. Whitey also knew when to put us in our place and when to pick us up – whether by means of a visit or a telephone call.'[18]

Some phone calls would present other challenges. Holtzhausen relates: 'John Coile, who was of Scottish origin, managed OK's Hyper-ama. Although he'd been in South Africa for twenty years, people still couldn't understand his Scottish accent. I could understand him, however, and each time after he'd phoned Whitey to discuss something, Whitey would phone me and ask if I could find out from John what the conversation had been about.

'So I would phone John and say: Whitey wants you to inform me as well about your discussion so that I can follow up on his behalf. Then I would relay to Whitey what John thought the two of them had decided. And it was not always how Whitey had understood it. John eventually realised what was going on and would just phone me directly,' Holtzhausen says with a laugh.

Saving jobs was still of great importance to Shoprite and Whitey. In March 1998 Carel Goosen told the magazine *FAS Retailer* that at store level, the options were basically either to reduce staff or to increase sales.[19] Naturally, Whitey and his team were working towards option two. Although some head office staff were retrenched, thousands of jobs were saved.

Callie Burger, head of human resources, recalls how he and a colleague were planning at the OK head office in Johannesburg how they should deal with the retrenchments. Meetings, conversations and letters were envisaged. One day Whitey bumped into them and asked: 'And what are you guys doing?' Burger told him what they had in mind. 'That's all well and good, Callie,' said Whitey. 'But I just want to tell you I'm switching off the aircons and the lights at the end of the month.' Needless to say, he and his colleague started handing out the termination letters at great speed without taking any other steps. 'When people from OK ran into me, they would just ask: "Where's my letter?" In this way we saved a lot of time and trouble, and had no difficulties – against all advice.

'Many people told us they could see it wasn't nice for us to do what we were doing, but that they knew it should have happened long ago. We had no time to work according to the rules. The decision was: we simply close the head office and deal with problems that may arise afterwards, while the business continues unhindered.'

* * * *

The acquisition of Checkers and, subsequently, OK were massive milestones in Shoprite's history, and Whitey handled the takeovers masterfully. In the view of Doug Parker, Whitey was also making a statement by rebranding most of the Checkers and OK stores as Shoprites. 'They were failed businesses, and Shoprite was successful.'

Whitey believed in cooperation towards a common goal, a mindset he had already instilled in his colleagues and employees. 'But he made it plain to all his consultants as well that they had to cooperate in the effort of getting the "monster" that was OK back to profitability – "so don't exploit me by making me pay through the nose for services". And everyone bought into it and did their bit, for they realised that if we did it right, we would have a big client for life as opposed to possibly no client,' says Parker. Whitey also handled the trade unions well. 'He said, we can either have thousands of job opportunities at R100 per hour, or no jobs at R101 per hour – take it or leave it. He was unyielding, and when he knows what he wants, he gets it.'

Another consequence of the OK takeover was that the group had expanded into a new product line, namely furniture. Mervyn Serebro, OK's managing director prior to the takeover, remained the head of Hyperama and OK Furniture, which would be run separately. At that stage Whitey was in two minds about the furniture division, but he retained it nonetheless. 'There was nothing wrong with the business or its brand. And, contrary to popular belief, furniture isn't a difficult business because there are few SKUs [stock-keeping units],' he says.

With the acquisition of OK, Shoprite Checkers took over the reins from Pick n Pay as the largest supermarket group in the country. The dream of surpassing Ackerman that Whitey had harboured while sitting among bags of flour and cartons of cigarettes in a tiny office in Lansdowne had been realised. According to the *Financial Mail*, Whitey 'had become the undisputed SA retailing master'.[20]

Raymond Ackerman writes in his autobiography that the merger between Shoprite, Checkers and OK 'had for the first time presented us with one large competitor as opposed to the several smaller ones we had become accustomed to challenging. Armed with firm new management plans aimed at countering the retail slump, the newly consolidated army of our opposition had marched forward confidently. Clearly, this was a time to keep a cool head.'[21]

For Whitey, however, there was no time to indulge in schadenfreude. Only a few weeks after the takeover he told *Finance Week*: 'I want this whole thing bedded down by June next year so that I can get on with my African expansion programme; that's what I'm really interested in.'[22] But it would take somewhat longer to get this problem child bedded down once and for all.

23

Full steam ahead

We didn't sink the Titanic, but it was an ugly leak.
– Whitey Basson[1]

By this time there was hardly anyone who didn't know about Whitey Basson. Even the family magazine *Huisgenoot* featured a story about 'the man who bought OK for R1'. Was it the bargain of the century – or a very pricey gamble? 'People in the industry said, Whitey has now aimed too high. This time he'll see his arse,' he said at the time.[2]

But he had done his sums. OK was making a loss of about R20 million per month. As part of the deal, SAB guaranteed a net asset value of R540 million – the amount by which the value of OK's assets exceeded its liabilities. Hence Whitey knew he had a little more than two years to return OK to profitability before it would really start costing him and his shareholders money.

However, OK's systems were in such a mess that no one knew which stores were profitable and which were loss-making, and to whom OK owed money. 'Don't ask me if I think I have snapped up a bargain. It's either the most expensive or the cheapest rand I've spent in my entire life. I'll only know in 27 months' time,'[3] Whitey told *Huisgenoot*. He would know sooner than that. Against all odds, OK was returned to profitability within a year. This time the posters read: 'Basson turns OK around'.[4]

But the OK transaction would also end up in court. Shoprite and SAB disagreed about the particulars. 'The one rand is also not quite correct,' Whitey explained.[5] For the sake of a valid transaction the nominal amount of R1 was chosen, although Whitey commented jokingly: 'We didn't pay too much, but SAB received too much!'[6]

The matter in dispute was how much money SAB had to pay Shoprite to comply with the guaranteed net asset value of R540 million. The agreement provided that if the statements as on 31 October 1997 were to show that the asset value was less than this amount, SAB would pay Shoprite the difference. The dispute was about accounting issues – among other things, the valuation of fixed assets and inventory, and the provision for creditors.[7] Shoprite believed that SAB still owed it R150 million to R200 million.[8] An independent expert estimated that the amount was much less, however, and Shoprite took SAB to court.[9]

The court case was such a source of stress that Whitey took up smoking again. He had started smoking at university but quit the habit when his younger daughter was born. 'During the court case, I became so incensed one day that I asked someone for a cigarette, and a few days later I was back to buying a packet,' he recounts. 'But I have long since stopped smoking again.' He told the *Financial Mail* at the time that he was annoyed with the situation. 'I am gatvol because this matter is hanging in the air.'

The dispute was later referred to arbitration. 'For a valid transaction one had to pay something, hence the token amount of R1,' explains Shoprite's company secretary André van Zyl, who also signed as a witness when the deal was closed. 'The first arbitration was in Johannesburg – there were files and files – and Whitey decided he wished to testify. But it was tricky, and all he wanted to know was whether SAB had cheated him.'

SAB had given them very little time to conduct the due diligence investigation. 'SAB hadn't put all their cards on the table and told us everything about what was going on in the businesses. And so Whitey thought they had misled us,' says Van Zyl. OK's reporting had not been up to scratch, and Van Zyl believes a proper valuation was in fact impossible. 'We had been allowed to inspect all the stores and the books. We couldn't prove in black and white that we had been misled, but we claimed that they owed us money.'

The arbitration proceedings dragged on. 'Closer to the end most of the SAB people who had been involved in the transaction were no longer there, and there was no enthusiasm left to take the matter further. But on our side, there was Whitey Basson!' The settlement came in 2017 – twenty years after the transaction, and after Whitey had already left Shoprite. 'The upshot was: You owe us nothing, and we owe you nothing,' says Van Zyl.

* * * *

'Is it about money for you?' a journalist asked Whitey some months after the OK transaction. He said no – the money was incidental. 'That was never part of my motivation. It's something else – maybe the people. Ask Annalise,' he tried to explain. 'I think one is born with certain drives,' Annalise added. 'Whitey quickly becomes bored with the same thing . . . life with him is never boring. But he has a passion for improving people's lives, whether it is by way of job creation, cheaper food, or even opportunities for employees' children.'

Whitey himself told *Rooi Rose* that he derived great satisfaction from turning struggling companies around. 'It gives self-respect to thousands of people when they make money from a business that is doing well. They are grateful if they can become shareholders. I conduct business with my heart *and* my mind. Retail is a very emotional business – it's a living organism.'[10]

His advice to anyone who intended starting their own business was to do their homework. 'You must practise all the shots so that you can react automatically when things happen. You must be 100 per cent prepared for everything that comes your way; you have to be able to cope with it both mentally and rationally.

'You must be able to think ahead. I checked out OK for a year. I dreamed about it. I agonise for days and months about decisions like that before taking the plunge. Before I bought OK, I literally went off to an island for a week to gain clarity in my mind. During the last two months before the takeover, it became an obsession. Even with my first takeover, that of Half Price Stores in 1973, I slept in a hotel for a while.'

Before long, however, Whitey was brought back to earth with a bump. Only six months after being dubbed the 'turnaround king' when he achieved what SAB had been unable to do in a decade, something emerged that he had not anticipated: stock losses on an unprecedented scale. And the question was: had there really been a turnaround at OK?

In the 1999 financial year – the first year in which OK's results were incorporated with those of the group for the full 12 months – the company's turnover increased by 19 per cent to R17,2 billion. But stock losses estimated at around R100 million came to light and wiped out a large part of the profit. It also caused the group's operating profit to drop by almost half (46,8 per cent) to R125,9 million, from R237 million the year before.

'I'm sitting here naked with only my socks on,' Whitey said at the time. 'They stole everything I've got.' The stolen items included Whitey's Superman cape, quipped one journalist.[11] Moreover, Shoprite had spent more than R370 million on the refurbishment of OK stores and, in total, stock to the value of more than R70 million had been written off since the takeover.[12] At the time of the acquisition, the joke had been whether the purchase price of R1 had been too high. The same question was being asked now, but no one was laughing.[13] Given the breakneck pace of the transition, it was probably to be expected that something would go wrong.

'There was an incredible amount of work that had to be done,' Holtzhausen recounts. 'The poor reporting and systems didn't help either. Everyone was occupied with changing stores, balancing stock and getting prices right, and the drastic losses were unexpected.' André van Zyl recalls that when the losses were discovered, the entire management team were summoned urgently on a Saturday afternoon. 'With the rapid switchover, balls were dropped. There were only so many hands.'

Shrinkage is a perennial problem in the retail industry. It occurs, for example, when goods that have been paid for are not delivered or are carried off from the delivery points. Cigarettes, razor blades, batteries, baby food and toiletries are popular targets. Besides shoplifting, there are also the food and drink that are consumed in the stores, mainly by staff but by customers as well. When staff and suppliers are in cahoots, the consequences can be disastrous. In Shoprite's case, it turned out that sophisticated gangs had exploited the restructuring and refurbishments to target the group.[14] The theft was mostly limited to Gauteng.

In the initial haste to stem OK's losses, certain 'internal controls' – practices on which Whitey and his team had always prided themselves – had suffered. The group had been particularly vulnerable during the restructuring and installation of new systems. OK's and Shoprite's computer and information systems were used in tandem for a while. To some extent, it was understandable – in the course of 18 months, 29 stores had been closed, 20 new ones had been opened, and the remaining OK branches had been converted into Shoprites. But the market was not so forgiving, and the news of the enormous loss caused the share price to drop to an annual low of R5,95.

He deserved a hiding, but not to be crucified, Whitey said in an interview. The events were 'one of those things that happen but it is not the end of the world. It is an unfortunate situation, and I pray that we can soon forget about the whole thing'.[15] He pointed out again that more than 20 000 jobs had been saved.[16] Besides, the theft had to be viewed in a context of nearly 80 armed attacks on Shoprite stores and trucks per year. A truck loaded with cigarettes was worth more than R1 million.

Today, Whitey recounts that there was 'enormous fraudulent collusion. I was eventually so despondent because we had tried everything to fix it. And I warned the suppliers that if we caught any of their trucks that were defrauding us, they wouldn't be allowed to supply to us for a year or two. Then the situation at least came under control.'

According to Holtzhausen, Barney Rogut used to say that success has many fathers, but failure is an orphan. 'It was a real shame that journalists and analysts reacted so quickly and aggressively. This was a one-time deviation that was swiftly rectified. Businesses like OK that had been dying a slow death for years received less criticism and deserved more.'

Whitey also said he would do it all again. 'These opportunities in a small market like South Africa come once in a century, and one must also consider that if we had left it [the OK] behind, the effect could have been more severe if, say, someone like Walmart had taken it over.'[17] The OK losses of R250 million had been stemmed, so if the loss of R100 million was added in, the group was still better off. At any other retail group pandemonium and panic may have erupted among the management team, but the problem was tackled resolutely, and steps were taken to prevent a recurrence.

Also, Whitey had Christo Wiese in his corner. 'Christo's biggest contribution was to trust Whitey, and Whitey always knew he had his support,' Goosen relates. 'And it was an enormous role, freeing Whitey's hands to let him do his thing, for if you wanted to stifle Whitey you had to come with all kinds of corporate governance stuff and red tape – remuneration committees and things like that drove him up the wall. Whitey also made very few mistakes, and he knew he didn't need external guys to check up on him.'

In any case, the whip was cracked, and the culprits were brought to book. They included staff members, supplier representatives and employees of outsourced security services.[18] Investigations showed the financial systems were of a satisfactory standard and that everything possible had been done to prevent a recurrence.[19]

Whitey, however, was impatient to reach his dream. 'We have a whole continent out there waiting for us,' he told Tim Cohen in 1999. He also berated himself and jokingly remarked: 'A proper price for OK was probably 99c!'[20]

24

Africa beckons

Our ambition is to provide all communities in Africa with a first-world retail shopping experience where food and household items can be obtained at the lowest prices, while contributing to the nurturing of stable economies and social upliftment processes.

– Shoprite's vision for Africa, 2003 annual report.

At the turn of the century, and with Y2K a storm in a teacup, the conversion of OK stores into Shoprite or Checkers stores had been completed. The stock losses, too, were a thing of the past. In fact, Shoprite boasted that shrinkage was now at its lowest level in 10 years, and also lower than internationally accepted norms.[1]

The year 2000 was the culmination of a 20-year period during which the group developed from the small 8-store Shoprite chain with a turnover of R12 million to one with 911 outlets (including franchises) and a turnover of R18,4 billion. Shoprite Checkers was also the preferred shopping destination of 64,3 per cent of South African households for food and groceries. Its closest competitor catered for only 28,3 per cent of South African households.[2] Over a 20-year period, turnover grew at an annualised compound growth of 44,4 per cent and earnings by 37,8 per cent. The tally of outlets on the scoreboard read as follows: Shoprite Checkers (349), OK (11), Hyperama (18), House & Home (20), OK Furniture (118), Sentra (148), OK Foods (19), Megasave (86), Value (65), Buying Partners (77), 8 Till Late (47) and Hungry Lion (30).

The group, known as Shoprite Holdings since 1994, now employed some 29 000 permanent employees and about 48 000 temporary and casual workers. It was not only the largest supermarket group in South Africa but also the largest retail company on the African continent.

And its expansion programme north of the Limpopo was well on track. Shoprite was the only South African food retail chain that was aggressively expanding into Africa, and it planned to capture 'the majority market share' on the continent. It was already operating 56 outlets in six countries outside South Africa. The long-term dream was to increase the operating income from other African countries to more than 50 per cent of group revenue.

PART FIVE

THE GOLDEN YEARS

25

Making his mark in Africa

There's no such thing as a free lunch.
– A regular saying of Whitey Basson's.

Whitey and Shoprite had already started putting out feelers towards the rest of Africa in the early 1990s. This project started taking shape after 1994 once the relaxation of exchange controls made it possible again to do business beyond the country's borders. Whitey had always wanted to expand to the rest of Africa. And he used to say one shouldn't be scared of dreaming, and of dreaming big. 'Once you have a dream, you define it and focus on it,' he told Tim Cohen.[1]

In 1997 he told *Finansies & Tegniek* that during South Africa's isolation years he had dreamed of pitting himself against the best international businesspeople, and he was now entering the ring against astute businessmen from other African countries. He hoped to create more wealth for Shoprite Checkers shareholders, and to drastically improve standards in Africa.[2] After 1994 he wanted to expand as fast as possible, before the rest of the South African business community woke up, with a view to earning just as much in Africa as they were doing locally. The long-term aim of the Shoprite team was therefore that the operating income from other African countries would make up more than half of the group's revenue by 2005.

Although Shoprite had already expanded to Namibia in 1990, Whitey did not regard this as his first step into Africa. Namibia gained its independence in that year but continued to use the South African rand as its currency. Despite the introduction of the Namibian dollar three years later, the rand was still legal tender and the new currency was pegged to it.

With this expansion, Whitey received anonymous death threats. 'When we opened the store in Windhoek, I had to wear a bulletproof vest and looked like Humpty Dumpty. I also wasn't allowed to give a speech,' he recounts. Nothing came of the threats, but they did result in Whitey's path crossing with that of Pieter du Preez. Du Preez was part of the security team Shoprite had hired to protect Whitey, and he subsequently stayed on to act as Whitey's bodyguard when he travelled in Africa. The death threats in Namibia would not be the last ones. The same thing happened each time they expanded to a new market in Africa – some of the role players who controlled the markets were evidently unhappy about Shoprite's entry. Consequently, Du Preez was constantly at Whitey's side in Africa – and Whitey saw potential in him.

'I liked him very much and he was a clever guy,' Whitey relates. 'So I told him, I'm going to appoint you – then you make my appointments and look after my security. And when you have nothing to do during the day while I sit and work, you use the time to swot.' Du Preez started studying law, completed an LLB degree, and became Shoprite's company secretary in 2008.

Shoprite's 'real' entry into the rest of Africa came in 1995 when it bought six stores in the state-owned National Home Stores chain in Zambia for R10 million. When Callie Burger, head of human resources, arrived at a management meeting one Monday, Whitey asked him: 'What the hell are you doing here?' 'What do you mean, Mr Basson?' a surprised Burger asked. 'I always attend this meeting.'

'Haven't you heard that we bought the stores in Zambia from the government?' said Whitey. 'What are we supposed to do with the stores if the employees walk out when they hear we're taking them over?

Jump on a plane and go talk to them!'[3] The employees did not walk out – on the contrary, they were only too happy to see the red colours of Shoprite. The state-owned retail group was collapsing, and Shoprite was a lifeline.

Whitey still likes talking about Shoprite's fact-finding missions to Zambia. He stresses again how difficult it was at times to do business in Africa, and that the continent posed unique challenges. 'Everyone thinks you just drive into Africa, and that it's easy,' he states. 'But when we did branch visits in Zambia, we only had old Cressidas to drive in. Before we set off, Freddy Niemand discovered some wheels had only one or two wheel nuts. We first counted how many wheel nuts there were among all the cars, and then divided them up so that each wheel at least had two nuts.

'They also told us that National Home Stores' trucks fell into three groups. "She's not well" meant there were a few things wrong with it, but at least the truck still worked. "She's buggered" meant there were more serious problems, but at least the truck could still be repaired. The third group of trucks was classed as "she's f*cked" . . . And that was the largest group!' Whitey recounts, and he still laughs about it when he thinks back.

The Shoprite group arrived on a greyish weekday morning at the store of Charles Bota, who was a branch manager in Ndola at the time. Years later, he wrote in Whitey's Tribute Book: 'With the sure and quiet confidence I later came to know him for, Mr Basson asked me questions about the economy, how we had managed to survive, the government, and if I thought there was any hope for business. My life, my family's lives, the lives of over 7 000 workers and countless local suppliers, the retail shopping experience and retail landscape of 13 million Zambians forever changed for the better because of this one man who came to Zambia in 1995; who saw where the vision of others was blurred, who conquered where many failed.'[4] Bota stayed on at Shoprite and later became the general manager in Zambia.

But the conquest was not a foregone conclusion. Whitey's sister Juel Starke relates that they were having tea at Klein DasBosch one Saturday morning after Whitey had attended the opening of the new Shoprite in Lusaka earlier that week. 'Whitey was very worried because there had been a crowd of people, but few sales. We were still sitting there chatting when his phone rang. I could hear it was business, and Whitey asked, "What do you mean, close the store? Are there no customers?"

'But imagine the speechless relief when the reply came: "No, sir, the store is completely empty, everything on the shelves has been sold out!" It was a big moment. After a subsequent visit to Zambia, Whitey also spoke excitedly about seeing people with Shoprite's red and yellow shopping bags everywhere along the road from the airport.'

* * * *

As the empty shelves indicated, the stores in Zambia created new logistical challenges, which would later also be the case in other African countries. In South Africa the full supply chains were already established and by this time highly evolved. But elsewhere in Africa, in a place like Lusaka, it was a different story. Fruit and vegetables were one of the biggest headaches.

Gerhard Fritz, head of Shoprite's operations outside South Africa, explains: 'Many farms were out of use, and where people did farm, it was with maize and soya beans. Potatoes were grown locally, but the quality was mostly poor. In the early years we transported produce by truck from South Africa to Lusaka, from where we distributed it further. We were the first company that started using refrigerated trucks.

'The Zambia Farmers Union was at first very sceptical, and we sent out people to encourage farmers to grow crops that had never been cultivated before, such as gem squash, carrots and salad vegetables. From the outset, Freshmark, our fresh produce supplier, played a major role in this by training farmers and supplying them with seed. Initially we sent probably ten to fifteen trucks loaded with fresh produce from Johannesburg to Lusaka every week. Today, more than 90 per cent of our requirements are sourced from local producers.'

The same approach was later followed in other African countries, with Freshmark initially importing fresh produce and then assisting local farmers to grow the crops and start supplying them. In countries such as Uganda, Angola and Ghana, fresh produce was flown in weekly and sometimes daily from Johannesburg. Countries that were situated on shipping routes were served from Cape Town, and road transport to Malawi, Botswana and Zambia took place from Johannesburg.

Companies such as Colgate, Unilever and Reckitt were already present in Zambia and manufactured a variety of products for the local market. The rest of the merchandise was supplemented from Johannesburg and transported with Shoprite's own trucks as well as by transport contractors.

Meat production, too, was a problem at first, but it became one of Shoprite's biggest success stories. Fritz continues: 'During our initial visits to Zambia it became clear that no one operated butcheries according to our standards. At that stage it was forbidden to export meat from South Africa to Zambia, and we were looking for a reliable local producer.'

Interviews were conducted with several applicants – including a dynamic young farmer who had studied in South Africa. He subsequently started expanding his family-owned farming operations and founded the company Zambeef. They were large cattle farmers and also operated a small butchery. Shoprite then gave them the chance to operate their in-store Meat Market butcheries on a concession basis.

'We invited them to South Africa and showed them what we required, and also lent them some of our best people to help them get the enterprise off the ground.' This was the start of a very good partnership. 'With our assistance and support they began playing a bigger and bigger role in the value chain, and with our help they started supplying eggs, milk, chickens, processed meat, yoghurt, cheese and flour as well.'

Zambeef is still one of Shoprite's largest suppliers today, and operates the in-store butcheries in Nigeria and Ghana too. It is listed on the Lusaka Stock Exchange and is one of Zambia's largest companies.

* * * *

But back to Shoprite's beginnings in Zambia. Whitey's team converted all six National Home Stores in and around Lusaka and other prominent towns into Shoprites, and Shoprite Holdings was listed on the Zambian stock exchange in 2003. The number of stores would later grow to 30. In a busy 1997, during which Whitey bought OK Bazaars, among other things, a Shoprite opened in Mozambique's capital Maputo as well.

The entry into Mozambique had a long lead-up. One Sunday Whitey was on a flight from Cape Town to Johannesburg, and he realised the man next to him was Chris Stals, governor of the South African Reserve Bank. 'He was reading his Sunday papers, just about every one that was on the market. His seat was 1A and mine was 1C. I thought, it's not really the right thing to talk to someone next to you who's busy, but about twenty minutes before we were due to arrive in Johannesburg I grabbed my chance.'

Whitey wanted to buy a site in Maputo on which he intended to construct a shopping centre, and the money had to be sent from South Africa to Mozambique. 'If I remember correctly, we wanted to transfer a few hundred thousand rand to Mozambique, and that for a few hectares of land with an excellent location. In those days, before 1994, it was difficult to send money from South Africa to the rest of Africa, and we asked various banks to assist. We would donate the money for the Mozambican "Peace Park" to the government, and they would then give us a 99-year lease. We also had to submit a development plan, and then we would be able to build the shopping centre.'

According to Whitey, he tapped Stals on the shoulder and said: 'Sir, I'm sorry to bother you, but my name is Whitey Basson, I come from Porterville, and I know you probably don't want to be disturbed, but I know you're the boss of the Reserve Bank.' And he told Stals his story. 'It's not really his department, he said, and I said, I know, but when you arrive at the office on Monday, please do me a favour – drop in on the guy whose portfolio it is, and tell him he should please approve it. Because we've now been struggling for several weeks to get approval.

'Naturally, I also told him that for every rand we would earn ten times more in foreign exchange. Early on Monday morning we received a message from two banks – they informed us that they had obtained the money and were patting themselves on the back. Then I said, nonsense, I had organised it myself with Mr Stals on the plane. So just pay your commission to me, since I did the deal!'

In the late 1990s, therefore, Shoprite's people were Afro-optimists – they believed the African Renaissance could become more than a political slogan.[5] But they were realistic too. Whitey wrote in the group's 1998 annual report that African governments needed to do much more to encourage investment. And he did not mince his words: 'Logistical delays remain a major problem. Bureaucratic red tape, a scarcity of suitable premises, depreciating currencies, and the insistence by some governments that the company's entry into the market be effected in partnership with local enterprises, complicate matters further.'

But Whitey still felt that Africa held great promise. The group's expansion into the rest of Africa only really started gaining pace after the turn of the century. The local market was saturated and the competition intense. Africa, on the other hand, offered less competition and higher profits.[6] The risk was high too – but as Whitey said, 'the more risk you assume, the greater the potential reward'.

At the outset, Shoprite aimed to expand into countries with strong economic drivers – such as minerals, oil and tourism – that could therefore sustain greater economic activity.[7] It sought to gain a foothold in the most profitable markets as soon as possible.

After the initial success in Zambia, 'we focused in earnest on the rest of Africa,' Gerhard Fritz relates. Within a few years, Shoprite opened stores where they could obtain premises and the governments of the countries concerned allowed their entry. 'News about our success in Zambia spread like wildfire, and we were invited at high level to establish Shoprite in other African countries.'

On a flight to Angola, Whitey told journalists that retail in Africa was like roulette. 'If you put all your money on one number, your chances of losing are that much greater than if you were to play eight numbers, for instance. With Shoprite I'd rather invest in 20 countries than only one.' But many other companies believed it was more like *Russian* roulette, he added.[8] In 2000 Shoprite expanded to Zimbabwe and Uganda as well.

Hennes Schreuder, a Pepkor man, was among those Whitey roped in to facilitate the African expansion. It was not always plain sailing. In Kampala, Schreuder recounts, they had selected what was in their view the best possible premises, which were located next to a central traffic circle. But it turned out to be a mistake – the traffic was too heavy, access was difficult, and parking was lacking. They vacated the premises and established smaller stores in other parts of the city.

Mistakes were inevitable – Whitey and his colleagues were trailblazers, after all. But they were not cowboys who simply invaded the rest of the continent. They did thorough planning before entering a country. First they identified certain countries with favourable macroeconomic factors and then conducted further consumer and market research.

In distinctive Shoprite style, they were also 'on the ground' and would stand on street corners counting the cars and taxis driving past.[9] 'I always conducted the first recce in an African country,' Schreuder relates. 'I would then compile an initial report, and we met every Friday to decide whether we would tackle the country or not. And I flew with obscure airlines. It was always nice when Whitey came along, as then we flew with the jet! And it made sense, because the man didn't have time to waste at airports.'

According to Whitey, Shoprite eventually bought a jet so he and his African team could travel faster and more safely from country to country. 'But we also had narrow escapes in the air on quite a few occasions. As you know, a plane can't see another plane among the clouds. But ours was equipped with the advanced TCAS (traffic collision avoidance system) that few other planes had at the time, hence our pilot could see other aircraft on the screen as well as their exact altitude and how far away they were from us. All aircraft are equipped with transponders that emit signals, which we could pick up.

'Once, after we had taken off at Luanda, we were heading for a mid-air collision with another aircraft. The pilot was a bit slow, whereafter the computer took over. It felt as if the TCAS system caused us to dive down a few thousand feet. It was quite terrifying, and everyone almost had two heart attacks. On another occasion, after we had landed in

Zimbabwe to refuel, an aircraft flew so low over us that we could just about read the writing under its wings.'

Malawi and Egypt followed in 2001. 'It was more of a culture shock to move from Porterville to Rondebosch than to go to the Egyptian capital, Cairo,' Whitey quipped.[10] But it was in Egypt where he failed for the first time. Jannie Holtzhausen vividly remembers their first visit to Cairo. It took place in the late 1990s. 'We arrived in the late afternoon and were astounded by what we saw and experienced. When you come from Outjo in Namibia, it's hard to grasp that more people live in one suburb in Cairo than in the whole of Namibia. The population density and poor distribution of food stores gave us cause to believe that the Shoprite formula would work there.' An office was set up in Heliopolis – on the outskirts of Cairo, near the international airport – and Holtzhausen and a team went there to set things in motion.

'Whitey is someone who believes what he sees and doesn't see what he believes,' Holtzhausen continues. 'That's important, especially when one enters a new market. Despite having done our research as well as possible, we failed to detect how basic the food culture of the majority of customers was. There were simply not enough people who were prepared to buy more than just the basic goods, and who could afford to do so.

'What we saw in Cairo was translated into good business in Soweto and other underserved areas in South Africa – but not in Egypt.' Schreuder adds: 'Moreover, they were the masters of red tape. As soon as we had complied with existing laws and regulations, they would come with new requirements.'

Holtzhausen admits today that with the bureaucratic red tape taking up so much of their time, they may not have picked up on all the negative signs soon enough. 'Shoprite was perhaps fifteen years too early in Egypt, and first-mover advantage isn't always good. It wasn't

214

easy to do business there. Contracts were difficult, business practices were incomprehensible, and as newcomers we were often exploited.'

The group entered into a partnership with the Egypt Kuwait Holding Company, a major player in the local consumer market. But that did not solve Shoprite's problems – on the contrary, it entangled them further in confusing and often murky local business practices.

In many African countries corruption and red tape were the order of the day, but in Egypt these phenomena were rampant. Whitey recounts: 'There was a legal system, but only for certain people and institutions. We were blocked from doing business properly. You want to import, say, batteries, but you're not allowed to because someone who knows someone has the contract to import batteries. It was a matter of who you know and who has the best connections.'

Other players, such as the UK supermarket chain Sainsbury's, had expanded aggressively in Egypt in the late 1990s, but Sainsbury's eventually pulled out and wrote off a whopping R1,2 billion.[11] 'At least we lost less than Sainsbury's – they lost as much there in the space of three months as we lost in the course of three years,' Whitey adds. Shoprite would finally divest from Egypt in 2006.

Whitey continues: 'Pieter Engelbrecht spent a lot of time in Egypt in an effort to turn the business around there. He even studied the Qur'an. At one stage it was very difficult because the engine of an Air Egypt plane had fallen off in South Africa, and I then forbade him to fly with that airline. So he had to fly via Dubai, which took a very long time.

'He really did excellent work there. We changed our entire strategy and put smaller stores at lower rentals in better locations – in more affluent and more densely populated areas, with thousands of houses and flats. But eventually I gave up and said, no, we can't carry on like this. Our business partners were responsible for the finalisation of contracts, but we couldn't really finalise anything. We are still good friends, but I think in the end Egypt remains a place the Egyptians themselves need to fix.'

Whitey and his team had better luck elsewhere. 'If you opened a store in Kuruman while living in Cape Town, you've already learnt how to cross rivers,' he remarks. In 2002 Shoprite expanded to Madagascar, Mauritius and Tanzania, and the year after that to Ghana.

Whitey's approach was that of 'testing the depth of the water with one foot before you jump in'.[12] In the early 1990s Shoprite began testing the Angolan market in association with a local businessman. A few container loads of goods were sent to Luanda and placed on premises that belonged to the businessman, and a Shoprite person sold the goods directly from the containers to street vendors. Although the relationship with the businessman did not work out, the initial profits were excellent. Consequently, Shoprite started opening stores, most of which were located in buildings it had constructed itself.

By the time Shoprite formally opened its doors in Angola in 2003, analysts pointed out that Shoprite's African operations were performing 'extremely well'.[13] Whitey explained at the time that it took 'three times as much energy to do business in Africa'. It took a pile of paperwork 15 cm thick to get a container across the Angolan border. The fastest freight transport to Angola was 28 days, and the slowest up to and including delivery was 160 days.[14]

But Whitey had energy in abundance. Jean Engelbrecht, owner of the Stellenbosch wine estate Rust en Vrede and a good friend of Whitey's, accompanied Whitey and his team on a business trip to Angola in 2010. He recalls not only Whitey's attention to detail but also his energy and enthusiasm. 'We spent a whole week visiting branches. I learnt so much, it was like doing an MBA. He knew his industry, he knew his products, and he had an eye for detail.

'His capacity for work was something to behold. I think Whitey crammed into a week what many others would probably do in a month. At six in the morning we would go to the first premises, and Whitey walks through to inspect everything. Next we go to the half-built warehouse to see how the building is progressing, then to the store in the local squatter camp, and then we fly off to the next town,' Engelbrecht relates. They kept up this gruelling programme for a week. 'But the team were very well prepared. No one stood around aimlessly – everyone knew what to do, and moved fast and efficiently.' And Whitey was busier than ever. In 1999 *De Kat* wrote that his colour-coded schedule for the year indicated a near-superhuman working programme.[15] There were business trips to Hong Kong, Chicago, Frankfurt, New York and Milan, but also to various African countries.

Whitey made sure he maintained contact with his head office while travelling. But in Africa telecommunication infrastructure was usually poor, which necessitated costly satellite phones. 'My first satellite phone was as big as a suitcase,' Whitey recounts. 'Later we bought smaller phones and tiny printers, which we used. To get a signal, we would often have up to ten different satellite dishes with us.'

'The signal still had to be linked to our laptops. I can still recall how Pieter du Preez and Wendy Truter had to crawl around in the gardens of hotels to get a signal so that we could receive and answer our emails. And then, if we did manage to get through to the head office, there was sometimes confusion about the passwords and our emails would hit a firewall. But at least Anita and Wendy managed to ensure that all the necessary information, emails and messages reached me every day, so that I could respond to it within 24 hours.'

Shoprite's people not only worked hard but also played hard. Whitey remembers an evening in a hotel on the banks of Lake Victoria in Tanzania when Freddy Niemand sat playing the piano until a late hour. Then a woman came up to him and told him to stop playing because the guests were unable to sleep. So he said: 'Don't give me a hard time, the manager asked me to play.' She looked down her nose at him and retorted: 'I *am* the manager!'

Doug Parker recalls a night in Kampala when they sat close to the orchestra in the hotel's dining room. Whitey asked Serge Martinengo if he could play an instrument, and he said he played guitar. Freddy Niemand offered to play piano and asked the orchestra whether they could play a song or two. Parker himself added the percussion with a knife and fork. Whitey grabbed the microphone, and the Shoprite orchestra got going. 'The other guests disappeared quietly, but it was great fun,' Parker recounts.

When the team travelled to Namibia, or other countries on the coast, they would often arrange 'own appointments', André van Zyl says. 'This was the codeword to indicate that we were going to do a spot of fishing. We had good times. When we got the chance, we would relax and enjoy ourselves.'

As time went on, Shoprite's strategy was refined. According to Gerhard Fritz, the focus shifted from 'opening as many stores as we can' to opening in mineral-rich countries such as Angola, Ghana and the Democratic Republic of Congo (DRC). The biggest challenge was Nigeria, which Shoprite eventually entered in 2005. 'It was a country with millions of consumers who had never been exposed to a formal supermarket culture. The legislation was based on an informal market, and we devoted much time to getting the laws of the country changed so that we could trade. Nigeria is but one example where Whitey was years ahead of the rest of the market. And what Shoprite did there to smooth the way for others can't be measured in monetary value.'

A big problem in Africa is that of securing suitable store spaces and appropriate premises. 'If we'd been able to obtain the premises, we could have been bigger in Africa than in South Africa,' Whitey reckoned.[16]

* * * *

In 1997 Whitey, André van Zyl and Philip van der Merwe travelled to Kenya to investigate opportunities there. 'We drove down Eldoret's main street, and Mr Basson inquired about a plot of undeveloped land,' relates Van der Merwe. They were informed that the land belonged to the Catholic Church and was not for sale – whereupon Whitey grabbed his Dictaphone and started dictating: 'Dear Pope, I am Whitey Basson from Shoprite . . .'

They had a good laugh at the time, but Van Zyl did post the letter. The request to 'His Holiness the Pope' John Paul II was for Whitey to be referred to the right channels so that they could discuss the 'piece of vacant land next to the church building that is known as the Catholic Diocese of Eldoret Sacred Heart Cathedral Parish . . . In its current condition the semi-developed structure serves no purpose, and we believe it should rather be converted into retailing premises to accommodate our group and others.' According to Van der Merwe, they are still awaiting a reply.

Whitey adds: 'One of our employees of Italian descent had an aunt who worked in the Vatican as a cleaner. I've always believed one shouldn't give up, so I asked him to send the letter to his aunt so she could leave it on the Pope's bedside table. But whether it was ever sent, I don't know . . .

'Jokes aside, there are so many beautiful pieces of land in Africa owned by the Catholic Church that aren't utilised at all. One day, when I find the time, I want to try and arrange an appointment with the church's high-ranking officials – maybe even the Pope – to see whether we can't perhaps do something with that land. There are really huge opportunities for the Catholic Church to make better use of its properties in Africa.'

Shoprite conducted some of its most intensive research in Kenya. 'Certain groups tried to stop all our moves because they controlled the retail industry,' says Hennes Schreuder. Shoprite finally opened stores in Kenya in 2018, but closed them again two years later.

Fritz, too, highlights the lack of suitable premises and infrastructure as one of the major challenges in Africa. 'Every store had to be provided with generators and clean water. In some cases we had to drill for water and even lay on sewerage works ourselves – just so we could open our doors.'

Another stumbling block was the rules and regulations governing trade among African countries. 'It's often easier to import goods from Europe than from other African countries,'[17] Fritz stated. 'When Shoprite started in Zambia, it was reasonably easy to import goods from South Africa – it sometimes took less than twenty days to deliver an order to a branch. Today it takes almost forty days – largely because of customs requirements, delays at border posts, and export permits.'

Today Whitey recounts: 'There were three big challenges in Africa – security problems, a lack of infrastructure, and poor communications. You couldn't simply sit in your office and press a button, and something would happen thousands of kilometres away. There wasn't decent accommodation either – hotels were often not up to scratch, and we sometimes had to make our own arrangements with regard to food and other services. When you start doing business in a country and you have no frame of reference like we had in South Africa, you have to redo everything from scratch. This made every process very complicated and difficult, and it took up a lot of time.

'In South Africa we were still busy and had already bought Checkers, but the expansion to the rest of Africa was a tough time. Few people realise how much the rest of Africa differs from South Africa, and what an enormous challenge it was to establish new stores there. But the plan with Africa was always to make a quantum leap in terms of size, and to put Shoprite firmly in the limelight.' Whitey and his team took this leap, came to know the stumbling blocks, worked at resolving them, accepted the risks, and remained optimistic throughout.

26

Global dreams are tempered

*One of my dreams is that my business will one day be all
over the world, even in America. I dream of exporting
South Africans. Of being able to ask them: 'Don't you
want to go and work for Shoprite in San Francisco?*

— Whitey Basson in 2001.[1]

By the time *The Economist* wrote a cover story about 'Africa rising' at
the end of 2011,[2] Shoprite was operating in fifteen African countries
outside South Africa where it served millions of customers annually in
more than 140 stores.[3] Whitey wanted to prove himself on the rest of
the continent and compete against the best international businesspeople, but it was also about more than that. 'When we arrived there, there
was nothing.' In addition to offering people a world-class shopping
experience, he aimed to create jobs and uplift communities.

Shoprite was making strides in Africa, but the continent also had its
unique challenges. Shortly after the turn of the century, the Shoprite
team flew to Equatorial Guinea to explore opportunities there. Whitey
was also supposed to meet with the then president of the country,
Teodoro Obiang Nguema Mbasogo.

The moment they touched down, however, the team found themselves in hot water. Three military vehicles brimming with soldiers
surrounded the jet. A few officers boarded the aircraft and insisted on
seeing the group's passports. The entire jet was searched too. Whitey
and the rest were then bundled out of the jet. There was a heated

exchange between Whitey and the senior officer, who did not believe Whitey had an appointment with the president.

For hours, the group had to sit waiting in the hangar in sweltering heat for some or other outcome. Eventually they were instructed to fly back at once. The reason for this hostile reception from the security force only became clear some weeks later. A plane carrying South African mercenaries who were on their way to Equatorial Guinea to help execute a coup had been intercepted in Zimbabwe.

Whitey remembers the events like this: 'All I know is that the government invited us to be there on that specific day. I was against it, because the people with whom I worked in France had told me there were serious divisions and that there was actually a president-in-waiting in a neighbouring country. Naturally, I didn't want to get involved in politics. But we decided to go nonetheless, and when we sat in the jet and no one wanted to allow us into the country, I just went to dance along with the local people. They all wore green T-shirts – it's quite a popular colour in Africa – and they gave me one too. Thereby I managed to relieve the tension somewhat, but it was quite hectic.'

The incident had an amusing sequel. 'After we had taken over Checkers, there was a strike at the Checkers Hyperama in Port Elizabeth. I was in Plettenberg Bay at the time, and then drove to Port Elizabeth. After about ten minutes of negotiations I saw I wouldn't get anywhere with the strikers. So I just started dancing along with some of the women to the music of "Gimme Hope Jo'anna". And after we'd danced for about half an hour, I'd danced the strike out of existence. I then dropped in at the store and made very good friends. So dancing helped me to resolve the strike, but it didn't get us through the gates of Equatorial Guinea . . .'

* * * *

Africa was not only dangerous at times, but nearly always onerous – Shoprite was a property developer from the very beginning and in many cases had to build its own stores. Logistical problems had to be overcome and, as mentioned before, the supply chains posed enormous challenges. According to the group's 2000 annual report, substantial investment in information technology over the past few years had resulted in streamlined procedures for ordering and stock control. A global tracking system provided up-to-date information of the whereabouts of its thousands of delivery trucks.[4] The encouragement of local manufacturers was regarded as key to the group's operations beyond South Africa's borders.

'The war for Africa is fought in the trenches and not in the boardrooms,' states Gerhard Fritz. 'People can sit here in South Africa and say, do this or do that, but if you're not there yourself, or haven't been there, you don't know what's going on. We physically built stores, and created something out of nothing. But African countries are at different stages of development, and we often had to construct our own infrastructure. So that makes things very difficult, and obviously expensive.

'And it's not a one-off expense but permanent costs. We train local guys as store managers. Then we leave, and he sits with all that machinery and equipment he has to maintain, and then he phones you because he has no electricity. The facilities we introduced there were state-of-the-art. That guy not only has to familiarise himself with your business, he is also responsible for a R3-million generator – and in the end someone has to fly there to help solve issues. Not everyone felt up to challenges like that.'

But Whitey has always been competitive and likes challenges. In Kitwe in Zambia they had to cart away tons of rotten cartons – 'which had already turned into compost' – from the building they had taken over. 'When we wanted to paint the building, we first had to get

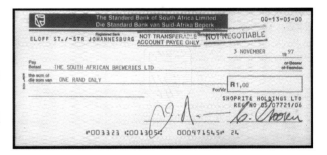

DR JOHANN RABIE
MB ChB (Stell) FCP (SA) MRCP (Edin)

PHYSICIAN/INTERNIS

107 Mediclinic 107
Rothschild Boulevard
Panorama
7500 Parow

PR. 1803123

Surgery/Kamers
Tel.: 930-4425/6

Res/Won
Tel.: 953-1854

Emergency/Nood
Tel.: 21-5400

Date: 20/5/92   Age if minor:
Datum: Ouderdom indien minderjarig:

Name: Mnr J W Basson
Naam:

Address:
Adres:

Rx
→ 2 weke vakansie
in rustige omgewing
met geneeg:
1) Slaap
2) Humor
3) Goeie wyn + lekker kos (matige hoeveelhede)
4) Musiek
5) Goeie geselskap
6) Oefening (stap/vis vang jag, swem)

In May 1992, Whitey's friend, physician Dr Johann Rabie, booked him off with this amusing prescription for a two-week holiday in peaceful surroundings, with generous doses of sleep, humour, good wine, delicious food in moderate quantities, music, good company and exercise.

The legendary R1 cheque with which Shoprite bought OK Bazaars from South African Breweries in 1997. It was signed by Whitey and Carel Goosen.

The Standard Bank of South Africa Limited
Die Standard Bank van Suid-Afrika Beperk

00-13-05-00

ELOFF ST./-STR JOHANNESBURG

Registered Bank

NOT TRANSFERABLE — NOT NEGOTIABLE
ACCOUNT PAYEE ONLY

3 NOVEMBER 19 97

Pay
Betaal   THE SOUTH AFRICAN BREWERIES LTD   or Bearer
                                                            of Toonder

the sum of
die som van   ONE RAND ONLY

R1,00

For/Vir

SHOPRITE HOLDINGS LTD
REG NO 05/07721/06

⑂003323 ⑈001305⑈ 0000471545⑈ 24

In the 1990s Shoprite snapped up Grand Bazaars, Checkers and OK Bazaars. Here Whitey poses with OK bags after his acquisition of that group in 1997.

A street scene in Angola. From 1995 Shoprite started expanding purposefully in Africa beyond South Africa's borders, but doing business in those countries was not always plain sailing.

Whitey and Christo Wiese, on a trip to expand Shoprite in Mozambique. They met at Stellenbosch in 1964 and later became partners in Shoprite.

Whitey and Shoprite's property team, Philip van der Merwe and Eugene Dreyer, studying plans for a new Shoprite somewhere in Africa, date unknown.

People often queued up when a Shoprite opened its doors. Here shoppers throng a store during its opening in Angola.

Photo by Obie Oberholzer taken in Kazimule, Zambia, with the handwritten annotation 'and Whitey Basson' added by GT Ferreira.

Whitey with some of Shoprite's no-name brand products, mid-90s. Today the Shoprite Group has more than 3 500 private-label products, both house brands and no-name brands, on its shelves, and sales of private-label products make up about 18 per cent of its total sales.

permission. So I said, paint, I'll take the responsibility. We then painted the buildings beautifully,' Whitey relates. 'Our month for cleaning and sprucing up was February, before the year-end, and then every store had to fix every cracked floor or tile, anything that was broken or faulty; if I walked in there on the first on March and it hadn't been done, there was hell to pay in that store.

'When we refurbished the store in Kitwe, we had to fix up the pavements and roads too. We planted trees, which were then stolen. So we made those welded cages that were put over the trees, and I had the road in front of the store tarred. Within a month, the neighbours on both sides were also painting their buildings, fixing up things and planting trees. When you plant a tree, you believe in the future because it takes time for a tree to grow tall. I always used to say, if you want to see progress in Africa, we and the hotels should move in there. And the rest will follow.'

Upliftment of communities and better access to food were other factors that inspired him to expand into Africa. Initially everything was imported, but local communities were developed systematically and local capabilities increased. 'People were poor where I grew up,' he told *Leadership* magazine in 2000. 'There was no guaranteed income. I can appreciate the fact that people can have nothing. The difference between having R10 and having nothing can be vast. There are lots of poor people among our customers, and we have to understand what their lives are like.'[5]

This was one of the reasons why Whitey believed it was so important to be on the shop floor rather than in the office, 'otherwise I would forget there are poor people out there and not only people in the boardroom. I have a need to see those areas upgraded and I feel depressed when I see poor people'.

When Shoprite entered a city or town, the standards people were accustomed to improved, and food became cheaper as well. This was notably the case in West African countries such as Nigeria and Angola, where Shoprite was the first retailer to introduce world-class supermarkets, compared to East Africa, where other supermarket chains were sometimes already operating.[6] 'We bring food prices down by 30 per cent, or 50 per cent, and occasionally more,' he told *De Kat* in 1999.[7]

'In Zambia an old man once came to shake my hand in the street. He said he was a grandfather, and for the first time in his life he could now buy apples for his grandchildren in a store. On another occasion I saw two hundred people queueing up for freshly baked bread.'

Whitey did not pretend to be running a charity. 'Naturally, my shareholders want to see the returns. But I would also feel good if someone were to stop me in Angola next year and say, thank you that you people have reduced the price of food by 30 per cent.'

To him, this kind of expansion was a win–win situation for his shareholders, the countries concerned, and consumers. At the time of his expansion into Africa food security was 'collapsing', and there was a need for better food retailing on the continent. 'You go to the big cities and see a metropolis with three million people who have no supermarkets,' Whitey said, 'and you say to yourself, "a certain percentage of them would surely have the need to shop at a smart, well-stocked supermarket and could afford to do so."'[8]

In the view of Prof. Nic Terblanche consumers were exploited in most African countries. 'Shoprite went in and provided food security – and did so continuously, 365 days a year. They experienced many problems but ensured that the stores always had stock.'

As in South Africa, job creation was also a key consideration elsewhere on the continent. It was vitally important to Whitey that local people should be developed and local talent exploited, Fritz recounts. 'We take delight in saying that the overwhelming majority of our employees are local. One of the aspects that stands out is how few people from outside we put in there and how many local people we developed. And when Pick n Pay and Game started following in our footsteps, they didn't train their own employees but appointed our people. It was actually a heck of a compliment.'

In 2004 Shoprite expanded to India – a huge step, but in its opinion a logical one. 'We believe the experience gained from managing the complexities of operating successfully in 16 countries has equipped the Group with the skills to do business anywhere in the world,' the 2004 annual report stated. This view underpinned their decision to expand to India, 'a country and a culture with which there exists a very special affinity through the large Indian population of KwaZulu-Natal, where the Group's predominantly Indian team trades very successfully'.

Despite certain restrictions concerning trading by foreign companies, Shoprite believed the potential in India was vast. Mumbai alone had double the number of inhabitants of KwaZulu-Natal, where at that stage Shoprite operated 61 outlets in a 'more strenuously contested market'.

Whitey was optimistic about the prospects. 'We can have a ball in the Indian market,' he told *Sake-Rapport*.[9] He compared the retail market in India at that point to the South African market in the 1960s. There were hardly any supermarket chains, and more than 90 per cent of the market was served by small businesses and hawkers. However, the scenario in the Indian retail space was changing with the establishment of shopping centres, where the need for anchor tenants would create opportunities for groups like Shoprite. 'I don't think we'll be able to occupy the market fully in my lifetime, because with its more than one billion people it's simply too big,' Whitey added.

When the first Shoprite in Mumbai opened in a cricket-mad country, the South African cricketer Jonty Rhodes and the former

Indian cricket captain Kapil Dev were invited to the ceremony, and the popular Indian singer and television star Raageshwari performed at the event. 'The store included all departments of international supermarkets, a concept that didn't exist there at the time,' relates Pieter Engelbrecht. 'Fruit and vegetables were especially popular because these products were mostly purchased from street vendors. The store was so popular that customer numbers had to be restricted over weekends. This led to the concept of "Wednesday market day", to relieve the pressure on weekends. Wednesdays then became the biggest trading day.'

The optimism, however, quickly had to make way for realism. India had all kinds of laws and regulations that made it difficult for foreign companies to do business. According to Whitey, one couldn't really trade freely in India. 'There were fixed selling prices for retailers, and we had to work through franchise partners. We had many customers and fantastic stores, but were simply unable to make a profit.

'But I still have regrets about it. If we could open again in India, I would do it – not Egypt, but I'd definitely return to India. It's an incredible country, with wonderful and smart people, but the tax structures are intricate and expensive, and the systems too complicated. At least we learnt a lot there, and the experience was good for us.'

Whitey recalls the day he and Pieter Engelbrecht realised their Eastern expansion had failed, and that they had to return home with their tails between their legs. 'We were sitting in the garden of our hotel in Mumbai. We bought a bottle of wine, polished it off between the two of us, and then became sorrowful because we had this wonderful opportunity here but were forced to close shop.

'I was very sad, because India and Egypt had been a dream of mine. I received many offers from overseas over the years. I always turned them down because I was very loyal to South Africa and its people, and

I love the country very much. But I always dreamed of arm-wrestling against the best in the world.

'I spent a lot of time in America – I used to go there every year for a week or two to see what was new in the retail industry. I always believed I would've done well there – I worked hard, and understood their culture fairly well. I was kind of in love with the country and its efficient management styles. But I never had the opportunity to compete there.'

He adds: 'I saw Walmart entering South Africa, and I think I will still see them exiting.' The American retail giant had made several attempts to enter the local market before its 2011 acquisition of a majority stake in Massmart, which owns, inter alia, Game and Makro.[10]

* * * *

In the 1990s there was speculation that Walmart was interested in OK, but like the rest, the world's largest retailer was not prepared to take on that challenge. Years later it was also being said that Walmart was making overtures to Shoprite. In 2010 a journalist asked Whitey whether Shoprite and Walmart were talking. Whitey replied: 'I can't speak on behalf of Walmart because I don't know what their plans are, but I definitely didn't receive a call from them or from Madonna in the past month.'[11]

But Whitey had never thought Walmart (which changed its name from Wal-Mart Stores to Walmart in 2018) would become the force in South Africa that it was in the United States. The South African market had its own challenges, and was among the most competitive in the world. 'Never fight a small war with your entire defence force,' Whitey always said, with reference to Walmart's entry into the local market.

As far back as 2008 Massmart had bought a smallish grocery chain,

Cambridge Food,[12] and also started selling food in its Game stores. In 2011 Walmart bought the majority stake in Massmart. But it was just another retailer that couldn't make headway with groceries. In August 2021 (after Whitey had already left) Massmart sold a part of its stable to Shoprite for R1,36 billion.[13] The deal comprised, of 56 Cambridge Food and Rhino Cash & Carry stores, which included 43 liquor outlets, as well as 12 Masscash Cash & Carry stores.[14] All these stores would become Shoprites or Usave.

Today Whitey recounts: 'I went to visit Walmart in America and even had an appointment to meet Sam Walton, in Bentonville. Darryl Fine, our advertising manager, and I had to spend the whole night in the hotel's ventilation shaft because there was a hurricane that we sat watching on TV. You weren't allowed to stay in your room, since you could be sucked out. We didn't have food either. So we went to the kitchen ourselves, took polonies from the fridges, made sandwiches and fried some eggs. And that was my night in Bentonville. But at least I spent quite a bit of time at Walmart the next morning.' Whitey's appointment with Walton, however, was cancelled at the last minute because Walton had fallen ill.

He also finally lifts the veil on Walmart's entry into South Africa, and his own strategic thinking: 'When Walmart came to South Africa to explore opportunities here, they approached us and asked whether we would sell to them. I said, the controlling shareholder is Christo Wiese, and you would have to ask him. But I don't think that is likely to happen, and I don't think we would like to be a subsidiary of an overseas company either.

'I then planned to get them off our back, and to prevent them from buying Pick n Pay. Because that was my biggest fear. So I talked to the Walmart team for almost two hours to convince them that Makro was their best option. Christo also said no – they couldn't buy Shoprite.

And thank heavens they didn't buy Pick n Pay – that would have been a major problem.

'All I needed to work on then was that they had to remain listed. If they had come in unlisted, they could simply have wiped us out with discount prices. It wouldn't even have made a dent in their books. But if you're listed, and your performance is constantly analysed in the press, it hamstrings you quite a bit.

'And then they did things that were really stupid. Game was a total disaster – they literally destroyed a good business within two years. But I don't think their entry into the South African market was well thought through. I do think their hardware stores are excellent and will do well in South Africa.'

Whitey says he is sad that he never met Sam Walton. 'They were very good to me – that is, before they came to South Africa. They had a file on us – I think they knew more about Shoprite than I knew about them. They took me through their warehouses, showed me all their systems, and showed how quickly they could replace the goods on their shelves. On my trips in later years I would always visit a few Walmart branches, and I was quite disappointed to see that the stores had deteriorated in some respects.'

In August 2022 Walmart announced that it had entered into a deal to buy the remaining stake (47 per cent) in Massmart too and would delist the company.[15]

* * * *

Following Whitey's retirement at the end of 2016, Shoprite's focus shifted back to the domestic market and it pulled out of certain countries. But the group still had a strong presence on the African continent outside of South Africa. In 2019 Whitey's successor Pieter Engelbrecht told the *Financial Mail*: 'If investors don't believe in Africa, they won't believe in Shoprite.' He acknowledged that the rest of Africa's contribution to the group was volatile, but he did not intend to change their strategy and planned to continue building on their African advantage. 'We have learned how to trade in the rest of Africa.'[16] Christo Wiese also reminded analysts: 'Shoprite is proudly African and South African, we're not put off by the challenges of this continent.'[17]

Both Fritz and Schreuder believe that, with its expansion into Africa, Shoprite did 'the right thing at the right time'. According to Fritz, premises had gradually become more easily obtainable, but the challenges had grown bigger in respect of the flattening of the economy, unemployment, and the strong American dollar. Africa's dependence on the dollar is one of the biggest factors that hamper expansion. Dollar rentals forced most international traders to close their doors, as the turnover in local currencies couldn't keep pace with the weakening of the currency against the dollar. In some cases, rental costs increased from 5 per cent of turnover to 20 per cent.

Fritz also elaborates on Whitey's eye for detail. 'Suppliers told us they once ran into Whitey by chance in a store in Nigeria. He started in the one corner, spent two hours walking through the entire store, and inspected everything. And the people were gobsmacked, for where do you see the CEO of a company walking through the aisles like that. And he did that right up to the end – up to the last trip we made. He would walk past every shelf, and if anything was in the wrong place, he noticed it. Afterwards, when he spoke to the manager, he would know exactly what was going on in the store. There are few CEOs who spend so much time on the floor – it's actually unheard of.'

* * * *

Whitey is still optimistic about Africa. However, he regrets the fact that the rest of the continent's contribution to the group's operations and profits has not grown as strongly as he would have liked. Nor has his dream of a presence outside of the continent been realised. Nonetheless, Shoprite is still the largest retailer in Africa today. At the time of Whitey's retirement it operated 475 stores in 15 other African countries,[18] and sales on the rest of the continent made up about 16 per cent of the group's total sales.

Shoprite's expansion into the rest of Africa has therefore been a partial success. Stores in some countries are still successful and profitable, and others not. But the first-mover advantage should not be underestimated. The experience Shoprite has gained and the footprint it has established give it a competitive advantage. Shoprite not only had to construct infrastructure in many instances, but also had to establish an effective supply chain and transportation network from scratch.

'This has created a barrier to entry as new entrants are discouraged from competing due to the large amounts of capital, time and understanding of operating in Africa that are needed,' Cadiz Asset Management stated in a research note in November 2019. They believed that in the long term, Shoprite would benefit from the high growth rates expected in Africa. The high barriers to entry would ensure that Shoprite retained its competitive advantage in the rest of Africa.

All of this has resulted from Whitey's vision and dreams of more than 30 years ago. And he is proud of what Shoprite has achieved to date. 'It gave me great pleasure to make a difference in the lives of millions of people who weren't used to a modern shopping experience,' he told Tim Cohen in 2010.[19] 'There were people who thanked us for just bringing food in at a reasonable price. We were generating sufficient return on investment for our shareholders and I felt we were doing a first-class job.'

'I'm still very positive about Africa,' Whitey maintains today. 'I actually think it's a pity that our stores in Nigeria were sold and often disagreed with Christo about that. None of our non-executive directors had ever visited Nigeria, and it beats me how you can sell a business if you don't even know what it looks like. I wouldn't have done it – I would've carried on with it.

'The new owners still send people to me to help them with certain strategic decisions, and they say they're doing excellent business. It's the second-largest economy in Africa – perhaps the largest – and it does go through its ups and downs, often because of the oil prices. But that doesn't mean Nigeria can't become a big manufacturing and agricultural country. In fact, I consider Nigeria and Angola the two best African countries to do business in.

'At one stage five or six stores in the rest of Africa were among Shop-rite's top ten in terms of turnover – and a store in Angola was in the number one position for a few years. This just goes to show how large those markets are – they just need to be utilised properly.'

27

Wine, meat and Gordon Ramsay

You can't build a brand without a point of difference.
— Whitey Basson

Wines of the World, Odd Bins, Championship Boerewors, Zip Cola, Lovies Nappies, Oralwise toothbrushes, and Nataniël and Gordon Ramsay in advertisements. These were all innovative ideas for giving shoppers more reasons to visit Shoprite or Checkers. While Shoprite's plans for the rest of Africa were ambitious, the local market was still its largest and most important. But competition was intensifying, consumer trends were changing, and the market was reasonably saturated. Consequently, fresh thinking was required.

After the turn of the century, the consolidation of OK was fully realised and its profit levels had been restored. The larger group was poised for further growth, both locally and internationally.[1] As part of its strategic positioning, the group now differentiated its most powerful brands more decisively from one another and focused separately on each of them.

The Checkers brand had become 'more viable' under Whitey's leadership and therefore needed more strategic focus. Hence it was decided that the Checkers format would join that of Hyperama, which would become Checkers Hyper, and be repositioned to cater for the middle-to upper-income market segment – that of more affluent consumers.[2] Shoprite was still the group's principal brand and was positioned on low-price leadership. Its primary customers were price-conscious consumers in the middle- and low-income market segment.[3] The brand capital-ised on South Africa's rising middle class and on increased government spending on social grants.

At the time of the acquisition of Checkers in 1991, there had been a debate about the name of the future company – should everything become Shoprite, or everything Checkers, or should they create a new brand name? Although it came up for consideration, a new name was not a viable option – it would be too expensive and establishing it would take too long. Checkers was a familiar name to consumers and although the company had been poorly managed in the past, it was unthinkable to simply ditch the brand. And as Shoprite was the brand where everything had started, there was no way Whitey would have allowed it to disappear. Hence Shoprite and Checkers 'were married', and 'together they offered more value'.

In 2010 Whitey explained on a television show that the group couldn't afford to advertise the two chains separately.[4] 'At one stage we divided our newspaper ads in two and said, these products are at Shoprite, these are at Checkers, and these are at both Shoprite and Checkers, and this is what they cost.'

But it was not ideal – two different brands, targeting two different markets, lumped together in one advertisement. Although 'Shoprite Checkers' had become a household name by now, it had always been the aim to differentiate the two brands from one another and give them each a distinct focus.[5]

'After the OK integration, when we did the repositioning, we started focusing separately on the different brands,' Whitey recounts. 'Retail is all about brand perception, what people believe your brand represents. Perceptions of Checkers' prices were poor, but perceptions of quality were reasonably good. One can't change the public's perception of a brand overnight. You do it bit by bit, slowly but surely.'

Checkers' prices were brought down in general, but they were not as low as Shoprite's. In the case of Shoprite, the message and the strategy were clear: 'We are the cheapest.' In order to succeed in the upper-income market segment, where other factors are important as well, Checkers had to be distinguished more decisively from Shoprite. Thus Checkers was firmly positioned as catering for the top end of the market.

'Shoppers still got value for their money, but they also had to be proud of buying there,' explains Neil Schreuder, Shoprite's former marketing director and currently managing director of ShopriteX, the group's new digital innovation hub.

This was where the concept of storytelling came into play. Whitey came up with the idea of 'Famous for . . .' 'These were the categories we would become known for, so that people could tell others around the braai why they shopped at Checkers,' Schreuder recounts. 'While Checkers' prices were still better than those of its competitors, those categories and the related stories also had to make people proud of buying at Checkers.'

Accordingly, Whitey and his marketing team started focusing on certain products with a view to changing customer perception. The targeted products were meat, wine, cheese and coffee. 'It was all aimed at showing why you should go to Checkers and not to a competitor,' Whitey says. 'For instance, we chose a boerewors champion to show we had the best boerewors in the country.'

Checkers' widely known 'Championship Boerewors' competition started as an internal staff competition in Shoprite and Checkers in 1992. The in-store butcheries of each brand's supermarkets could develop their own recipes, and the best boerewors was chosen from among these entries. In 2001 the competition was opened to the public, and since then a winner has been crowned annually.

Everyone gains from the project. The winner receives prizes and the right to be known as South Africa's 'boerewors champion'. The company can pick and choose from thousands of recipes, and the winning recipe is used for the 'Championship Boerewors' for a year. In this way, the competition markets itself (and the boerewors).[6] Today it is the biggest boerewors brand in the country, and sales have grown from about R500 000 per year to over R300 million per year.[7] Put differently: a year's Championship Boerewors would stretch from Johannesburg to London and can be used to make more than 56 million boerewors rolls.[8]

Checkers also launched the 'Steakhouse Classic' range – steaks of restaurant quality at a fraction of the price. 'The customer sees we have the best boerewors and vacuum-packed steak, and therefore starts believing we have the best butcheries,' Schreuder explains. In 2007 Checkers became the first retailer to stock 'certified natural lamb' from the Karoo and the Kalahari – another drawcard for the carnivores.[9]

Special wine ranges added to Checkers' appeal. In the past, supermarkets used to offer you a choice of a few boxed wines, but Checkers became the first supermarket to offer estate wines at affordable prices.

Whitey initially raised the idea of producing a private-label wine specifically for Shoprite and Checkers with the winemaker Jan 'Boland' Coetzee. 'He said it wasn't possible, as you could never get the taste and quality of such large quantities of wine to stay the same year after year. Only Distell has ever managed to do that in the case of Chateau Libertas.'

But Whitey made a plan nonetheless. He had seen the name 'Odd Bins' somewhere while on a trip to England. When he came up with the idea of selling good wines without the labels of the estates, the name occurred to him again. The Odd Bins collection consists of limited-edition vintages from famous South African wine estates that do not carry their original labels but are sold anonymously and at lower prices in numbered Odd Bins batches. Consumers are invited to try and discover the 'secret' of each Odd Bins number. Once the bin is sold out, the number is never repeated.

The liquor division was run as a specialty division. Wine experts and specialist buyers visited farmers and wine cellars, collected candidate wines and started negotiating about prices. Whitey and a team headed by Jan 'Boland' Coetzee would then hold 'blind' wine-tasting evenings at Shoprite's head office to decide on the best wines (according to quality and price) they would include in Odd Bins.[10]

Whitey wrote the publicity material together with Wilhelm Landman and called it 'Discover the Secret of the Bin'. The golden rule was: never say whose wine it is. The labels were also designed in such a way that they appeared to have been handwritten by the winemaker. Shoprite's wine experts would visit various wine estates and negotiate to sell some of their wines as Odd Bins. The estate still makes a profit, albeit less than on its own labels, and gets its surplus wine sold.

'The "Secret of the Bin" was very important,' Whitey says. 'A customer once came to me and said he knew what wine a certain number was. He was wrong, but I played along and said: "How did you know that? Don't tell anyone!"'

The next step in the marketing of wines was the creation of a 'wine route' where consumers could buy estate wines at good prices. The wine buyers bought the estate wines at discount prices, to which Shoprite would add its profits. The winemakers then had to sell the wines at the same prices in their own cellars. According to Whitey, millions of customers pass through the stores every week, and only a few through the cellars. 'They had to be stupid not to see the benefit in it.'

Shoprite subsequently also launched Wines of the World, a collection of top-quality wines from countries such as France, Spain, Argentina and Australia, which are purchased for them by the wine connoisseur

Michael Fridjhon. Whitey got the idea from a store in Dallas, Texas. 'We marketed Wines of the World in bright colours to create a fiesta feeling,' he recounts.

Checkers started offering a larger variety of cheeses as well. Whereas your choice was previously between Gouda and Cheddar, you were now able to choose from a wide range of over 400 local and international cheeses – including Emmental, Boerenkaas, Gorgonzola, Camembert and Pecorino. 'Today this has become commonplace, but we were the first,' says Schreuder. 'And again, it didn't necessarily make us a lot of money, but it was a big drawcard from a lifestyle perspective, and therefore very good for marketing.'

Whitey elaborates: 'The question was always: are we giving people good reasons to buy from us rather than from Pick n Pay? Everything was done with the aim of changing customer perception. Your market isn't necessarily the same in every town – it shifts. And you need to stay just above your customer's aspiration level, but not too far above it. Your threshold is always slightly above your market's aspiration – you should never go below that either. I didn't position Checkers as a direct competitor of Woolies – I wanted the top end of the mass market, the middle market, to perceive Checkers as being just above their aspiration level. Shoprite, on the other hand, targeted the middle- to lower-income market with the promise of lower prices. And Usave was there to serve the bottom end of the market with low prices and simplicity.'

Charles Back, the wine and cheese producer, and owner of Fairview adds: 'I was very excited about the fact that cheese was one of Checkers' focus areas because it had a huge ripple effect. Consumers were introduced to a wide range of cheeses they would not normally have seen in a supermarket. It also put pressure on us as local producers to start competing with the imported cheese varieties.'

But the biggest impact was on the competitors of Shoprite/ Checkers – suddenly Pick n Pay and even Woolworths were obliged to improve their cheese offerings as well. 'So the specialist cheese industry profited a lot from this new emphasis on exotic or special cheeses. In fact, the cheese industry ought to erect a little monument to Whitey because of his decision to exploit special cheese varieties as a growth opportunity.'

Checkers also expanded its coffee offerings considerably, by launching its own range of single-origin coffee called Foreign Ground.

* * * *

Another trend that took root in South African retail was the establishment of private labels. These are products such as toilet paper, tinned food and disposable nappies that are sold under other brand names than those of the manufacturer. When they are manufactured or packaged for a particular retailer, they are known as 'house brands' or 'own brands'. These brands are often slightly cheaper than the well-known national brands. A third variant is generic 'no-name brands', which have very basic packaging and are even cheaper than house brands. Whitey embraced this trend to offer his customers better value for money and more choices. Private labels also offered higher margins for retailers as they could be marketed more cheaply.[11]

The difference between private labels (house brands) and no-name brands is that while both are owned by the retailer, more attention is given to the establishment and marketing of the former. Hence you can also ask more for the product as it carries a brand name instead of 'no name'.

In retail, your shelf space is one of your biggest assets. Shelf placement helps to determine customer perception of a given product and ultimately its sales. If you put your private-label product next to a better-known brand, it shows the customer they are equally good. 'Nobody necessarily knows that it's Shoprite's or Checkers' own brands, but you give attention to the brand, and you put it on the best places on the shelves,' explains Whitey.

'I did it in Angola after Distell made me cross. They had started producing J.C. Le Roux there, but then wanted to charge more for it than it would've cost to get it from the Cape. So I said, surely it can't work like that – I have to buy at the best price. But they wouldn't budge. We then produced our own sparkling wine and called it Don Carlo. And it was given a larger facing [shelf placement] than J.C. Le Roux. Within six months it was the biggest sparkling wine in Angola.' Today the group sells enough sparkling wine in Nigeria to fill 3 166 424 champagne glasses annually.[12]

The group initially introduced private labels as a cheaper version of branded products – with Shoprite's Ritebrand and Checkers Housebrand – but in time also introduced new private-label brands such as Oh My Goodness and Simple Truth to appeal to the premium market segment.[13]

The private-label sector would grow rapidly, and house brands are no longer viewed as inferior.[14] 'It's incredible how far people will drive to find disposable nappies like Huggies or Pampers. So we just started our own product line, Lovies,' says Whitey. They did the same with toothbrushes, dental floss and mouthwash – Oralwise was Whitey and his team's answer to the better-known Oral-B brand.

'I spent a lot of time on purchasing,' he continues. 'Renier always said: "You don't sell yourself rich, you buy yourself rich." We visited all the trade fairs and went to China for toothbrushes. At a point, toothbrushes cost R2 but were sold for up to R80. The price of our own toothbrushes was first R5,99, and then R7,99, but they still sold badly. We then pushed up the price to R19,99, and they flew off the shelves! Today Oralwise makes a lot of profit for Shoprite.'

They followed the same approach with a carbonated soft drink. 'We made our own Cola, called Zip. We got an American group – one of the largest manufacturers for house brands – to help us with this.' According to Schreuder, everyone said a private-label brand for a carbonated soft drink was a non-starter as Coca-Cola was so dominant. 'We went through probably 700 different options for the packaging and had a variety of syrups flown in from Atlanta. Whitey was dead set on it, and when people told him it couldn't be done, it just spurred him on even more.'

Finally, everything was ready – the can had been designed, the colours selected, the taste perfected – and Zip Cola was launched. Whitey boasts: 'At one stage our sales of Zip Zero exceeded those of Coke's sugar-free alternative in some of our stores – and it tasted like Coke.' The group still sells Coca-Cola, of course, and annually sells enough Coke to fill 62 Olympic swimming pools.[15]

Today the Shoprite Group has over 3 500 private-label products on its shelves, and sales of these products account for about 18 per cent of its total sales.[16] 'All these categories showed how we were different,' Schreuder explains. 'No one wants to go to a braai and say, I shop at Checkers because the Ricoffy is cheap; you'd rather say you shop there because they sell the best wines. It's a clever way of signalling that we are in the top market segment, but our prices are still low. And it has been very successful.'

Whitey also rolled out a new store format that targeted a market below that of Shoprite and was based on what he had originally envisaged when he left Pep. He initially intended to establish the concept of limited assortment in South Africa. But then Shoprite came into the picture, and the idea was put on the back burner.

In 2001, however, Shoprite opened its first Usave, which was based on the concept of limited assortment, in Stellenbosch. The Usave chain, which comprises no-frills small-format stores with a limited range of low-cost products, 'is positioned below the Shoprite store profile, enhancing the Group's price perception at the bottom end of the market where price is all-important'.[17] The stores were mostly opened in or close to townships. The group also viewed this format as the ideal vehicle for their expansion into Africa.[18]

Whitey says he is 'mad' about the Usave concept. 'If I had to open anything again today, it would be Usave with its limited assortment. It's easier to run, and you don't have to search far and wide for premises because the stores are smaller. And Usave was profitable from day one.'

According to Prof. Nic Terblanche, the 'totally divergent retail groups' Whitey eventually drew together under one umbrella placed him in a class of his own. 'Shoprite, Grand Bazaars, OK, Checkers, and 8 Till Late – from a cultural perspective, these businesses differed completely from each other. They actually had nothing in common, but Whitey managed to refine each one neatly, and successfully integrate it into the group.

'The dilemma with OK at the time, and the reason why it went bust, was: what was the brand perception of OK? Was it clothing, groceries, or furniture? The moment you don't have clarity about who and what a store is, there is trouble. The consumer should know exactly what a store's brand represents. And Whitey and co. separated the elements very neatly and retained some of the brands and dropped others. Given the diversity of target markets, you have to understand retail very well to be successful.'

Whitey may have understood retail very well, but he never rested on his laurels. He was constantly on the lookout for ways to innovate and keep the business fresh. In the early 1980s, he and other Shoprite people started undertaking regular trips to America. 'I was always worried that I would miss out on some or other trend others were able to spot,' he recounts. 'I took trouble to study successful trends and ideas from across the world and would then apply them in Shoprite.'

Consequently, Whitey also realised he should offer his customers not only cheaper chicken and baked beans but also services that had not previously been available in a supermarket. Value-added services provided an additional avenue to differentiate Shoprite from its rivals and give people another reason to visit his stores.

Since 1998 the Money Market counter has been offering Shoprite's customers a simple, convenient and cheap way to send money to other people via cellphones. Shoprite was the first retailer to introduce such a low-cost service.[19] The service developed over time into one where customers can also buy tickets for various leisure and sporting events, pay their municipal bills, buy airtime, renew their TV licences, and book bus tickets and flights. Today the Money Market account is a full-fledged transactional bank account, and customers can withdraw or deposit cash at Shoprite, Checkers or Usave stores, receive their salaries, and send money to someone.[20]

The first Medirite started trading in the Checkers Hyper in Brackenfell in 1999, making Shoprite the first retailer to establish pharmacies in its supermarkets.[21] Ten years later the group bought Transpharm, a pharmaceutical wholesaler. In 2005 Computicket was acquired, and the first Shoprite LiquorShop was opened. The LiquorShops are separate stores, but they are usually located close to the entrance of a Shoprite or Checkers outlet. Among other things, a new emphasis was put on whisky. 'We knew whisky was important to the emerging market and we went big with it,' Whitey relates. 'So we launched the House of Fine Whisky, where you could buy the best whisky at supermarket prices.'

Joseph Brönn, deputy CEO and responsible for whisky and wine, tells an amusing story. He was a member of a team that accompanied Whitey to Scotland in order to look for a whisky that could be bottled for Checkers. There they met Billy Walker, a famous name in the whisky business, who had two whisky cellars. Walker and Whitey hit it off and eventually he said Whitey could select any cask of whisky, which he would then bottle for Checkers. Whitey walked through the cellar and chose a cask. They were back in the office when a man who worked in the cellar came to tell them apologetically that Donald Trump had bought that very same cask for his golf estate a week before. So Whitey had no choice but to play second fiddle – albeit to Trump – and select another cask.

* * * *

There was a high appetite for risk, and although Whitey wanted to have his finger on the pulse everywhere, he encouraged his staff to take risks and try out new things. During one of his trips to America, Whitey experienced the Black Friday phenomenon – the first Friday in November after Thanksgiving Day, on which retailers offer huge bargains – and he discussed it with his marketing team on his return. In 2014, Checkers became the first retailer to introduce South Africans to Black Friday deals on the last Friday in November.

'He challenged us to think big,' Neil Schreuder says. In one case, the marketing team had an idea to make retail exciting for children and harness a degree of 'pester power'. Research was done into collectibles for children and into mini products, including ones that carried the suppliers' brand names. 'Many people thought it wouldn't work, but Whitey said we should give it a go.'

The result was Little Shop, one of the best promotional campaigns Checkers ever ran. 'Within a month our stock had run out, and our sales had doubled. A conservative CEO would have turned down the proposal. But Whitey said we should try it, and it worked.'

Another idea was a humorous television ad in which children would mimic the celebrity chefs Gordon Ramsay and Jamie Oliver. 'So Whitey said, if you want to do that, why don't you get the real Gordon Ramsay?' Schreuder recalls. The marketing team cast their reservations aside and recruited Ramsay – the world-famous chef who is notorious for his outbursts and swearing on his television shows – for the advertisements.

Three television advertisements were produced – in the first one Ramsay said he would use Checkers' meat products in his restaurants. In the second ad, he and Nataniël looked at Checkers' wines and cheeses and Ramsay stated that these were world-class products at supermarket prices. In the third one, Ramsay and his daughter Matilda launched the Oh My Goodness range of kids' convenience meals they had helped to develop. 'One of the world's best-known chefs recommending our meat and other products by name. That was worth its weight in gold,' says Schreuder. 'It helped change the perceptions of people who were still shunning Checkers at the time. And it was driven by Whitey, who always challenged his people to think bigger.'

28

Building for the future

Actions matter. Words matter less. Score the try.
— Whitey Basson

The mammoth American online retailer Amazon is one of Whitey's favourite companies.[1] Amazon's founder, Jeff Bezos, says he frequently gets asked the question: 'What's going to change in the next ten years?' It is an interesting question, he states, but he is almost never asked what is *not* going to change.[2] In his view, 'that second question is actually the more important of the two – because you can build a business strategy around the things that are stable in time'. In ten years' time customers will still want low prices and fast delivery, and '[w]hen you have something that you know is true, even over the long term, you can afford to put a lot of energy into it'.[3]

At a time when Bezos was still selling books from his garage, Whitey already knew that the control of distribution networks was crucial. Today, Amazon's distribution model is unparalleled. 'The success and ultimately the survival of South African retailers will in time depend on their ability to control the supply chain,' Whitey noted in the group's 1998 annual report.[4]

Shoprite was the first food retailer in South Africa to set up distribution centres (DCs) and thereby centralise the supply chain. From early on, the group put a lot of energy into this idea because it translated into better control, greater efficiency, and lower prices. In this way Whitey could ensure that the group maintained its low-price leadership through low-cost leadership. With this model, suppliers delivered their products to a DC and the retailer itself distributed the goods to its outlets. It was much more efficient than the old system where suppliers themselves had to deliver their products to each individual store.

Whitey does not think centralised distribution is really innovative; it is actually nonsensical to do it any other way. 'I knew as a kid already that it must be cheaper for one truck to go to one store with a full load than to have 1 000 trucks waiting to deliver one box each,' he told Tim Cohen.

'If you are trading in high volumes that justify a warehouse, then you can take truckloads from suppliers, store the stock and take one truckload to a store. Central distribution was never optional for Shoprite, and it was never a debate in any First World country. It's a best-practice concept worldwide.'[5]

Today he explains further: 'If we buy, say, baked beans from Langeberg, there is also a big saving for the supplier in only having to come to the depot. There are no significant handling costs, and of course he can sell to us in bulk. So we would buy 60 000 tins, and they are delivered at the depot. But then we also negotiate a discount and the suppliers also save.'

Today Shoprite's centralised distribution model is unrivalled in South Africa and Africa, and among the best in the world. The group's largest DC is in Centurion in Gauteng, but the one in Brackenfell outside Cape Town is the newest and most technologically advanced. It is now known as the Whitey Basson Distribution Centre. In 2021 it won the South African Property Owners Association (SAPOA) Award for Innovative Excellence in the 'Industrial Development' category.[6] The dry goods warehouse in Cape Town has a floorspace of nearly ten rugby fields, and nine giant Airbus A380 passenger aircraft could fit into it.[7]

All the products consumers find on the shelves of Shoprite, Checkers, OK or Usave outlets are first delivered to a DC by hundreds of suppliers. Each store places its orders via a computer system. 'The warehouse operates in near total silence, thanks to voice-enabled technology fed to staff through earpieces, and fully electric forklifts.' Order pickers select the correct items, which are then loaded onto the trucks in a specific order so that they can be unpacked systematically at each store. Once the trucks leave the centre, another computer system guides and tracks them to ensure they use the most efficient delivery routes.

Within walking distance of this warehouse is the cold storage unit, also a massive structure, where goods are stored at low temperatures – from ordinary 'fridge' conditions to sub-zero temperatures. Tollie Lewis, one of the warehouse managers, recounts that despite the thousands of products moving in and out daily, individual customers still receive attention. There is a woman in Sea Point, for instance, who buys salmon every week at her closest Checkers. The crate with cold products destined for that Checkers branch contains her package of salmon.

Prof. Terblanche explains again: 'Your logistics chain is of crucial importance. Competition is so fierce and the profit margins are so small that you have to manage your business very efficiently, and you need enormous volumes to make any impact at all. Stock must move and not lie on a shelf. There Whitey and his colleagues have excelled, with the DCs they started, and how technologically advanced they are today. All of these initiatives were Whitey's brainchildren.

'The introduction of distribution centres was an excellent move. What goes onto the truck must be absolutely reconcilable with the demand on the other side. The DCs are something incredible, and they were not simply cut and pasted from an overseas model. Yes, the concept and systems originated overseas, but the level at which Shoprite Checkers' DCs are run is something else.'

Today Shoprite has 29 DCs, from where 1 234 drivers with a fleet of over 800 trucks deliver almost 340 million cases of products per year to the group's stores[8] in order to provide the 2 159 customers they serve per minute with goods. The group sells 250 products a second, and in 2021 it sold a mind-boggling 7 billion individual items.[9]

* * * *

After the turn of the century, Whitey also started delegating more, knowing that one person could do only so much. Accordingly, Carel Goosen was promoted to deputy managing director.[10] 'I always had Callie,' Whitey says. 'When I walked out of the door, he was the boss – he was my 2IC [second in command].'

Goosen became responsible for Information Technology, Financial Management, Logistics and the OK Franchise division, which included OK Foods, Sentra, 8 Till Late and Megasave. Other heads who reported directly to Whitey were Jannie Holtzhausen (Operations: North Africa), Mauritz Alberts (Operations: Sub-Saharan Africa), Callie Burger (Human Resources), Barney Rogut (Buying and Merchandising), Brian Weyers (Marketing), André van Zyl (Statutory and Legal Services), Philip van der Merwe (Properties), and Etienne Nel (Portfolios, which included OK Furniture, Freshmark and Meat Markets). Succession planning was important too, hence Whitey and his team identified successors for most of the senior executives and showed them the ropes.

'The plan was of the course that when I retired, there had to be a working team who could take over from me, and I had to make sure that it happened,' Whitey states. 'And I knew that if a bus were to run me over, the company would be able to carry on equally well.'

Pieter Engelbrecht, who took over from Whitey as chief executive, had started at the group in 1997. He was appointed as a director of Shoprite Checkers in 2003, and became an alternate director of Shoprite Holdings in 2005 and a director in 2012.

The company prided itself on the fact that only three levels of management existed between Whitey and store employees.[11] According to the 2000 annual report, Shoprite had always had an 'open-door policy' and embraced an informal work style. 'Whitey frustrated me at times,' Goosen admits. 'But in general we had a very good relationship. He trusted me, and he supported me as well.

'Now and then we disagreed, but it never caused problems. What did annoy me sometimes was that he was so outspoken when you'd messed up – he would give you a dressing-down in his office or in front of other people. He could be abrasive, not only with me, but with other members of his staff. And the less confidence he had in you, the harsher he could be. Some days it upset me. But what I learnt from him is that a boss can get angry, he just needs to restore that relationship. If he wants it to be restored, that is.

'You would never go to bed that night without Whitey having called to tell you what a great guy you were and what good work you were doing. And he did that with all his managers – he would uplift them in the evenings after having trampled all over them in the course of the day. And then you would go to work the next day with renewed passion and motivation.

'I learnt from him that you don't have to be nice or popular to build or to lead a team, you just need to maintain that balance. But he was very good at managing relationships – and whether it was me, or a store manager who may only have passed standard eight, he worked with all of us in the same way. He was always fair, and a good boss.'

As far back as the 1980s, when it was expanding to other provinces, Shoprite had divided the rest of South Africa into different divisions.

Whitey says he is a great believer in the idea of breaking down larger parts or projects into smaller and more workable parts. The head office in Brackenfell in the Western Cape still had overall control over properties, finances, personnel and marketing, but each region was effectively a decentralised division with its own general manager.

Shoprite had a 'strong discipline structure within the business' and no one encroached on another person's terrain, but they had retained 'that one crucial aspect that people shouldn't lose their entrepreneurial skills', Whitey told Theo Vorster. It was not a case of Whitey managing thousands of stores and 150 000 employees. 'When you eventually have your structure in place, you are managing a lot of small businesses' that together make up your employees and company.[12]

Whitey visited each division once a month and met with the general managers. 'But anybody could sit in, even the tea lady. For instance, I would fly to Bloemfontein in the morning and then to Johannesburg in the afternoon. I would do one division in the afternoon and two the following day, then I would fly to Durban, and the day after that to PE. And of course, I visited Namibia every three months, and the African markets on a regular basis as well. I looked at everything when I arrived there, from sales to the electricity bills, and I was able to spot quickly if something was wrong or needed attention.

'My dad used to tell the joke about the guy who is walking down the street and someone asks him, how's your wife? and he replies, compared to what? You can't analyse any financial information if you don't compare it with something.' Thus, Whitey would rapidly analyse all the key financial indicators and point out the items that required attention. 'Speed was paramount to me – we had to wrap everything up fast.'

This was all part of Shoprite's culture. You had to be prepared for Whitey's sharp eyes, and fix things quickly if you had messed up. 'Retail's culture is incredibly important,' Whitey emphasises once again. 'Now and then someone else took charge of the meetings and I would go to inspect the stores, since the bosses weren't there. Then I would ask the employees how things were going, and I looked around on the floor myself. I did many surprise visits. I would say I was coming to Bloemfontein but then fly to, say, Namibia instead. Because I felt I had to experience the stores like an ordinary customer – they shouldn't spruce up the place for my benefit. In that way I managed the business hands-on, on a day-to-day basis.'

He was so 'hands-on' that he even tested the apples. If there is something Whitey detests, it is a floury apple – 'and if there happened to be one floury apple among twenty others, you could be sure that would be the one Whitey picked up', relates Johan van Deventer, general manager of Freshmark.

'One morning old Sampie Lourens, the apple buyer, was summoned to the corner office. A nervous Sampie arrived there an hour before the time and smoked ten cigarettes before he'd gathered the courage to knock at the door of the famous office. He suspected it might be about a floury apple.' His suspicions turned out to be correct. Sampie still tried to explain, but Whitey was not interested in the technical considerations and reacted like a customer. 'Just give me a fresh and tasty apple,' he said.

Sampie was crestfallen, but Whitey asked: 'Do you have a pocket knife? I'll buy you one, then you cut open the apples and taste them yourself.' According to Van Deventer, Sampie arrived back at the office pale-faced and asked: 'Does Mr Basson now want me to cut all the apples in half?' From that day on, Freshmark buyers carried pocket knives with them.[13] And Freshmark sells a lot of apples. If all the apples the company sells annually had to be packed next to each other, the line would stretch around the globe.[14]

Freshmark is responsible for the procurement, buying and distribution of all the fresh produce sold at the group's stores.[15] It is one of the largest buyers and distributors of fresh fruit and vegetables in Africa, and up to 95 per cent of the fresh produce is sourced directly from local producers in each country. Today, it sells enough avocados annually to make 11 million bowls of guacamole, and enough iceberg lettuce for 260 million hamburgers.

Van Deventer also recalls his first meeting with Whitey in the late 1990s. He was the branch manager of Freshmark City Deep at the time, and eager to impress the 'big boss'. 'This was still in the wild days when we simply traded – doing calculations on the back of a cigarette pack,' he recounts. 'So I decided we needed to start improving our image and at least get uniform labels. Barcodes didn't exist yet. I therefore had labels printed for each line that carried a picture of the product type, as well as the name Freshmark, the address, and the well-known slogan: "We Sell Freshness".'

A chuffed Van Deventer thought it looked very grand. He and his team prepared thoroughly for Whitey's visit – they scrubbed, swept and tidied up. 'So I walked with him to the production area where we did all the pre-packaging, and rolls of my new labels were hanging neatly in a row. Then he said: "Yes, they look nice. But have you been to one of our magazine sections? You'll find comics there too. Why would you put a picture of sweet corn or strawberries on a label if people can see for themselves it's sweet corn or strawberries?"

'I couldn't win that one. The lesson was, reflect carefully on what you do and why you are doing it,' says Van Deventer.

* * * *

In 2011 Shoprite acquired the franchise division of Metcash, which included brands such as Friendly Grocer, 7-Eleven and Price Club

Discount Supermarket. The 150 stores were integrated into the group's OK Franchise division.[16] In the same year Shoprite entered the hospitality and catering sector by launching the business-to-business brand Checkers Food Services, which services customers in the hospitality and catering industries.

Under Whitey's leadership, Shoprite also introduced a project department and began exploiting talent at Stellenbosch University by means of the 'Brightest Young Minds' programme. Whitey asked Pieter Engelbrecht to lead the project office.

'People were always too busy for projects, or too prejudiced, so we recruited smart people from the university and put them on various projects,' Whitey recounts. 'That was how Neil Schreuder started at Shoprite, and to my mind he is the best marketer in the country today.'

Shoprite's innovation department was created in 2005 with the sole brief of identifying new opportunities and new possibilities, and seeing how these could be successfully integrated either into the group's main business or within a broader framework of retailing.[17] Most of the senior managers were shopkeepers who had worked themselves up over the years and concentrated on day-to-day operations. Given Shoprite's rapid growth, and a changing retail landscape, Whitey started developing talent to sustain the company for the next few decades. It was obvious that technology would play an increasingly important role and require new skills and experience.

Schreuder was one of the first of the new generation with a 'quick mouth and strong opinions' who had no qualms about arguing with seniors. And that appealed to Whitey. At the age of 28, Schreuder became marketing director as well as the only English-speaking member of the senior executive management. 'Whitey knew I was determined, dedicated, and a hard worker, and he gave me a chance,' he recounts. 'I was apprehensive about the challenge, and felt I was not yet ready for it. But Whitey said, Neillie, you don't need to have all the answers. You just have to ask the right questions. Everything will be okay.'

Today Schreuder is Shoprite's chief of strategy and innovation. 'We have done incredibly well, and, among other things, left Pick n Pay in the dust,' he says. 'For an accountant and shopkeeper, Whitey was very, very creative. He had a brilliant eye for design, for packaging, and a strong feel for marketing and how to position things and tell stories.'

* * * *

According to analysts, two of the Shoprite Group's key competitive advantages are its economies of scale and its supply chain that has been built up over decades.[18] Owing to its extensive footprint throughout South Africa and the large volumes of goods that go through its stores, Shoprite has been able to source goods more cheaply than its competitors and can therefore keep its prices low. This resulted in increased customer loyalty and demand lead to further scale advantages. The greater scale, in turn, allows the group to spread its fixed costs over a larger number of products, which reduces its overall cost per unit. Shoprite's lower prices also make it harder for new players to enter the sector, as they struggle to compete.

Shoprite's centralised supply chain has resulted in lower transport costs for suppliers, while ensuring the quality of products. The group's fleet of trucks are used more efficiently and follow optimised routes to the stores. Consequently, there is 'an improvement in the lead time of products to the stores, and on-shelf availability. The DCs also enable better space utilisation within the Group's individual stores. The efficient use of space results in cost savings, and increased sales,' Cadiz Asset Management stated in 2019.

By the turn of the century Shoprite's profit margin had returned to 2 per cent, which was considered standard for retailers. Over the following decade it improved to an unprecedented 5 per cent,[19] and this level was maintained up to and including Whitey's retirement. By 2018 the group's market capitalisation was R122 billion, its turnover over R145 billion per year, and its market share in South Africa nearly 32 per cent.[20]

In 2019 Shoprite celebrated its 40th anniversary. According to Deloitte's *Global Powers of Retailing*, the group was the 86th largest retailer in the world, and the only South African retailer in the top 100. 'When I started out, Pick n Pay was my main rival – it was at that stage the largest in South Africa,' Whitey says. 'But I believe we won the contest – with a core team of hard-working and smart people around me, and a board that was supportive and didn't interfere unnecessarily. We just did things differently.'

29

An aversion to rules

My board must look like my business. Why would I sit with a clergyman on my board? I'm not in the church business, am I?

– Whitey Basson

Whitey has little patience with committees and the excess of rules and regulations that go hand in hand with corporate governance. He also believes that too many rules and regulations smother small businesses. In 1997 he was already openly opposed to excessive business regulation. 'Only in a deregulated environment can a true culture of entrepreneurship be created. In our country we have far too many meetings and seminars, and too little real action to create a business climate and encourage a culture of entrepreneurship,' he told *Finansies & Tegniek*.[1]

Things sometimes got heated at Shoprite. Neil Schreuder writes in Whitey's Tribute Book about an incident at a strategy meeting after someone had quoted a 'stupid' rule that everyone followed blindly. The issue of Shoprite's policy was then raised, whereupon Whitey replied: 'I *am* the policy!' (This statement was subsequently printed on a number of T-shirts.)

Over time, the rules and regulations proliferated. And Whitey still gets hot under the collar when talking about the subject. 'Christo always said the guys don't want to serve on my board any more because they only get braai grids every year. But now directors have to be paid in accordance with the size of the company, and not the size of your brains and what you contribute.'

This brings him to another core principle: his unshakeable belief in merit-based appointments. 'People should only be appointed in positions on the basis of their skills. This applies to general staff members as well as directors.

'Government officials regularly visited Shoprite's personnel department and tried to demand that people be appointed in certain categories on certain job levels. I then took a stand and said: My task is to make sure that the company is run as well as possible, in the interest of its shareholders, its customers *and* its employees. Therefore, we appoint people who have the requisite skills, and not because they are women, men, white, black or whatever.

'Every year I sat at human resources and said, nothing would give me greater pleasure than giving a chance to people who haven't previously had the opportunities. But just give me competent people with the requisite skills and experience. We can't be held responsible for our poor and unequal education system. People will eventually come through from below. And that did happen – the company has been properly transformed up to senior management level.'

'We were also criticised about the composition of our boards. And yes, my directors were for a considerable time mostly white males, but they were people with the necessary experience – they all came from retail. I couldn't replace them with people who knew nothing about the business.

'There was also a difference between the boards of our unlisted companies – the companies at operational level –and the board of our listed company, Shoprite Holdings. There have long been quite a number of women on the boards of our unlisted companies.'

Nonetheless, Shoprite Holdings appointed its first black and Indian directors in 2003.[2] Reggie Hlongwane, a businessman with diverse interests in Gauteng, was appointed as non-executive director. He also served on the board of Pepkor. Hlongwane was a past president of the Foundation for African Business and Consumer Services (Fabcos) and managing director of Pep Reef, an affiliate of Pepkor, in which black business held a majority stake. Hlongwane eventually stepped down as director in 2010.

Ram Harisunker joined the board as executive director in charge of KwaZulu-Natal, India and the Indian Ocean Islands. He had started working at Checkers in 1969 and was appointed to the board of Shoprite Checkers (a subsidiary of Shoprite Holdings) as far back as 1999.

Whitey believes it is self-evident that people from different cultures, backgrounds and genders can bring different views to the table, which can only be good for a company. 'Ram had worked himself up, he was experienced, and he also thought differently about certain things, and conveyed his ideas to the board.'

There is an amusing and instructive anecdote in this regard. Harisunker once bought a blood-red Mercedes-Benz sports car. Shortly afterwards, he and Whitey sat eating their lunch somewhere in a small store office. 'I wanted to show him that I, too, liked samoosas, and I polished off about ten. "Aren't you having one?" I asked. And he replied: "Are you mad? That stuff gives me heartburn!"' The conversation then turned to Ram's red Merc. 'With Mercedes cars also available in silver, black and white, I asked him, why did you choose a red one? And who's going to buy it from you one day? No one wants a red Mercedes.'

Harisunker replied: 'That's where you're wrong. It's almost the only red Mercedes, so the Indians in Natal will be queuing up to buy it from me. Don't think that what works in the rest of South Africa is how things work in Natal and for Ram Harisunker!'

In 2012 Dr Anna Mokgokong was appointed as a director of Shoprite Holdings. Among other things, she had been South African Businesswoman of the Year in 1999 and was the co-founder and executive chair of Community Investment Holdings. She was also chair of Rebosis Property Fund and Jasco Electronics, as well as a director of Afrocentric and Medscheme. Whitey emphasises again: 'She was not appointed because she's a woman.'

* * * *

After leaving Shoprite, Whitey served for a few months as independent non-executive director of the dairy group Clover. 'One of the biggest investors in Clover inquired whether I would take over as chairman of the company,' he recounts. 'Because in their view the current chairman wasn't necessarily impartial as he was a big farmer and one of Clover's largest suppliers. So I said, but that's exactly the person you want there. What can he do that will harm the shareholders? He has a wealth of knowledge and experience that will benefit the company. That's why companies go bust – it's when they shift their focus away from the customer to corporate governance.'

According to Whitey, all the additional rules regarding corporate governance arose after the Enron scandal in the United States. The energy giant Enron, which was a Wall Street darling in the 1990s, was declared bankrupt in December 2001 as a result of large-scale accounting and corporate fraud. At the time, it was the biggest bankruptcy in history.[3] The scandal also led to the collapse of Arthur Andersen, one of the 'Big 5' accounting firms, which as Enron's auditors been signing off the company's books for years despite all the irregularities.

Whitey believes he may have a solution. Audit committees, corporate governance and all the accompanying rigmarole can demand excessive attention and divert businesses' attention from their core operations. Wouldn't it be cheaper to rather just take out insurance against an Enron incident?

Whitey is also very vocal about the King Code. The King Report on Corporate Governance provides guidelines for the governance structures and operations of companies in South Africa. It is issued by the King Committee on Corporate Governance, which was established by the Institute of Directors in South Africa and is chaired by former judge Mervyn King.

The King Report and King Code set out what 'ethical and effective leadership' for South African companies involves. Among other things, it includes standards of conduct for boards and directors of listed companies, banks and certain state-owned entities. The first King Report was issued in 1994, followed by King II in 2002, King III in 2009, and King IV in 2017. Compliance with the principles and code is largely voluntary, but certain aspects are binding for entities with a primary listing on the JSE.[4]

Whitey believes King has a brilliant legal mind, but questions 'the kind of unnecessary red tape he introduced. We had a very simple policy on compliance with the King principles. Some of them are enforceable, and others not. We complied with the enforceable principles. But the others are merely recommendations, and if we didn't benefit from such a principle, we didn't comply with it. The chairman supported me. But this was not only our view – it was company policy. We didn't want to let senseless things hamper us.

'The same applies to the IFRS (International Financial Reporting Standards). Some of the accounting standards are right, but most of them are far too difficult to implement. How is it possible, with King and all the committees, that a company like Steinhoff goes to the dogs and no one picks it up?'

In Whitey's view, a committee is a good place to 'park' something you don't actually want to get finished because all the members start calling for new information and fight among themselves. 'But it's a waste of time when it comes to business. People are always telling you what to do, or how they think things should be done, and there are 60 different things you can think of. I always believed in prioritising things, and speed was always important to me. For when it comes to business, you have to do things fast and get them finished, win or lose. But you need to make sure you win more than you lose. It's as simple as that.'

According to Whitey, one of South Africa's biggest problems is the plethora of regulations that makes life difficult for entrepreneurs – there are far too many rules they have to comply with.[5] Besides taking up too much time, compliance is also expensive. 'I have a passion for people who not only work hard but also get things done. That's why I've always had a big problem with bureaucratic red tape and stuff like corporate governance. I'm not saying it's wrong – generally it's a good thing – but there's just too much of it. After Enron, it simply got out of hand.

'My view is that one needs it, but you must ensure that the people making the rules and regulations really know what's going on in the industry. Although these things are right in general, one size doesn't fit all. All the rules and regulations – including those of corporate governance – protect inferior people. It's actually absurd.

'I don't know what the solution is, and I'm worried about it. The structures that are being put in place may be good for well-developed countries like Switzerland, but not for developing countries such as South Africa where economies need to grow fast and many jobs have to be created. And all the rules and regulations in South Africa are suppressing entrepreneurship and economic growth.'

30

The Shoprite family

Whitey Basson's rivals in the business world say the softest part of his anatomy is his teeth. But to his employees, he's the man with the big heart.

— *Rooi Rose*[1]

Job creation has always been extremely important to Whitey, and improving people's circumstances is close to his heart. 'Shoprite is one of the largest employment creators in South Africa and in Africa. And it's not only the people who work for Shoprite,' he says. 'Think also of the secondary impact, the downstream employment that is created. There are many cases where the mother started working as a clerk and worked her way up, her children went to university, and now they work for the company. I wanted us to offer people new opportunities.'

Today the Shoprite Group is indeed the biggest job creator in the South African private sector. In 2017, when Whitey retired, the group had close to 150 000 employees, and it also creates thousands of new job opportunities every year.

In 2000 a journalist asked Whitey if the responsibility ever scared him. 'I get scared speechless,' he said. 'You must remember that to the people who work in this company I am their friend, and their prosperity depends on how this company is steered. I must ask myself whether I am delegating enough so there's someone to watch the ship all the time. There are icebergs around. But the employees have to be as responsible as I am. I could be wrong, but they could lose their jobs.

I am only there to lead the way. In the end it's all about people. The people make it work.'[2]

Jimmy Fouché, a former company secretary and director, also says Whitey always had the interests of his employees at heart. Many people who started at the bottom of the business as shelf packers, for instance, now occupy high positions. One of them is Ben Alexander, who began his career as an order picker in the early years. Today he is head of the non-foods distribution team. In 2017 Alexander wrote in Whitey's Tribute Book: 'When I walked in at Shoprite on the morning of 15 January 1981, you took my hand and asked, "What is your name? What do you do?" I'll never forget how you added, "Welcome to Shoprite!"'[3]

Charity Malope from Dennilton, Mpumalanga, started at Shoprite in 2008 as a till packer. 'I was unemployed before I started working at Shoprite, but always saw the Mobile Soup Kitchens serve in my community. It became my mission to work for Shoprite, a company that looks after communities,' said Malope. By 2019 she was a branch manager.[4]

According to Whitey, 'from day one it has been the policy of our group to improve people's circumstances and give them better opportunities'. In 2011 he told Theo Vorster that they give their employees' children 'first option, if they are sufficiently qualified to do the work', and 'make sure that all people within the group are evaluated and that they can move to better positions'. The 'nicest thing' for him was that some of his employees' children had become doctors and professors, 'and you know that you've been part of the process' of helping people grow and giving them opportunities. He valued the fact that 'it gives you that loyalty of the people who work with you, plus that unbelievable satisfaction when you walk past someone and he says, "Meet my wife and my son, who has just completed his studies."'[5]

When Whitey retired, he requested the board to establish a bursary fund for employees and their family members. Since then the Whitey Basson Bursary Fund has granted many bursaries – also to matriculants from Hoërskool Porterville in Whitey's old hometown. The acting principal wrote: 'You have given five young people the opportunity to pursue their dreams and to create a future in South Africa. The future of our country lies in the hands of our youth, and opportunities of this kind provide hope for a stronger economic outlook.'

To Whitey, Shoprite and its employees were like family. Despite the enormous growth of the company, he always tried to retain the 'sense of family' that had been characteristic of Pep's early years. 'Today you would probably be charged,' he muses. 'But at the head office I always used to give people hugs, ask about their husband, wife or children, and joke about them turning grey. It was an intimate bond with people who worked with me, from the directors and senior staff to my driver. In fact, my driver and I had nicer conversations than you'd get in board meetings – and he could at least tell me what was really going on in the business.

'Open doors are important, and the guy above you not only issued instructions, but there were also friendships too. It's like a rugby team that loses every Saturday and then, under a new coach, suddenly starts winning. He can't really coach them differently. But he can motivate them better, give them a sense of solidarity, a common goal – and then you win again.'

* * * *

Stories about Whitey's relationships with Shoprite's people are legion. Some have been recorded in his Tribute Book. In 1990 Moereeda Davids, who worked at Shoprite Somerset West at the time, went to help with the opening of Shoprite Kimberley. On her way home she was involved in a serious car accident and spent a long time in hospital. She was subsequently offered a job at the head office. One day Whitey bumped into her and asked why she was still limping – didn't she have physiotherapy while she was in hospital? She told him the hospital staff had tried, but she had still been too weak at that stage. So Whitey arranged for her to get physiotherapy treatment again, and also for his personal driver to take her to all the sessions.[6]

Another head office employee, Jo-Anne Collison, recounts: 'When I turned 21, Mr Basson – our managing director – personally came to congratulate me with a bottle of champagne. I'll never forget that . . .'

* * * *

Losing key personnel was upsetting to Whitey. Even though it seldom happened, it was, to him personally, a much greater disappointment than when a promising business deal fell through, he said in a 2002 interview.[7] His philosophy was also that talent should bubble up inside the company, and not bubble out of the door. When people left the company, it meant that their voices had not been heard.

'If you say that you would like an appointment with the MD because he is going in the wrong direction and you need to get your career going – you will be given an appointment with him, or with the GM of that division. I encourage such an approach because if you don't get competent people coming through then there is a problem with your business.'[8]

One Sunday, Whitey phoned Hennes Schreuder and got straight to the point. 'What the heck is your daughter doing in Johannesburg?' Whitey asked. 'She's working there,' Schreuder replied.

'But why isn't she working for us?' asked Whitey.

'Whitey, don't ask me, ask her. And why do you want to know?'

'She should come and work for us,' Whitey said, and ended the call.

Schreuder's daughter called her dad five minutes later. 'Who's Pieter Engelbrecht?' she asked.

'He's Whitey's executive assistant.' He wanted to meet with her.

Whitey's younger daughter, Mari, and Schreuder's daughter Ciska had been fellow students at Stellenbosch. On that Sunday, Mari had remarked at the Bassons' family braai that Ciska used to have the best notes on campus and that copies of her notes were circulated among the other students. 'That was when I received the call out of the blue,' Schreuder recounts. Soon afterwards, Ciska started working at Shoprite.

Later, she went to work for Marks & Spencer in London. When Whitey discovered this, he was quick to call Schreuder again and ask why. On returning to South Africa one holiday, she happened to be on the same flight as Whitey. 'He doesn't easily accept a loss,' Schreuder continues, 'and this was of course a loss – she'd ditched Shoprite for Marks & Spencer. So Whitey wanted to talk to her. They didn't want to allow her in the first-class section, but Whitey said she was his secretary and that they had to discuss work. Whitey, the relentless negotiator, did all he could to win her back. Shortly afterwards someone resigned, and she returned to Shoprite. It's a very big organisation, but Whitey still wanted to help families and have family members working there.'

Whitey also had the ability to spot talent early, as he did with the people he took with him to Shoprite from Pep, and the 'troopers' he recruited everywhere who ended up staying with the company for decades. One such recruit was Photy Tzellios, Shoprite's supply chain director. 'The year was 1991 when Anita [Whitey's long-standing secretary] set up a meeting for us at the local Spur in N1 City,' Tzellios wrote in Whitey's Tribute Book. 'What convinced me at the time was your ability to recognise talent; your impressive management team;

you, the maverick, and the clear challenge to beat the opposition!'[9]

Fritz, too, relates that Whitey was 'pro-family'. 'When your child finished matric or their university studies, he would always say there was a place for that child at Shoprite. And he always inquired after people's children – what is he studying, is she an accountant, why is she working for PwC and not for Shoprite? And many people's children and family members became very successful and made their mark in Shoprite.

'It's been several years since Whitey left us, but he still calls you when you're ill, he knows what's going on, and he cares – what other guy would bother to do that? That's the type of man he is; every person who worked for him is on his list, and he stays in touch.'

In 1985 Whitey appointed Allen Johnstone, who became the managing director of Shoprite Butcheries. When Allen decided to retire in 1997, he wrote to Whitey: 'It was an absolute pleasure and privilege to serve under you . . . What I enjoyed the most was the freedom you gave me to do the job without looking over my shoulder every five minutes. It takes a great man to delegate to such an extent.

'I would also like to thank you for the true friendship over the past twelve years. It meant a lot to me that I could consult you when I needed advice, not only when it came to business but also in my private life. I will soon be leaving Shoprite with a heavy heart but, at the same time, with a sense of pride. Looking back on what we have achieved in a very short period, one can't help feeling pleased with oneself.'

André van Zyl believes Whitey knew how to work with people. Part of it was that he always showed respect for others, especially older people. 'When we stopped at the Shoprite in Goodwood, all the cashiers would spontaneously hug him.' Many of them were coloured people, and Whitey was specifically intent on creating better opportunities for members of the coloured community. This stemmed from his childhood years in Porterville when he had coloured playmates and couldn't understand why they had to walk to school while the white kids were transported by bus. 'I tried to help people who hadn't had the same chances as others.'

In his pursuit of this goal, Whitey's efforts were not limited to the provision of employment. In the Pep days he had already been involved in projects aimed at providing new business opportunities to members of the coloured community.[10] 'Renier was very philanthropic and cared a great deal about the coloured community,' Whitey recounts. The Group Areas Act not only prohibited coloured and white South Africans from living in the same residential areas; it also barred them from owning businesses in group areas that had not been assigned to their own racial group. To Renier and Whitey, the legislation was not only morally untenable but also prevented the company from properly doing business with its largest customer base.

Consequently, in 1974 Pep established a separate company, Pep Peninsula, in which Pep held 49 per cent of the shares and coloured shareholders 51 per cent. By 1979 the company was operating twelve stores and had 800 coloured shareholders. 'I even sold shares in the evenings to people such as teachers and explained what we were going to do,' Whitey recalls. 'When the Group Areas Act was repealed, many guys made fortunes.'

Suppliers and consultants, too, benefitted from Shoprite over the years. Many of them grew along with the company. One example is Laura Kotze from Golden Grove, who supplied chickens to Shoprite.

Whitey always says you shouldn't do business just with your head, but also with your heart. This is clearly illustrated in a story about a small advertising agency that has become 'one of the ad industry's trade legends'. Shortly after the turn of the century, Mad Ad founder Adelaide Potgieter, in her twenties and very ambitious, sent an arm and a leg of a mannequin to Whitey with a note that read: 'Dear Mr Basson, I would give an arm and a leg for a minute of your time.'

The note piqued Whitey's interest. He sent her the bust of a mannequin, accompanied by a note: 'Thank you for the arm and the leg, but you have forgotten the most important part of the body – the heart!' But this gimmick gave Adelaide a foot in the door, and eventually Shoprite became a client.[11]

'I also believed in taking our suppliers with us,' Whitey says. 'Our architects, our engineers, our quantity surveyors were with us from day one. They gave me a discount and had to work hard, and I looked after them. Steve Barclay, the fridge mechanic at a big company, came to us and said he wanted to start a business but had no money. And I said: Let's give that damn Englishman a chance!' He started a company and serviced and repaired all our fridges, countrywide.'

In 2000 Shoprite instituted the Supplier of the Year competition to recognise 'exemplary service and commitment'.[12] Most of the award ceremonies were held at Klein DasBosch.

'Whitey and Annalise Basson have the great privilege of inviting you to attend the Shoprite Checkers Supplier of the Year Gala Evening,' read one year's invitation to a formal function. But these events were usually big and jolly celebrations that have acquired legendary status. Hundreds of people were invited annually – the one evening was for suppliers and the other for employees – and your chances of sitting next to either a senior board member or a store manager of Shoprite were equally good. In 2007 Arch Chemicals was named Supplier of the Year in the category for non-food products. Ironically, one of its most important products is HTH pool chlorine, which the then tiny Shoprite had struggled to buy or sell years before.[13]

Whitey also helped people who did not do business directly with Shoprite. Former Springbok cyclist Chris Willemse operates one of the country's most successful cycling businesses, Chris Willemse Cycles. In 1977 Willemse opened his first shop in Paarl and then moved to Bellville. But he still lacked operating capital. In 1979 he had a lucky break. En route to a bicycle show in Taiwan he met Danie Roux from Shoprite, who suggested that he travel with the Shoprite group. Roux also wanted to introduce him to his boss. That was how Willemse met Whitey, who asked if he could help him select some bicycles for his children.

Whitey asked him about his business and his plans, and which bicycles he was going to buy. Willemse admitted he was only going to buy bicycle parts. The minimum order was 200 bicycles, and he could only afford 20. Whitey offered to lend him the money but he declined, as he did not want to owe money to someone he barely knew.

Two months later, he received a phone call asking him to go and see Whitey Basson. At Shoprite's offices, Whitey told him he had ordered the cycles Willemse had shown him in Taiwan and that they had landed in the country, ready for collection. Willemse could pay him back, interest free, after each weekend's cycle sales. 'This was the biggest break in my business career,' Willemse told *finweek* in 2017. 'To this day Whitey is one of my greatest heroes.'[14]

31

Virgin Cola and Madiba

If you look at the history of South Africa, there were
lots of Rubicons and many mistakes. But there's always
a solution at the end of the road.

– Whitey Basson[1]

Whitey did not hold back when it came to renowned businessmen such as Richard Branson, or even statesmen such as Nelson Mandela. In September 1997 the eccentric Branson, founder of the Virgin Group, was in Cape Town for the launch of his modelling agency, Storm. Supermodel Kate Moss was one of his guests, and the fashion magazines were full of photos of Branson and Moss.[2]

Whitey wrote to Branson a month later. He had already tried to make contact with Branson a year before in an attempt to bring Virgin Cola to South Africa. Branson had not replied, and Whitey was outraged when someone else approached Shoprite and said he had acquired the franchise for Virgin Cola in South Africa.

So Whitey wrote to Branson that he did not want to do business with agents. It was obvious to him that Branson had only been doing some 'tyre-kicking' in the period between Whitey's first letter (in July 1996) and this one a year later. He ended with a postscript: 'Maybe next time you visit South Africa, I should look after Kate Moss while you are doing some work!'

Branson would only reply in 2001. He realised the relationship between Virgin Drinks and Shoprite Checkers had not started off on a good note, he said, but he would like to meet Whitey 'to put the past behind us'. They met in May 2001, during another Branson visit to South Africa, whereafter Branson wrote to Whitey: 'Many thanks for giving us a second chance and I very much hope this is the start of a long-term relationship.'[3]

But it was too late – Virgin Cola never appeared on Shoprite's shelves. Virgin Drinks USA, which distributed the drink in the United States, failed to make headway and closed in 2001. Production of the drink ceased in the United Kingdom in 2009, and Virgin Cola was a thing of the past.[4]

Someone with whom Whitey did have a long-term relationship, however, was Nelson Mandela. As Shoprite grew, it played an increasingly significant role in building and supporting the resilience of the communities in which its stores operate. The group was one of the first donors to the Nelson Mandela Children's Fund.

Adèle Gouws, Shoprite's PR and communications manager, wrote in Whitey's Tribute Book: 'How wonderful it was to arrange the handover and to witness how you [Whitey] and Madiba started a friendship of mutual respect from that day that would last for years to come.'[5]

There were occasions when Whitey made Madiba laugh. In 2004 Shoprite donated a number of prefabricated mobile classrooms to the Free State Department of Education, and in May a plaque was unveiled at the Rebatla Thuto Secondary School at Koppies in the Free State. Both Whitey and Madiba attended the ceremony.[6]

'We were sitting next to each other and my bottle of water stood in front of us,' Whitey recounts. 'I took a sip of the water and asked him whether he also wanted a sip. He was about to take it when his security detail almost dive-tackled us and said he wasn't allowed to drink from my bottle. 'So I said, the world has really changed, hasn't it. Here we have a white guy trying to give a black guy some of his water, but it's not allowed! We then had a good laugh. He was always so easy-going and relaxed.'

After Madiba's retirement, Whitey once went to see him at his house in Houghton, Johannesburg. Whitey then told him there were rumours going around that Pick n Pay had been supplying him with free food since his retirement. 'We talked about various things, and I remarked: gosh, Madiba, you've lost weight. You can't get any thinner – you'll collapse. So I said, it's because you're eating that Pick n Pay food – you should rather buy your food from Shoprite or Checkers. He then pressed his bell and told his secretary: 'Do you hear what Mr Basson is telling me – he says I'm too thin because of Pick n Pay's food. We must buy our food from Checkers!'

Madiba's life and values have always resonated with Whitey. Over the years, they met numerous times and joined forces for various initiatives aimed at uplifting communities. One day Madiba phoned Whitey to invite him to a handover ceremony. After the proceedings, Madiba took him by the arm and they walked together to a man in a wheelchair. Whitey would only find out later that the man had been the victim of a hijacking, and Madiba had wanted to wish him all the best. 'He was a wonderful person who made time for everyone,' Whitey stated.[7]

According to him, Madiba played a vital role in the saving and reconstruction of South Africa. The way in which he steered the transition – without violence and without an economic collapse – deserves lasting praise, Whitey believes. 'With modesty and humanity, he devoted his life to changing and shaping our country for the best. Let us continue his Long Walk and climb every great hill with his devotion and acceptance of the responsibilities freedom brings,' Whitey wrote in a statement issued on 6 December 2013, a day after Madiba's death.[8] On the day of Mandela's funeral, Shoprite and some of its competitors closed their doors. Shoprite alone lost about R260 million in sales.[9]

In June 1996 Shoprite Checkers launched the national Woman of the Year Award in partnership with the SABC. The competition was aimed at recognising achievement by women and encouraging women to play their rightful role in the reconstruction of South African society. 'With this Award the Group is able to do something concrete for its most important constituency: 80 per cent of its shoppers are women.'[10] Members of the public could nominate women in six categories: business entrepreneurs; arts and culture; health; sport; community affairs; and education. A panel then selected winners in each category, and an overall winner was chosen out of these six.

When a barefooted Selina Maphorogo, the very first overall winner, walked onto the stage, Whitey involuntarily 'burst out crying'. Despite her limited schooling, Maphorogo, a community health worker, helped set up and run a healthcare project at Elim in the Northern Province (today Limpopo). As a result of this award, she became a popular international speaker on the problems of developing countries and their solutions.[11]

In 2007 Shoprite launched its Soup Truck Initiative. The soup trucks distributed soup and bread to underprivileged children and elderly people, and fed some 200 000 vulnerable people in the first few months of the project. Today Shoprite's Mobile Soup Kitchens serve nearly 5 million hot meals annually.[12] Whitey believes, however, that there is only one real solution to South Africa's problems. It is to create employment – as Shoprite did over the more than 30 years with him at the helm.

As ever, he is an optimist about the country's future but does not hesitate to point out its problems. For instance, he told *The Money Show* host Bruce Whitfield: 'South Africa has all the elements in it to be a world-class country. And it can, or rather should, provide a decent standard of living for everyone concerned. I'm actually very positive about the next twenty or thirty years. The younger generation of South Africans . . . will stand up and get [the country] back on track.'[13]

But the right structures need to be in place to get things done. 'Whatever our president says, unless he fixes the structures, from the issuing of driver's licences to employee remuneration, people on the ground won't have better lives in our lifetime,' Whitey said in an interview with CNBC Africa.

He believes in capitalism and the creation of wealth, and that this capital can in turn be invested. 'You can give indigent people money, and I do that from time to time. I'm not saying that's wrong, but you can use that same money to raise your dam walls on your farm by a metre and a half and thereby create jobs for more people.

'In Stellenbosch there are many people with a lot of money, but they don't use it to buy chewing gum – they employ people,' he says. He used his salary and dividends to give people jobs.

Whitey also convinced Pieter Engelbrecht to stay in South Africa after he got a tempting offer from elsewhere. 'I said we need competent people here to grow the pie – not slicing the existing pie so we can gobble it up and it's Friday afternoon.

'People should stop complaining. Let us say: these are the areas we need to tackle, and then we tackle them. The only way to solve the problems of poverty and inequality is by creating jobs,' he reiterates.

Today the Shoprite Group provides employment to about 150 000 people, but it also ploughs back hundreds of millions into communities. In 2021 the group served nearly 153 000 meals per day to vulnerable communities through its corporate social investment (CSI) programmes, in addition to the 5 million hot meals to people in need through its Mobile Soup Kitchens.[14] This is an impressive example and legacy.

PART SIX

THE RECENT YEARS

32

Whitey hands over the reins

I have been privileged to lead the Shoprite group from small beginnings to one of the continent's greatest companies. After so many years with the group, it's time to pass the baton to a new generation of leadership.

– Whitey Basson's statement about his resignation.

It was the sort of announcement one could see coming but which still came as a shock. On 31 October 2016, Whitey announced at Shoprite's annual general meeting that he would be stepping down as CEO at the end of the year. He had been a key figure in South African retail for more than 40 years, and suddenly an era had come to an end. 'A retail landscape without the charismatic Whitey Basson is almost inconceivable,'[1] *Rapport* wrote on the announcement of his retirement. Whitey told reporters he was 'tired' and had had enough of 'the nitty gritty stuff' that stood in the way of Shoprite's growth. 'I'm constantly fighting on several fronts . . . I'm gatvol of it all now. You need to be young,' he said.[2]

His replacement was Shoprite's former chief operating officer Pieter Engelbrecht, who was just 47 years old at the time. Whitey himself had anointed him as his successor and had taught him the art of retail. Engelbrecht had also spent years as Whitey's executive personal assistant. Whitey said: 'Pieter is a very driven guy. I'd say about 50% of the operating issues he's already taken over. So it's not a new job for him.'[3]

Today, Whitey says: 'Pieter has all the qualities a good chief executive should have, and he's hard-working and ambitious, with the requisite experience and qualifications. As Carel Goosen always said: you don't have to urge him on, you rather need to hold him back!' To ensure an orderly leadership transition, Whitey would stay on as non-executive vice-chairperson and would be available to management to share his knowledge and experience, the company said in a statement.

At the same time, questions were being raised about Whitey's remuneration. Christo Wiese told the *Financial Mail* at the time: 'I would pay R1 billion in the middle of the night for another Whitey.'[4]

At the same 2016 AGM where Whitey announced his resignation, 'testy' investors objected to his remuneration package of R100 million (which included a cash bonus of R50 million) for the past year. Christo again jumped to Whitey's defence, saying that Shoprite 'would have been happy to pay him much more'.

Regarding the controversy about his pay, Whitey told the SABC: 'I don't fix my own salary. We have contractual arrangements that are based on international standards and practices. It's not that nice going into Africa for the first time, and no one else has been out there, and the hotels aren't good. So those elements do compensate you at least for the effort you put in.'

He added candidly: 'It's not nice to hear that all the time. It's not nice walking past the people you work with and love, thinking they earn x and you earn much more. That's not something that makes you feel proud – it's just . . . it's there.

Then came the wisecrack: 'But I can also run Shoprite like the SAA [South African Airways], if you want to pay me a small salary.'[5]

During May 2017, Whitey exercised a put option to sell some of his Shoprite shares back to the company. The repurchase transaction was approved by a large majority of the shareholders at an extraordinary general meeting. For the rest, fund managers reacted positively to this development and showed understanding that it was reasonable for Whitey to diversify his interests. They also acknowledged the enormous value Whitey had added to Shoprite over many years.

In fact, the big salaries and bonuses had a history stretching back nearly 40 years. The initial agreement between Whitey and Renier van Rooyen – that he would in the end own 25 per cent of Shoprite – had not worked out as Whitey had expected it would. And when Christo returned to Pep and bought Van Rooyen's shares, he became the single largest shareholder in Pep, and consequently also in Shoprite. 'He [Christo] and I concluded a deal in terms of which I would get a certain percentage of the pre-tax profit,' Whitey explains. Everything is relative. Whitey's salary was enormous compared to the average salary, but R100 million was small change in comparison to R30 billion – roughly what that 25 per cent would have been worth today.

Whitey also says that over the years he received many offers from foreign companies who wanted him to work for them. His answer was always no, because he loved his country, and Shoprite, too much. Besides, his zeal and ardour were never associated with money. 'What drove me was the desire to be successful and to build a business. It was more of a human goal than a material one. I wanted to outperform other people, and not necessarily become richer.' On the sale of his shares, however, Whitey became richer than most people could ever dream of.

* * * *

If the 'good job' Simon Raubenheimer referred to is measured by the company's share price, Whitey certainly delivered on the expectations.

When Shoprite listed in 1986, the company had a market capitalisation of R29 million. Thirty years later, by the end of 2016, it was R100 billion. For years, however, Shoprite failed to attract attention on the JSE. During most of the 1990s and early 2000s, the share more or less moved sideways.

But from about 2005, its price was on a steady upward trajectory. With the acquisitions of the 1990s under control, the company's investments in technology, its people and its systems started paying dividends, and Shoprite began leaving its competitors in the dust. Owing to the pioneering expansion into the rest of Africa, as well as good profits, the market began to take note. In 2008, Shoprite was included in the JSE Top 40 Index, which comprises the 40 largest companies on the JSE in terms of market capitalisation. In the nearly twenty years since Whitey had acquired OK, Shoprite's profits had also only grown every year.[6]

Shareholders laughed all the way to the bank. If one had bought shares valued at R100 000 at the time of Shoprite's listing, they would have been worth more than R11 million by the end of 2016. This is a compound annual growth rate of more than 17 per cent, compared to that of the JSE All Share Index of 12 per cent. The same investment in Pick n Pay over the same period would have grown to R4,5 million (a growth rate of 13 per cent). And by the end of 2016, Shoprite's market value was three times that of its once largest rival.

An analysis of Shoprite's performance measured by shareholder returns (share price growth and dividends) against that of its big rivals – Pick n Pay, Spar and Woolworths – during Whitey's 'golden years' revealed that he 'crushed' his competitors. According to Daily Investor, the annualised return for Shoprite shareholders achieved by Whitey from 1 January 2001 until his retirement was 22 per cent, and the other CEOs could not hold a candle to him.[7]

Furthermore, Whitey had said at the start of Shoprite that he wanted to be 'as big in groceries as Pep Stores was in clothing'. Eventually, Shoprite would also become much bigger than its counterpart in clothing. Today, Shoprite is no longer a discount share on the bourse but a favourite: a so-called 'blue chip'.

When Whitey's retirement was announced in 2016, Christo Wiese said he fully deserved his reputation as one of South Africa's retail giants.[8] 'Whitey has been a very strong and charismatic leader, who has managed the company through market transitions and challenging times, taking calculated risks to turn the supermarket group into the leading food retailer on the continent.'[9]

Maria Ramos and Wendy Lucas-Bull, CEO and chairperson respectively of Barclays Africa (previously Absa) at the time, wrote to Whitey that his 'leadership and vision have been the main reason Shoprite is the retail and corporate giant it is today'. Ironically, Lucas-Bull would succeed Christo as chairperson of Shoprite a few years later.

* * * *

A year later, on 25 October 2017, Whitey also stepped down as vice-chairperson and non-executive director of Shoprite Holdings, thereby walking away completely. He acknowledges today that it was not easy to retire. 'Walking away from a business you had built up was very, very hard.'

Shareholders and others had often asked him whether he would consider returning to retail, perhaps as chairperson of Shoprite in the place of Christo Wiese, Whitey said during a television interview in October 2019.[10] 'I said no, there's just nothing in it for me except to destroy me, because it's like going back into the ring for a second time for a boxer.'

He also did not want a conflict of interest between Christo and himself, 'and quite frankly, I don't think I would fit into resurrecting something which probably needs different strengths and different capabilities'. If they really needed his help, he would rather assist Engelbrecht or Wiese from the sidelines. However, if a possibility should arise that the people of Shoprite 'that I dearly love' would be harmed or that the company would falter, 'I will regard it as my duty to stand with the people', he said.

Although he did not refer to it at the time, another big factor in Whitey's decision to walk away was the pressure to merge Shoprite with Steinhoff, a move he had been trying to prevent for years. The matter would cast a great shadow over Shoprite, Whitey himself, and his relations with Christo Wiese.

33

The Steinhoff debacle

You don't need to have all the answers, just ask the right questions.
– Whitey Basson

In August 2016 Whitey visited Christo Wiese at the wine farm Lanzerac, outside Stellenbosch. Their get-togethers were usually convivial – but this time harsh words were exchanged between the two friends and business partners of 40 years. The disagreement was about Steinhoff, the controversial company run by Markus Jooste that would have a massive impact – at first apparently positive, but later disastrous – on Christo, Pep Holdings, as well as the entire South African and even the international investment and business community.

Christo was dazzled by Jooste and had already folded Pep Holdings into Steinhoff. He was still the largest single shareholder in Shoprite and now wanted to sell the supermarket group, too, to Steinhoff. But there was just one obstacle – Whitey was implacably opposed to it. He knew precious little about the proposed transaction – but he thought Steinhoff was a bad company, that Shoprite and Steinhoff were not a good fit, and he had no time for Jooste.

He did his best to warn Christo against Jooste and Steinhoff. But for the first time in many years, Christo's renowned power of judgment had failed him. The issue remained unresolved and soured their relationship.

Whitey still finds it difficult to talk about Steinhoff, but he has finally lifted the veil on some of the things that happened behind the scenes

– particularly regarding his partial falling-out with his long-standing friend and business partner. In the end, Steinhoff's wheels fell off very quickly. But the company had a long and interesting history.

* * * *

When Renier van Rooyen was establishing Pep, a young man in the town of Westerstede in the then West Germany was also planning his retail business. The Iron Curtain was still closed, a situation that also created opportunities – Bruno Steinhoff realised he could source furniture cheaply in communist East Germany and sell it to richer West Germans. This was the foundation of the company that would later become known as Steinhoff Europe.[1]

German industrialist and businessman Claas Daun, a contemporary and friend of Bruno Steinhoff's, would also play a prominent role in the expansion of Steinhoff. In 1995 Daun invested in a small furniture manufacturer, Gommagomma, in Ga-Rankuwa, north-west of Pretoria, an area that formed part of the then homeland of Bophuthatswana. The company's financial director was Markus Jooste. Daun introduced Bruno Steinhoff to Jooste, and in 1997 Steinhoff bought a large interest in Gommagomma. They took over another furniture company, Bakker & Steyger, which they merged in 1997 with Gommagomma and Daun's furniture group, Victoria Lewis, to form one company named Steinhoff Africa.[2]

Steinhoff Africa and Steinhoff Europe also consolidated their operations, and in September 1998 Steinhoff International listed on the JSE at R4 per share. Jooste had meanwhile become the group's CEO. Following the acquisition of the Cornick Group a year later, Steinhoff became the largest furniture manufacturer in South Africa.[3]

Steinhoff expanded rapidly, mostly via mergers and acquisitions.

The period up to and including 2015 constituted the company's glory years; in the eyes of the majority of business analysts and asset managers, Steinhoff could not put a foot wrong. Its share price soared to more than R60, and Steinhoff and Jooste were hailed as a shining South African success story.

* * * *

The euphoria around Steinhoff took Christo Wiese in as well. In 2011, Wiese had crossed paths with Jooste when the former sold the historic Lanzerac estate outside Stellenbosch in exchange for shares in Steinhoff to a consortium of overseas investors. Christo also subsequently swapped a block of PSG shares for more shares in the furniture manufacturer.[4] He had watched the evolution of the company and believed it would be a good investment.[5] Two years later, in 2013, he became a director of Steinhoff.

Christo started working towards consolidating his interests. His masterplan was ultimately to house all his retail interests in Africa, including Shoprite, under one umbrella – that of Steinhoff. The first step was to sell Pepkor to Steinhoff.[6]

The R62,8 billion deal took place in 2015 – one of the largest acquisitions in South African business history. Steinhoff now owned more than 92 per cent of Pepkor, with the rest in the hands of Pepkor management. Christo held a direct and indirect interest in Steinhoff of about 20 per cent, which made him the largest single shareholder.[7] The deal made Steinhoff even bigger, and the company also listed on the Frankfurt Stock Exchange at the end of 2015.

At that stage Whitey was no longer a director of Pepkor, hence 'I had nothing to do with it,' he confirms. In August 1972 Whitey had been appointed as alternate director of Pep Stores Limited and its subsidiaries, and on 1 September 1975 as director. In 1999 he had been appointed as non-executive vice-chairman of Pepkor, but he had resigned in 2004 to focus exclusively on Shoprite. 'Christo was very pleased with the Pepkor deal,' Whitey continues. 'He was obsessive about it, and just talked constantly about how well Steinhoff was performing. So he wanted to do the same with Shoprite.'

Consequently, Whitey soon became caught up in the second phase of Christo's plan: to have Shoprite join Pepkor under the maroon umbrella of Steinhoff. While there had previously been speculation about a merger between Shoprite and Steinhoff – it was even the subject of a *finweek* cover story in 2009 – nothing came of it at the time. But Christo now saw a golden opportunity to consolidate his interests. Having already exchanged his interests in Pepkor for a stake in Steinhoff, he sought to do the same with Shoprite.[8]

At that stage, Shoprite's shareholding was as follows: Christo owned nearly 16 per cent, the Public Investment Corporation (PIC) just over 11 per cent, and Whitey about 1,6 per cent. Banks, unit trusts and retirement funds owned about 70 per cent.[9] But Christo also held special deferred shares via another investment vehicle, Thibault Square Financial Services. These shares were not entitled to dividends, but carried the same votes as ordinary shares. The deferred shares carried about 32 per cent of the voting rights of Shoprite, which meant that Christo effectively had a voting interest of just under 50 per cent in Shoprite.[10]

Whitey was fiercely opposed to such a merger. As far as the deal itself was concerned, there were two major reasons for his opposition. First, he saw no sense in combining the two companies. 'I still remember saying at a point that it would be like putting Anglo American and Toyota together. I thought it was ludicrous.'

The second reason was the nature of the proposed deal. Christo proposed that they do a share swap again, as in the case of the Pepkor and Steinhoff transaction. Whitey was dead set against that.[11] He considered Shoprite a better company and investment than Steinhoff.

'Shoprite didn't need the deal. It went back and forth. And I talked to friends and other big shareholders in Shoprite, and inquired who would help me oppose the deal.'

The proposed transaction would mean that Shoprite would be controlled by Steinhoff – and under Jooste at that. As chairman of Shoprite, Christo had served as a sounding board for Whitey but had never meddled in the affairs of management or in Whitey's decisions. After 40 years at the helm, it was unthinkable to Whitey to report to anyone – let alone Jooste.

* * * *

According to Whitey, he had also never got on well with Jooste. 'I didn't like his style. But that was just my personal feeling. What worried me more was that I didn't think he was a good businessman.' Whitey remembers vaguely that he might have met Jooste on occasion in earlier years. But his memory is much better when it comes to a Wilgenhof reunion in the school hall of Paul Roos, in the form of a dinner and auction.

'Not far from us sat a man who bought paintings at ridiculous prices. It was obvious to me that he wasn't only bidding to buy a painting or to push the price up a bit – he wanted to be seen and heard. I've bought many paintings at auctions where you pay perhaps ten or fifteen per cent too much because it's actually a donation, but this looked to me like an unnecessary show of bravado.'

Whitey was sitting next to Christo, and he asked him who the man was. 'He said it was that Jooste chappie, but he didn't know him well either.' Whitey already knew then that they could never be friends.

It was rumoured that Steinhoff 'blew' between R60 million and R80 million on treating clients and partners to an excursion to Britain to attend the 2015 Rugby World Cup tournament.[12] Wasteful extravagance like that made Whitey break out in a cold sweat. 'I almost couldn't believe the Steinhoff board would've approved something like that,' he says. 'In fact, Christo couldn't tell me whether Jooste, Steinhoff, or the guests themselves paid for the trip. The only person I know of who paid for himself was GT Ferreira [a co-founder of Rand Merchant Bank], who said even if they give it to charity, he wouldn't accept a free trip.'

Whitey cautioned Christo, and anyone else who wanted to listen, about Steinhoff, but few of them listened. In his opinion, swapping your Shoprite shares for Steinhoff shares was like trading a champion horse for a donkey. 'Why would I have wished to be involved in Steinhoff?' he asks again today. 'I didn't think it was a good company, and I didn't want to waste my energy on it. I said, it wouldn't work for me because then I'd have to listen to a bunch of nincompoops.'

As always, Whitey did his homework thoroughly. He thought some of Steinhoff's companies were poor-quality businesses and that the company was not sufficiently focused. He did not have a high opinion of the management, and was simply unable to get financial figures that made sense to him or proved that Steinhoff would be a good investment.

'Furniture is a simple business,' he remarks. 'Your job is to sell things and make a profit from it. So what is the profit, and what is the cost of capital? And Steinhoff just had too much debt. The share price did well, but what was the bottom line? In my view, it was purely greed . . .

'I first asked colleagues in Shoprite – amongst others Joseph Brönn – to look into Steinhoff, and he couldn't see anything that made sense.

Then I asked Johann Rupert: am I missing something, or am I being too critical? He said, if you could get Jooste to keep his year-ends the same, you would be able to analyse the company and try to understand what's going on there, but unfortunately that's not yet possible.' In fact, Steinhoff regularly changed its company's year-ends, which impeded year-on-year comparisons. Whitey also called in other experts, who did all kinds of valuations. 'So I said, let's start from the beginning and do it the "boere" way. What is the return on capital, and what is the cost of capital?'

As a 'laaitie' in Porterville, Whitey had won cooldrinks or ice creams for his skill at doing sums, but *these* numbers simply did not add up. 'I was bemused by how all the analysts had arrived at their valuations – I just couldn't see what they saw,' he says, almost in disbelief. 'In fact, I got Sanlam to help me with the sums. Their answer was the same as mine.'

Whitey was one of the few voices against Steinhoff, but not the only one. As far back as 2007, Sean Holmes, an analyst at the local arm of the American bank JP Morgan, had advised investors in a research report to steer clear of Steinhoff.[13] And in 2009 an investment manager, Craig Butters, had requested a meeting with Christo to warn him about Steinhoff.[14] But the warnings fell on deaf ears.

Among other things, Whitey asked Christo to first meet with the senior executive team of Shoprite to hear what they thought of his plans. 'He came back and said, the executive team support the plans because it's time that we revamp the company. I then called the executives together and said: listen guys, this is what Christo tells me. Our understanding has always been that if I fail to see something, you should tell me. And if that is how you feel, go for it. But I'm not going to support the deal. They then said as one: no, Christo is talking nonsense.'

Whitey went back to Christo to sound him out about this. 'He asked me, do you think I'm lying? I said, no, I don't think you're lying, but those nine or ten guys I saw this morning think so. Again, we had words about it, and I said: well, this is where I draw the line.'

A few days later, Whitey again went to see Christo. 'I told him that I didn't feel like starting a second life within Steinhoff in any case. I felt I'd achieved everything I wanted to, and I didn't see my way clear to carrying on working. I'd been under a lot of pressure, and at 70 I no longer had the stomach for it. When Steinhoff came along, I thought: I've built up Shoprite. Why should I now have to play on someone else's team? And that's why I resigned. I'd wanted to resign for a long time before that because of all the corporate red tape, and this was now the right time.'

'We argued so much that I told Christo: I've never differed from you in public, but this time I'll definitely do so. I told him it would be a death knell for Shoprite, and that there were no benefits in a deal like that, except perhaps to get his personal affairs in order.'

* * * *

Christo, however, steamed ahead. Shortly after the announcement of Whitey's retirement on 31 October 2016, analysts said such a merger was now 'not only likely but could happen in the near term'.[15] On 14 December 2016, Steinhoff and Shoprite issued a joint cautionary announcement on the JSE's news service, SENS, in which they set out the details of the proposed transaction.[16] Shoprite would acquire Steinhoff's African retail operations, collectively known as Steinhoff Africa Retail, or STAR, which consisted inter alia of Pepkor Africa, including Pep and Ackermans; the JD Group, including Bradlows and Hi-Fi Corporation (now HiFiCorp); Steinbuild, with Pennypinchers and Timber City in its stable; and Tekkie Town. In exchange for STAR,

Shoprite would issue new shares to Steinhoff, which would give Steinhoff a material interest of nearly 40 per cent in Shoprite.

At the same time, the Public Investment Corporation (PIC) and the Titan Group (the investment company of Christo's family trust) would exchange their interests in Shoprite for Steinhoff shares, which would ultimately result in Steinhoff owning Shoprite and its new stake in STAR. The envisaged company was to be known as Retail Africa and would be an 'African retail champion'.

Only three months later, in February 2017, Shoprite and Steinhoff announced in a second statement that the deal was off – the PIC, Titan and Steinhoff had terminated their negotiations because they could not reach agreement on the value of the share exchange.[17] The *Financial Mail* asked Whitey if he was pleased that the merger had not happened. 'Are you asking if the Pope is Catholic? Well, he is!' he quipped.[18]

The minority shareholders were delighted. Their complaints had been 'that the deal was sparse on details, lacked obvious costs-savings overlaps and would mean exchanging a stock with bigger potential for what they called inferior businesses'.[19]

Simon Brown, a well-known market analyst and investor, told James-Brent Styan, author of *Steinhoff: Inside SA's biggest corporate crash*, that minority shareholders (including himself) specifically wanted Shoprite shares and were not really interested in Steinhoff.

'Shoprite is the world's best retailer focusing on lower-income groups. I did not want bits and pieces of other companies such as Bradlows and all the rest through Steinhoff shares. I only wanted my focused, excellent asset, Shoprite,' Brown said. Executive teams of some of the other companies concerned, particularly those of Pep and Ackermans, had also been unhappy about the proposed transaction.[20]

* * * *

But Christo, who had been elected chairperson of the Steinhoff board in May 2016, made another attempt. He saw a merger as a 'natural development',[21] he had confidence in Jooste and his team, and the prospect of becoming the single largest shareholder in the second-largest global retailer was just too enticing.[22]

This time, Wiese followed a different approach. 'He then talked to me again about his decision,' Whitey recounts. 'And I said, I can't be angry with you if you want to sell your shares – it's your choice – but I won't be part of it. The same goes for my executives and other shareholders, because now they don't have to sell all their shares either. And according to him, Shoprite would remain listed.'

Meanwhile, in the year between his retirement announcement and his last day at Shoprite, Whitey felt he had been sidelined. And he kept warning. Whitey refers to Tekkie Town, which he did not consider a good buy, and definitely not at the price that was paid. 'In fact, I don't know if a due diligence was ever done on Tekkie Town. I asked Pieter Erasmus about it, and although he was Pepkor's managing director, he said he hadn't been involved in the deal – it had been handled by the 'Bentley brigade'.

'I talked to Christo again and said, you need to be extremely circumspect because these things are obviously so wrong. But I knew that was what would happen – Christo was going to do what he wanted to with Shoprite and with Steinhoff. So I just carried on with meetings where I could help keep Shoprite on the right track.'

In September 2017, Steinhoff listed its African retailers separately on the JSE as Steinhoff Africa Retail (STAR).[23] It announced that Christo and the PIC would exchange their shares in Shoprite for shares in the new company. STAR also acquired a block of shares from Christo that carried the same votes as those of ordinary shares (at a 'ridiculous' price, according to Whitey). It would mean that STAR effectively gained control of Shoprite. On 30 November 2017, with Whitey already having left Shoprite, STAR issued a SENS statement to the effect that the group planned to acquire a controlling shareholding in Shoprite.[24] But the merger would never happen. A week later, the Steinhoff bomb exploded.

* * * *

There had been red flags earlier. Following allegations of tax irregularities, the German tax authorities raided Steinhoff's offices in Westerstede in November 2015. The board subsequently appointed German forensic investigators to look into the allegations. In August 2017, the German business magazine *Manager Magazin* published claims about fraud at Steinhoff. But everything was denied.[25]

The first big alarm bell sounded on Monday 4 December 2017. Steinhoff was due to issue its 2017 consolidated financial statements two days later, but said in a statement the statements would be released in unaudited form. It explained that the board and the auditors, Deloitte, had not yet finalised their review of 'certain matters and circumstances, most of which were raised by the criminal and tax investigation in Germany'.[26]

Deloitte was perturbed by these allegations and claims. There was talk of non-compliance with tax requirements and the incorrect application of accounting principles – specifically revenue recognition and related-party deals.[27] Deloitte received the forensic report, but it wanted Steinhoff to commission another forensic investigation. As auditors, they had to be satisfied that the company's financial statements were free of material misstatement, were presented fairly and in conformity with generally accepted accounting principles, and reflected a true representation of the company's financial position and results. Otherwise they could not give a 'clean audit report'. And Deloitte refused to give its approval – it had not received sufficient information from Steinhoff to sign off the statements.

On Wednesday 6 December, the board of Steinhoff announced in a grim statement: 'New information has come to light today which relates to accounting irregularities requiring further investigation.'[28] They added that Jooste had resigned as CEO, and also announced that the publication of the audited financial statements would be delayed (they were eventually only released in May 2019). This news caused Steinhoff's share price to plunge from about R50 to R6 in the course of five days, and to drop further to just above R1 over the following few months. That was 99 per cent lower than the peak of close to R100 in the stock's glory years.

Wealth was destroyed on an unprecedented scale. Christo's investment of more than 40 years in Pepkor was almost wiped out. When the 'accounting irregularities' came to light, Christo owned about 20 per cent of Steinhoff. His stake, which at one stage was worth almost R90 billion, plummeted to around R176 million.[29] The PIC, as well as the country's largest asset managers, suffered huge losses. According to Rob Rose's book *Steinheist*, more than half of South Africa's 1 651 pension funds had exposure to Steinhoff.[30] Many other investors, too, had allowed themselves to be duped by Jooste and co.

* * * *

Still smarting a bit as he thinks back, Whitey relates: 'I fought with him [Christo] about Steinhoff, but instead of listening to me he ignored my concerns. I warned him again, as I'd done before, that Jooste couldn't run such a large and diversified business. So don't put your money into it – keep your money in Shoprite and Pepkor.'

He grouses again about corporate governance in South Africa, and refers to the fact that highly qualified, smart and experienced business-people were serving on Steinhoff's board at the time of its collapse. 'Steinhoff's single largest business was retail. But how many of them were retailers? And what did Markus Jooste do?' he asks.

'I said to Christo: Are you guys in your right minds? In Steinhoff there were simply not enough people with a sufficient grasp of the business. There were many bankers and accountants, because they are two a penny, but retail is an art of buying and selling you need to be skilled in. There aren't many people who can do it because you work yourself to the bone – and it's a combination of white collar and blue collar, from day to day.

'Boards in South Africa have become a joke. Look at Steinhoff's board – you couldn't have asked for better professional directors. But unless they've previously been involved in the industry, outside directors don't know the business. A company in the retail industry needs retailers on its board too – it's as simple as that.'

* * * *

The Steinhoff collapse meant the end of any merger plans. In March 2018, Pieter Engelbrecht told Netwerk24 that on a scale from one to ten, his relief about the fact that Steinhoff and Shoprite had not merged was a full ten. 'There's no sense in it now – it's off the table for good. With the benefit of hindsight, one sees it's better that it didn't happen.'[31]

To an extent he was 'lucky' that he 'only lost R59 billion', Christo told Rob Rose in 2018. If 'this thing' had happened a year later, he would have lost everything, he said. In other words, had Jooste's financial tricks only come to light after Christo had already swapped his

Shoprite shares for those of Steinhoff, the jewel in his crown – Shoprite – would have gone down the drain too. After having lost his dollar billionaire status for a few years, Christo won it back early in 2022, according to Biznews – ironically, thanks to a considerable increase in Shoprite's share price.[32]

As mentioned previously, Christo had been a member of the supervisory board of Steinhoff since 2013 and served as its chairperson from 2016. After Jooste's resignation, he initially stood in for Jooste as acting chief executive but resigned a week later from the temporary position and also as chairperson in order to affirm the principle of 'board independence' and to prevent any possible conflicts of interest.

He provided a glimpse of his philosophy in this regard in a radio interview in 2016.[33] The fate of a company is to a great extent in the hands of its top executives, including the CEO, he explained. As chairperson and the largest shareholder in Pepkor, Shoprite and other companies, he had to trust their top executives. Had he been unable to do that, Pep and Shoprite could never have grown. If you want to be involved in a global firm with hundreds of thousands of employees, you need to have trust, he stated.[34] At the same time, boards should not blindly accept executives' actions and decisions.

Thus Christo's approach to corporate governance – in fact, his philosophy – is: The only thing you can do when you are building large businesses is to work together with people, get to know them, and – if you share the same values – put your trust in them.

* * * *

Whitey and Christo still talk to each other often, but their relationship will probably never be quite the same. They rarely butted heads, and Whitey believes one of the reasons for Shoprite's success was that

Christo never interfered in its management. For nearly 40 years they had a rock-solid relationship and trusted each other completely.[35]

'Christo actually tried to get me off the Shoprite premises because I stood in his way,' Whitey discloses. 'But we've been friends for more than 40 years, so I'm not going to continue holding it against him. I just avoid saying anything about it – I make jokes and talk about other things. He admits at least that he was wrong and should have listened to me.

'Besides, one has to remember that Christo isn't really a retailer and never occupied operational positions at Pep and Shoprite. Make no mistake, he's a brilliant investor – the most brilliant investor I know. But he's not a retailer, and doesn't really like it!'

The Steinhoff debacle also reopened old wounds. The 40-year-old issue of Whitey's stake in Shoprite reared its head again. 'After we had a quarrel, and he said there was a difference between the controlling shareholder and the chief executive, I said it's actually a pity, because I could've been the controlling shareholder if Renier had kept his word. And Christo too – he was on that subcommittee [of Pep], so he made that decision along with the others.

'I'm not going to write him off as a pal now. But he wanted to sacrifice me and sell a business that he knew had been built up 100 per cent by me and my team. Fortunately, I was able to prevent it.'

34

Farmer, investor and family man

When I visit friends, I have a tendency to open their fridges and check whether they're not perhaps buying from the opposition. I have no qualms about scratching around in their second and third drawers too.

— Whitey Basson[1]

Following the crash of the Steinhoff shares, Stellenbosch was abuzz with talk about the fallout. Who had taken hits and who had survived? But for the rest, Whitey took little notice of it. He had meanwhile exchanged his office in Brackenfell for an office in the Old College Building in Stellenbosch's Church Street, where he could now devote more attention to his own business interests and his family's investments. Anita van Rensburg, who had been his secretary for 30 years, moved with him to the Stellenbosch office.

His office was an informal place where people constantly dropped in for a conversation or to ask advice, or just for a cup of tea. Over the years Whitey had become good friends with a considerable number of Stellenbosch's prominent businessmen, and they would regularly have lunch together.

In the wake of Steinhoff's collapse, the term 'Stellenbosch Mafia' was on everyone's lips.[2] The label refers to a generation of Afrikaner business-people who are extremely successful, have become very wealthy, and are in some or other way connected with Stellenbosch. A name that features regularly when this 'grouping' is mentioned is that of Johann Rupert, controlling shareholder and chairperson of the luxury-goods group Richemont and the investment holding company Remgro. His father, the legendary Anton Rupert, founder of the Rembrandt Group that was the forerunner of Remgro, had established his enterprise in this Boland town and lived there himself. Although Richemont is based in Switzerland, Remgro's corporate head office is still located in Stellenbosch.

Christo Wiese's name also crops up. Pep, however, operates from Parow, a short distance from Stellenbosch. Ironically, neither Rupert nor Wiese lives in Stellenbosch. Other names that are mentioned include Jannie Mouton, founder of the investment group PSG, and GT Ferreira. And then, of course, there is the infamous Markus Jooste, who lived in Stellenbosch as an 'inkommer' and established Steinhoff there.

Critics of this 'billionaires' club' believe they do big deals only among themselves, conspire to keep new entrants out of the market, or are even pulling the strings of government and the South African economy from their adjacent offices in this town. But Whitey dismisses the concept as a load of nonsense. 'There is a sizeable circle of friends and acquaintances who studied at Stellenbosch University at roughly the same time. Some guys are not friends in the least, but they happen to have been contemporaries at Maties and have built up large businesses. And now they're suddenly something akin to the Illuminati.

'There's really nothing to it except sensationalist journalism. We may eat out together occasionally, or you bump into someone and talk some business, but there are no deliberate plans to act in concert or to do business together.' After the Covid pandemic, Whitey decided to establish his office at Klein DasBosch.

Many aspirant entrepreneurs come knocking at Whitey's door for advice. He has always been interested in talented, young entrepreneurs and people with ambition, and feels heartened when they become successful. Some are in search of seed capital but he would rather help with advice, and particularly 'people who pursue their trade and would like to stand on their own feet', he explains. 'The banks don't want to help them – they don't help you when you need money, only if you already have money. But I didn't achieve much success with guys who are looking for R10 million for 10 per cent of a business they believe to be worth R100 million, and then there are no numbers that support the valuation.'

Whitey is now also a wine farmer. He has always had a yearning to produce top-quality wines, a passion he could not pursue while he was at Shoprite. Klein DasBosch has only five hectares of vineyards, but in 2002 he bought an additional farm directly opposite Klein DasBosch on Blaauwklippen Road, which he named Mont Marie.

'I always tried to give my full attention to Shoprite, so I was never able to be involved in the farm on a day-to-day basis. Once Mont Marie was added, I could appoint a full-time manager and run it like a proper business.'

Whitey makes his wines with the help of expert winemakers, including Jan 'Boland' Coetzee. 'I'm a novice in the wine industry, but I have a good mentor in Jan Boland, one of the best winemakers,' he says. Coetzee, a rugby legend and winemaker extraordinaire who was also born in Porterville, played in 127 matches for Western Province as flanker and in six tests for the Springboks. In 1980 he bought the Vriesenhof wine estate, a neighbouring farm to the one known today as Klein DasBosch, and produced his first wine there in 1981.[3]

Today they produce, inter alia, a Merlot, a Cabernet Sauvignon, a Malbec and a Chardonnay under the Klein DasBosch label, as well as a rosé called Maude's (named after Whitey's mother). The Mont Marie range includes the Director's Reserve, which is a Bordeaux blend, and a Rhône blend called Manna.

Owing to their limited quantity, the wines are only available for sale internationally and in selected restaurants and stores. 'I want to build the brand so that it can stand on its own feet,' says Whitey. 'That's what I wanted for Shoprite too – that it would still be a strong brand 100 years after my death. All my life I've sought to create things that can survive for longer than one's own lifetime, and it was nice to transform the farm and to figure out how to make it successful.'

Whitey also had a tasting room and a cellar built on Mont Marie. 'I used to keep my vats with Jan Boland at Vriesenhof and my bottles at Lourensford. I won't say I'm a control freak, but I wanted to have everything close to me.'

Given the beautiful view from Mont Marie, the architect convinced Whitey to have a full-fledged restaurant built – but when it was almost completed, he realised he was not really cut out for the restaurant industry. So, he asked the talented young chef Pieter Vlok to pay him a visit and offered him the restaurant. Vlok is the son of long-standing family friends, Louis and Mariechen Vlok. Among other things, he had worked for a few years under the famous chef David Higgs at the Rust and Vrede Restaurant and then ran the Overture Restaurant together with the equally renowned chef Bertus Basson.

'You don't have to put in any money, you just pay me a percentage of your turnover,' Whitey told him. Vlok grabbed the opportunity with both hands. He and Annalise worked together on the design and planning of the restaurant, which has since become a popular destination. 'We're very proud of Pieter and what he has achieved at the restaurant – for years it's been among the top ten restaurants on Tripadvisor,' Whitey boasts.

Besides the winemaking, Whitey's attention is particularly focused on looking after his family's investments and other interests. After his retirement he sometimes still attended meetings at Shoprite's head office, but nowadays he works mostly from his office at Klein DasBosch. There are full-time farming operations on the farm DasBosch outside Porter-ville as well. In the early 1990s Whitey's parents retired to Strand, where Captain Jack died in 1993. DasBosch now belongs to Whitey and is managed by Simon Coldrey.

Simon, who has been running Whitey's farming operations for more than 40 years, plays a special role in Whitey's life. Their relationship came about in an interesting way. Simon, who grew up in Cape Town, matriculated at Rondebosch Boys' High in 1980. He and Whitey's nephew André (Juel's son) were classmates and André asked him if he would be interested in helping his grandfather on the farm during the holidays. That was when Simon met Whitey for the first time. Although he was a city boy, he immediately took a liking to farmwork. After Jack left the farm, Simon continued doing holiday work for the Basson brothers, Jan and Whitey, and was appointed permanently in 1985. After the dissolution of the brothers' partnership in 1995, Simon and Whitey carried on farming as DasBosch Boerdery.

According to Simon, Whitey has a deep-seated interest in farm-ing and is very involved in the development of his farms. He farms with grapes and wine on Klein DasBosch, with game on his farm in Bushmanland in the Northern Cape, and with citrus, table grapes and avocados, primarily for export, on DasBosch itself.

He relates that Whitey is passionate about the appearance of his farms, which have been transformed through the planting of shrub-beries and trees. 'When we develop or beautify a new area, he often says we're working too slowly, and that we're not getting any younger – the trees must get into the ground so we can still appreciate them when they're fully grown. Thousands of trees have been planted on the different farms over the years.'

As a young farm manager, Simon frequently accompanied Whitey on a drive through the orchards on Saturday afternoons. One day Whitey stopped the vehicle, climbed out, bent down among the trees in a wind-break, and reappeared with a small piece of black plastic pipe someone had discarded there. 'Then he took out his pocketknife, cut out a con-nector that was attached to the pipe, presented it to me and said: "I've now saved you 75 cents." It was a lesson I'll never forget.'

In addition, Whitey owns a large hunting farm, Dagab, in the Bush-manland region between Brandvlei and Kenhardt. An invitation to Dagab is a sure sign that you are in Whitey's inner circle. This is where many stories originated, and Whitey acquired another nickname – 'One-Shot Whitey' – which refers to the occasion when he brought down two buck with a single bullet. Since then, Whitey has boasted that he needs only one bullet on a hunt. Pieter Engelbrecht tells of the first time he went hunting with Whitey: 'He told me a lot about hunting, and that he actually needed only one bullet. I was walking behind him, and he dropped a bullet. So I said: "Wait, Mr Basson, you've just lost a year's ammunition!"'

According to Christo Wiese, Whitey is the ideal hunting partner. 'One of Whitey's many attractive qualities is his ability and willing-ness to make fun of himself – to the great amusement of his audience. For that reason, among others, I can't imagine a better hunting partner than Whitey. On our long-standing annual trips to my Kalahari farm, he would regale all of us with his stories about his rugby career and his exploits as the Don Juan of Porterville. He recounted, for instance, that when Porterville's school rugby team ran onto the field, the crowd would shout as one: "Pass the ball to Whitey!" How big such a crowd could have been in Porterville in those days, one can only guess.'

Obviously he would like his farms to stand on their own feet and be self-sustaining, Whitey says. But farming as such is not a good in-vestment. 'I've even told cabinet ministers, rather give people Shoprite shares than a farm. But people's connection to the land is an emotional thing. I went to look at my grandfather's farm in Calvinia. I feel connected to that land . . . My mother's childhood footprints lie there.' After his father's death, his mother, Maude, moved to Stellenbosch and regularly visited the family at Klein DasBosch. She died in Stellenbosch in 1998.

Whitey especially enjoys seeing that the people who work on the farms are prospering. 'There are many people in my employ, and it's satisfying to see them doing well. I always say to people who complain about my money: so what do you think I did with it? Gambled it away, bought Lamborghinis, splurged it on overseas holidays? No, I reinvested it, in listed shares or private enterprises. And, in the end, it creates jobs.'

He also does not fritter away money carelessly. 'Whitey is one of the stingiest people I know,' Engelbrecht jokes. 'Yes, I'm stingy,' Whitey confirmed in a television interview. 'I don't waste a cent on nonsense. The moment you leave, I'm going to turn off all these lights that have now been switched on [for the television team].'[4]

Whitey has a love for old cars and does not easily sell them. He tracked down a special Chevrolet Fleetline which was his father's very first car, and the one in which the young Whitey learnt to drive.[5] To him, the cars are not a sign of status and luxury. They are rather a symbol of the excellence he has always aspired to. 'Each component fits perfectly into the car as a whole, and the perfection is an incentive to me.'[6]

* * * *

Nowadays, Whitey is also able to spend more time with his family. It was a difficult balancing act during his Shoprite years, when he would often be away from home for more than half the year. His family was always important, but so was Shoprite. 'The whole week, 24 hours a day, I belong to my job, but on Sundays I'm completely relaxed and I spend time with my family and friends,' he told *Rapport* in 2000.[7]

Even if you have all the money in the world, you can't buy joy and happy relationships, he told the magazine *Rooi Rose* a year later. Because he travelled so much, it was important to him to be with Annalise and the children as often as possible. 'This is where my solid ground lies, here where no one walks around sulking for longer than two minutes before we clear the air and laugh. We can fight, I tell you!' he said. 'You should embrace every opportunity and every moment to the full . . . I take nothing for granted, whether it be in my work or in my personal life.'[8]

During those Shoprite years, when he was away from home regularly, he would talk to his family every day, regardless of whether he was in Kuruman or Cairo. And he always tried to be at home over weekends, although it was not always possible.[9] 'My family say the reason I was such a good dad was that they saw so little of me,' he said jokingly to the television presenter Jak de Priester. 'I worked very hard and spent a lot of time away from home, but I endeavoured to give them everything I could.

'From the time I got married and we had children, I tried to work twice as hard because I wanted to give them the best. I always had the motivation to achieve things that would probably not have been achievable if I hadn't put in the hours . . . I also never left things half done – I finish something once I've started with it.'[10]

But Whitey's weekends at home were not your average 'two leisurely days at the end of each week. That is a luxury one cannot afford while working in the retail industry,' he said in an interview at the time. 'The reality is that stores in the Shoprite Group trade every weekend and therefore it is business as usual for me. Mentally I am on duty for most of the weekend. Come Saturday afternoons I slow down a bit, through to Sundays, but then on Sunday afternoon after 6 my mind is back in full focus on our business.'[11]

The city was not for him. 'I like to walk outside and smell the grass as I do when I walk on the farm, or go horse riding. For me, life is close to the ground when I can enjoy a book while seeing the horizon in the distance and bright skies above me, with a braai looming. That makes me happy. My childhood on a farm has influenced my thinking a lot on how to enjoy a weekend. I want to be in harmony with nature and close to water. That is how I relax.'[12]

Today Whitey feels he would have liked to spend more time with his children, but it would have been difficult to do things differently. As he put it in 2003: 'As an entrepreneur, I thrive on the excitement of business deals and risks. That's who I am; that's the way I was made. I know that if I hadn't put so much effort and time into my career, I would never have been able to play this role in the establishment of a successful business.'[13]

'Whitey did his best to attend the children's school and sporting events,' Annalise recounts today. 'In later years he unfortunately had less time to spend with us. Shoprite demanded most of his time and attention. Our home was an extension of his office. There was always a work atmosphere, with people coming and going at all hours of the day, seven days a week. If there was a problem, anywhere in the world, everything would come to a standstill until it was resolved. He would never wait until the following day. There were constant telephone discussions with colleagues about all aspects of the business, from chickens that had made someone ill to the dominee's wife who'd stolen something!

'I also listened to how people were bawled out over the phone about some or other mistake they'd made, and I would think: if I were that person, I'd resign on the spot. But a short while later that person would get another call, which motivated him again to carry on,' Annalise says.

When Whitey was with his children, however, he made sure he gave them his undivided attention. 'Of course, they say that's not true, but I tried my best,' he says. He always believed that when you are at work, you should devote 100 per cent of your attention to it, and when you are with your family, you should give them the same amount of dedication. He also taught them to assert themselves.

According to Annalise, Whitey taught the children to hold their own in any company – but without being pushy. 'He taught them that people in high positions aren't necessarily right. If they disagreed with such a person, they should get the opportunity to state their case.'[14]

Whitey believes being a good father is not about the number of rugby matches, hockey matches or school concerts you attend. 'What matters more is teaching your children good values by setting an example . . . and commitment to that which you consider important in life – such as realising your dreams and never quitting when you believe in a project or an idea.'

Whitey realised his dream of becoming Africa's largest retailer. But in 2001 a journalist asked him about his other dreams.[15] 'Being a better golf player,' Whitey said with a laugh. 'But no, jokes aside. That my children would use their talents and opportunities.'

According to Whitey and Annalise, both their sons have an inborn business sense. As a child, Adrian picked the green figs from the neighbours' tree, put them in bags and tried to sell them in the neighbourhood, Annalise recalls. When the family went camping at Keurboomstrand during December holidays, he would ask the fishermen for the small fish they threw out and sell these to people at the campsite.

She continues: 'I also remember the times we had family meals at the Spur above the Grand Bazaars in Bellville, and Adrian would buy himself a bottle of Coke beforehand because he didn't want to pay so much for a glass of Coke in the restaurant. His dad would then be very proud of him and couldn't understand why the other children weren't able to reason like that too.'

After graduating with a BCom, Adrian went to work in London for a while and then joined Shoprite as divisional manager of the fast-food business, Hungry Lion. He was also Shoprite's chief digital officer for a period, and was appointed as alternate director to the board in 2005.[16] Jacob Wiese, Christo's son, was appointed as alternate director at the same time. Naturally, the appointments raised eyebrows. 'We are privileged to show our children the ropes in the big business world. It's not anything underhand . . . even though it may sound like something from a soapie,' Whitey said at the time. Today, Adrian is the CEO of Hungry Lion.[17]

Annalise relates that their younger son, Cornell, imported BB guns from China and sold them at a profit on home soil while he was still in primary school. He also entered into a deal with Shoprite to replace the batteries of all the watches customers returned. Cornell has never been attracted to large companies. Nowadays he helps to manage the family assets, along with Adrian and a couple of other institutions.

Whitey and Annalise's elder daughter, Nikki, also studied occupational therapy – according to Annalise, from an early age she wanted to help people with disabilities. Today she is partially involved in the marketing of Klein DasBosch wines.

'The years of growing up in Welgemoed remind me of rooibos tea and rusks with my mom and dad and my brother as we sat watching *Dallas*,' Nikki recounts. 'At the end of every episode, we all first had to analyse what JR had got up to. It was relatively unheard of for kids to watch TV programmes such as *Dallas*, but my dad is certainly not the conventional parent. He encouraged us to think for ourselves and stand up for what we believe in, even if it meant there would be many different opinions, and that's how I try to teach my own children.'

She and Whitey had planned to start playing golf after his retirement – it was something they could do together, and that would give them time to enjoy each other's company. So once when it was her birthday, she asked for a set of golf clubs. 'That same afternoon, a set of clubs was delivered to my home – not new ones, but the clubs my mom had played with 35 years before. My dad said there was nothing wrong with the clubs. They were "more than good enough", and there was no reason to buy new ones.'

Mari, the younger daughter, has a law degree, but has been interested in the fashion industry since childhood. When she finished studying, she worked in Truworths' purchasing division to learn more about the industry. In 2010 she opened her own business, a boutique called Mari and Me, in Sea Point and later another branch in Cavendish Square, but after the birth of her second son she gave it up.

According to Nikki, after the birth of her elder daughter, the first grandchild, Whitey was upset about being referred to as 'Oupa'. 'We used to call his dad, my grandfather, Dakka, and it was then decided that the grandchildren would call him "Dadda".'

In 2001, Mari also provided a valuable glimpse of the Bassons' family life for the magazine *Sarie*.[18] 'We're a close-knit family, and I talk daily to my parents on the phone. During the years when I was growing up, my dad travelled a lot. Although I didn't see him every day, we still have a close relationship, and we share a great interest in retail.' On Sundays at their family braais, or during their family holidays, they would reason with one another at length. Debating was one of their hobbies.

'People always think I must be spoilt because I'm Whitey Basson's daughter,' she added. 'That I grew up with designer clothes, for instance.

That's not true. My dad used to call my friends' parents to ask how much pocket money they got in order to decide how much he would give me. I got my grandmother's old car when I went to university. I had to work during university holidays, and cut my teeth at Shoprite's purchasing division.

'We always discussed business in our house. My dad taught me that it's important to do good research and start a business enterprise you're passionate about. Another thing he always says is that you have to want to live your work. You must be *so* passionate about it that you can't help making a success of it. You must be involved in every aspect of your enterprise – from customer service to money matters. You can ask him right now how much a tin of baked beans costs, and he'll know.'

35

Whitey's success factors

It is said that good companies do well in difficult times and exceptionally well in good times . . . We believe we are a good company. But good companies comprise good people and we are fortunate in having those in abundance, people who put their shoulders to the proverbial wheel on a daily basis and do what is required of them, and more.

– Whitey Basson, Shoprite Annual Report, 2015

Whitey Basson is certainly the greatest retailer South Africa has ever produced. For nearly four decades he wielded the sceptre at Shoprite and irrevocably transformed the retail industry in South Africa and the rest of Africa. What made him so successful? 'I was a 24/7 CEO. The saying goes, don't sweat the small stuff – but I did. And someone who can see the bigger picture *and* is concerned about the finer details will make an ass of you,' he warns.

'Of course the overall strategy is important. But retail is a huge business with millions of small interactions, the circumstances change on a daily basis, and there are constantly fires to put out. Consumer preferences keep changing too, and you have to stay abreast of those changes.

'In the first place, you need to know: why is someone buying from me? If I don't know *that*, I can't do my job. Sam Walton, Raymond Ackerman, Renier van Rooyen – look at all the best retailers, they were all hands-on, and they all knew exactly what went on in their stores.

You have to know what's going on on the floor – you can't run your stores from an office or boardroom. And I ran the business fearlessly and didn't mince my words either.'

In particular, he was quick to reprimand people about drivel and nonsense. One of his regular sayings was: 'Bullshit baffles brains'. Neil Schreuder explains it like this: 'Whitey had a masterly way of expressing very complicated ideas in plain language, so that anyone could understand it. This characteristic was extended to how to serve our customers and keep things in the company simple.

'Today one calls it customer-centricity, or reducing friction in customer experience, but Whitey reckoned much of the boardroom talk, or MBA jargon, was a load of hogwash. In his experience, the failed businesses he took over, such as Checkers and OK, had been run by people who didn't do their job but talked about "business theory". He realised early on that to run a successful business, the top executives also need to be on the floor, there has to be an open-door policy, and you have to look at the detail.

'His maxim "bullshit baffles brains" refers to the talk of people in ivory towers, consultants, and businesspeople who theorise. No matter how smart they may be on paper, they won't realise it when the business runs into difficulties. Hence, it was a warning: know your business, so that no one can bullshit you – and also a philosophy of no bullshit in the business, no nonsense, and no hierarchies.'

* * * *

Everyone who knows Whitey well tells the same story – about his eye for detail, and how he made no bones about putting someone in his place if his standards had not been met. Peter Solms, a Shoprite colleague, recounts: 'Around 1992 or 1993, at the opening of the revamped

Shoprite Plumstead, Whitey decided to walk down the aisles. Suddenly he stopped and said, "They're doing it just to irritate me!", and turned one tin around – among hundreds of others – whose label was facing the wrong way. It was then that I realised the company was destined for great things.'[1]

According to Andrew Gardener, the opening ceremony of the Shoprite in Dube, Soweto, in July 2001 was 'colourful, chaotic and packed with thousands of people'.[2] In the confusion, he was unable to accompany Whitey on the traditional walk-through before the opening. 'When we were sitting on the stage and a dignitary was giving a speech, Whitey leaned over to me and said: 'There aren't any yellow dusters at the shoe-polish section. Go put them there quickly.' This reminded me again of his incredible eye for detail and his determination that all of us should constantly improve our standards. It was the "Basson factor" that spurred us on and inspired us.'

There are a good many stories about Whitey's 'blunt' approach, which also show that people were sometimes wary of him. Johan van Deventer, general manager of Freshmark, relates that after the dissolution of the control boards, including the Deciduous Fruit Control Board and the Banana Control Board, the marketing of many fresh products was opened up. They could be freely marketed within South Africa and exported as well. 'Freshmark jumped in and recruited a man who was only going to export, because we already had good relationships with the producers. But he simply couldn't get moving – there was always a reason why nothing had been shipped yet.' Naturally, Whitey was not happy about this, and one day he summoned the man to his office.

Word has it that Whitey said to him: 'You can just remain standing, because this won't take long. The question is: why haven't we exported anything yet, and when will the first ship depart?' The man launched into a litany of reasons and excuses – wind in the harbour, payments, specifications, prices, congested markets, and more.

'So Whitey just stopped him in the middle of an excuse and said: "Hold on!" He picked up the glass of water that stood on his desk, turned it around in his hand as if admiring it, and said: "You've now told me in great detail that the glass comes from Venice, the water comes from Franschhoek and the pH is perfect, and the ice is just right too . . . But where's the effing whisky?"

'Needless to say, the man left the office ashen-faced and resigned shortly afterwards. The lesson: talk less, and deliver the goods!' Van Deventer explains.[3]

Another story that went around was that the safest place at a meeting was next to Whitey, 'otherwise he looks you in the eye all the time'.[4] Tom Voges was one of the poor souls who once sat opposite Whitey at a meeting to discuss Housebrands for the Sentra group. 'I proposed that we give the Sentra stores access to Shoprite's Housebrands,' Voges says. Whitey looked up, glared at him a few seconds over the top of his glasses, turned to Carel Goosen and said: 'Carel, buy this man a bicycle, because with that type of proposal he'll be of more use to us as a cyclist than as a marketer.'[5]

Willem van Rensburg was on duty in the warehouse in Brackenfell on a summer day when Whitey called him from a Shoprite in Strand. He said there were no umbrellas. Van Rensburg immediately sent someone there with a number of umbrellas, and called Whitey to tell him the crisis had been averted. 'I then sort of expected a compliment, but he made it plain to me in no uncertain terms that there should have been umbrellas in the store in the first place, and that I shouldn't expect compliments merely because I'm doing my job.'

In 2010, Whitey told *Leadership* magazine: 'I guess I am abrasive at times, but I mean it without malice. If someone doesn't do a job

Whitey with Selina Maphorogo, the first winner of Shoprite's national Woman of the Year Competition, in partnership with the SABC.

Whitey and Nelson Mandela in a jovial mood during the handover of a classroom at the Rebatla Thuto Secondary School in Koppies in the Free State, 31 May 2004. In that year, Shoprite donated a number of pre-fabricated mobile classrooms to the Free State Department of Education.

Tears of joy! Whitey hugs Jaco Labuschagne (13) who won a bakkie in the annual Shoprite Checkers Championship Boerewors Competition, Sun City, 2010.

In October 2014, Whitey was nominated to participate in the Ice Bucket Challenge, which resulted in charitable donations. Here the singer Kurt Darren douses Whitey with ice water during the annual Shoprite Checkers Championship Boerewors Competition at Sun City.

The Basson family – *from left,* Cornell, Nikki, Adrian, Annalise, Whitey and Mari.

Whitey on horseback at Klein DasBosch, and on his ski boat on the Langebaan Lagoon.

Whitey, his son-in-law and whisky adviser Hein, and Joseph Brönn, head of Shoprite's liquor division and currently the group's deputy CEO, during a visit to the Talisker ageing cellar in Scotland. The purpose of the team's visit was to buy single casks for Shoprite Checkers' whisky range.

Whitey might not have become a medical doctor, but he did receive an honorary doctorate from Johann Rupert, then chancellor of Stellenbosch University, 2010.

Although Whitey kept an eagle eye on his rivals, there was never ill feeling between them. Here he is with Gareth, Wendy and Raymond Ackerman outside the restaurant at Mont Marie, May 2021.

Whitey, aka 'Dadda', and Annalise with all their grandchildren on the occasion of their 51st wedding anniversary. *At the back, from left,* are Cara, Lise, Kohl and James.
In the front, from left, are Henk, Jack, Whitey, Kira, Annalise and Camron. Whitey was given the puppy, Elvis, as a birthday present.

properly and isn't earning their keep or doing their bit for the team, I'm not merely abrasive, I'm actually ruthless. However, I don't think I've ever gone to sleep at night worrying that I haven't solved a personal problem with staff.'[6]

Whitey's pursuit of excellence was non-negotiable. The standards were equally high for the company, its employees and himself. 'The blunt manner, honesty and unbiased opinions were part of the culture Whitey created,' Schreuder recounts. 'The people who work together have a right to say: I don't like this idea, you're not doing a good job, or this isn't going to work – you tell it like it is. And this led to trust and loyalty. You knew where you stood. If you didn't perform well you knew it, and you had to fight your way back. If you did perform well, you knew that too, and Whitey supported you all the way.'

Although Whitey does not believe there is a recipe for success, there are still principles that can improve all businesses. 'Number one is hard work. What is your punching rate, as they say in boxing? The more punches you can throw per minute, the better your chances of winning the fight. In the business world, the person with a higher punching rate, a higher level of commitment, will always do better than the other person.'

Hard work was par for the course at Shoprite. But Whitey enjoyed it because he was passionate about retail. During his television conversation with Kobus Wiese and Toks van der Linde, he said his advice to young people was that they had to be energetic, and you could only do that if you had passion. 'No matter how smart you may be, you can't be successful if you don't play better and work harder. You must have that energy, so don't do something you're not passionate about or that doesn't really interest you.'

He told the magazine *Maksiman* there were three principles that applied to his life as a whole: vision, optimism and integrity. 'For me, these principles have always guaranteed a winning recipe. And you must expose yourself to all levels of the business – you must constantly keep abreast of what is happening in your business, in the industry and in the world.'[7]

Today, he recounts: 'I chopped cabbage in Shoprite so that I knew what the product I was giving the customer should look like. How soon does it spoil, and when do you start selling it at the discounted price? My operating profit was two per cent higher than that of my competitors because I knew the nitty-gritty.

'If you get to know the business from the ground up, you make decisions with the right information. That's the difference between successful and unsuccessful businesses – you have to know about the customer, and know about the product. That you learn only at ground level. A computer printout that shows you have 10 000 packets of cornflakes and a shelf in a warehouse with 10 000 packets of corn-flakes – which physically shows you the extent of it – are two different things. I regularly walked through my warehouses – row by row – and therefore knew by how much we were overstocked or understocked. People always ask me what my formula was. I didn't have a formula. I knew my business, and lived my business – day by day.'

Whitey also made decisions fast. 'Speed has always been important to me – I make decisions like *that*,' he says, clicking his fingers. He believes you should work hard every day of your life, and that a prob-lem should be solved immediately. What it comes down to for him is 'tackling a problem, solving it, finalising it and putting it away', he told Theo Vorster.[8]

Deon Minnaar confirms this. He crossed paths with Whitey in the late 1990s when Whitey and a planeload of executives visited the Middle East – where Minnaar was working at the time – in search of new markets outside South Africa. 'Whitey's questions were probing, extensive, direct and detailed – as only he can do it,' Minnaar recounts. 'One thing I learnt from this remarkable man is that he doesn't make notes – he does something right away or delegates it right away. The only note I ever saw was a folded slip of paper in his shirt pocket. It contained his itinerary for the week, which Anita, his secretary, constantly had to update.'[9]

* * * *

Whitey kept to the following principles throughout: keep things simple, avoid hierarchies, empower your teams, establish a single point of accountability, and prioritise a culture of thrift – because what you are spending is your customer's money, and the margins you are losing are someone else's opportunity. Marketing is of course a key role of a good retailer, and Whitey sometimes referred to himself as a 'marketer'. According to him, marketing requires you to think differently: not to do what you have been taught, but to think of that which has not been done before.

Schreuder explains it like this: 'It's about the art of the possible – it calls for imagination, and for waking up and thinking I shouldn't do the same thing better, but should do something that is completely different. It's hard to find people who can do both, who have that balance. But Whitey was such a person.

'Every day you're only as good as the last tin of baked beans you sold. Retail can be monotonous, but Whitey was also able to switch to another gear instantly and think of a crazy idea for an ad.'

Thus Whitey regularly had new ideas, and also encouraged others to come up with new ideas. 'It's quite a modern leadership quality – you encourage curiosity in order to see if things can be done differently or better. And for Whitey, it came naturally. He could go to twenty divisional financial meetings and at each one ask the same question about every expense, but at the same time come up with creative ideas. He applied his principles consistently, and it paid dividends – tell it like it is, debate ideas and obtain multiple perspectives, make a decision, and stick to it. It means bad ideas don't get very far, and you don't waste money on them.'

* * * *

Whitey also understood that you cannot expect to win if you do not take risks. He took calculated risks – such as the acquisitions of Grand Bazaars, Checkers and OK – and the results were spectacular. 'It's my policy – I don't take on something unless I have a good chance of winning,' he told *Maksiman*. 'In the business world you must be specific and take on things where you feel your chance of success is better than fifty per cent.

'I learnt a few things the hard way, with time and effort. Be original, and don't be afraid of taking risks and nurturing big dreams. Think big, and don't be scared off by hard work. Learn to trust your sixth sense, your gut feel, and not to let golden opportunities slip through your fingers. Lastly: don't let a disappointment get the better of you or make you throw in the towel too soon – persistence wins the race!'[10]

As an optimist, Whitey saw the opportunities in risks rather than being put off by the potential pitfalls. Had he not stuck his neck out to buy Checkers – and OK as well, without the support of the bigger Pep group – Shoprite would not have been where it is today. In 1997 he said in an interview that luck might also play a role, and that there were brilliant businessmen who had never really had a lucky break.[11] A few years later, a journalist asked him: 'Have the dice landed well for James Wellwood Basson?' Whitey replied: 'I think so, but if they hadn't fallen the right way, I would've made sure I got to the places where they do fall the right way!'[12]

After every calculated risk, and every strategic decision, Whitey focused entirely on it. In his autobiography, Jannie Mouton writes that at a dinner William H Gates, the father of Microsoft founder Bill Gates, once hosted for a number of hand-picked businesspeople, he asked those present to write down a single word that they deemed to be of utmost importance in the business world. Coincidentally, Bill Gates and the legendary investor Warren Buffet chose the same word: focus. 'When I read that story,' Mouton writes, 'I realised how important focus was for discipline and success. I always admire Whitey Basson, chief executive of the Shoprite Group, for the same thing. He is incredibly attuned to trends in the retail industry.'[13]

One evening at a dinner, Jannie's wife Deidré mentioned to Whitey that Checkers's lettuce sometimes went bad before the expiry date, and before that of the opposition. 'That resulted in a huge research project in our fridge, because Whitey wouldn't believe her. He also had packets of all his main competitors' lettuce delivered to her, and Deidré faithfully jotted down changes in colour and freshness for the duration of the shelf-life of every packet of lettuce. In this process Whitey determined his lettuce had indeed been kept at too high a temperature, by 2°C, and special lettuce refrigerators were installed throughout the group.'

* * * *

A colleague of Whitey's once remarked that 'walking in at the back door' formed part of his management style.[14] He admitted to Theo Vorster that he loved to drop in at his stores unannounced, especially when he was on holiday. 'It's my passion to make sure that my stores are in order.' If he didn't drop in at the stores himself, 'there were usually people dropping in on me to tell me what was wrong'.

Consequently, everyone was always on their guard because the big boss could pitch up unexpectedly at any time. But it was also during one of those visits that Whitey's interest in his people, and his predilection for giving them a chance, manifested itself. In 1994, Charles Ochse, who later became chief foods buyer for Shoprite, met Whitey during an unexpected branch visit to Checkers Moreleta Park. 'As young branch manager, I said to myself it was now or never, and I told him I wanted to become a buyer. Two weeks later, I reported in Cape Town as a trainee buyer. I will always be grateful for the opportunity he gave me and the trust that was placed in me.'[15]

Other colleagues, employees, friends and acquaintances still speak about Whitey with awe, and with great admiration for his interest in everyone's lives. 'I've always experienced him as sincere and someone who is genuinely interested in his people and their families,' Gerhard Fritz says. 'He taught us that Shoprite is the most important thing in your life after your family – nurture it, look after it, and Shoprite will look after you. All of us who worked with him knew we could call him at any time, and he would always listen. I know of many people Whitey helped to get back on their feet, and also of others he offered a chance to prove themselves. With the opportunities he gave us to advance in Shoprite, he changed our lives and those of our families for the better, permanently.'

'Whitey still calls me every year on my birthday,' says Tollie Lewis. 'He has done so much for so many people – not only his employees, but the suppliers too. There are many suppliers who started small and grew along with us.'

In 2015, Whitey told Jak de Priester he 'enjoyed' the people around him and derived great satisfaction from improving ordinary people's lives and seeing how communities benefitted from that. Building a shopping centre in a town, establishing the first supermarket, seeing other businesses arising as a result, the shelf packer becoming the manager and years later the regional manager – these were the things that mattered to him.[16]

He believes every person has a talent or particular skill but not everyone has the opportunity to develop it, which is why he is so keen on helping people to help themselves. 'I'm very serious about my job. I hate slackness, and I'm uncompromising when I do business,' he told *Rooi Rose* in 2001. But he said the future of Shoprite's people was his responsibility. 'That's why, when I do business, Shoprite and its people come first.'[17]

Someone once described his management style as one of 'chaos', but Whitey's actions and decisions were not chaotic in the least. He did his research and carefully reflected on strategic moves. 'With the acquisition of Shoprite, I immediately appointed an American company that conducted research on customer needs. They used a methodology whereby they removed bias from the responses. Then they basically said – price is 70 per cent of people's needs. There may be other motivating factors as well for different people, but low prices will always be a need.'

Whitey never forgot this. 'Lower prices you can trust, always' is Shoprite's slogan, and for him that was non-negotiable – the chain's low-price positioning was maintained as he was 'willing to sacrifice profits in favour of affordability'.[18]

According to Doug Parker, Whitey's decisions were never rash. 'He is thorough, both in his research and his reasoning, but one aspect that makes him stand out is his ability to read and sum up a situation, and to realise what is really going on. Whitey is just different. I was used to working with the CEOs and senior executives of nearly all the large retailers in South Africa, and when I met him, he was initially hard to gauge. But to my surprise, he had a good instinct for retail and thought 'out of the box' in an unexpected way – he would come with a view or standpoint you hadn't anticipated at all.

'He simply had a different way of thinking about things. Most executive directors in retail, especially your accountants, don't understand the sector, but Whitey did, and he also understood his market perfectly – what they wanted, and how to get them to shop at his stores. He had a razor-sharp grasp of his business and his market. These were critically important factors. He was resolute and unwavering, and had a clear idea of what he wanted to achieve.'

Parker also says Whitey was a strong, autocratic leader. 'But his employees respected him – they respected his abilities, and what he demanded and expected of them. He had high expectations of his staff. And he never accepted second best – it was all or nothing. He was hard on his staff and pushed them, but at the same time he was incredibly loyal and supportive.'

Jimmy Fouché paints a similar picture. 'The feel for retail is in Whitey's blood . . . He is someone who's interested in his business, knows what goes on in the business, and wants to have things done right. In retail, you must have your finger on the pulse. Whitey wasn't a textbook participative manager. He certainly took his team's views into account, but he didn't rely on democratic team decisions. He would talk to his people, get people on his side, listen to their input and make a decision, and then allow everyone to implement it. But he's not someone who sits down at a table and asks everyone to vote on what should be done. He's an entrepreneur – so you have a clear idea of what you want to achieve, you listen to other people and discuss it with them, but in the end, you are the decision-maker and the doer.'

Whitey himself says: 'I tried to continue Renier's management style at Shoprite. I was often accused of not consulting others, but I don't think that's true. If you have so little time, and Renier's drive, as I also had at Shoprite, you tend to make decisions you have reflected on for a long time and that you know are right for the business.'

According to Fouché, Whitey is not a committee person either. 'But that is not to say that he doesn't take his team into consideration and work together with them. It's not a committee decision but a team game. And there was no doubt about who was the captain. But it probably also starts with assembling the right people around you, so that you can depend on what they think and say, and on them doing what they say they will.

'He relied on people, because of course he knew he couldn't do everything himself. You have to draw in people in whom you can trust, but you don't delegate the final responsibility or accountability. You delegate the duties but retain the responsibility. And when you do that, you will also insist that things be done the way you think they ought to be done. But he has always been someone with an appreciation for other people's contributions.'

* * * *

'Everyone has the right to walk through the door; everyone has the right to complain as long as the common goal of the company is to grow, to create new jobs and ensure a better future for all its stakeholders,' Whitey once told Tim Cohen.[19]

Fritz says Whitey has the ability to motivate you and spur you on to attain success. 'Sometimes you get very angry with him, but when you reflect on it afterwards, you realise he is actually right and that there are other ways to do things.'

According to Schreuder, Whitey cared a great deal about his people but 'used to highlight mistakes and make an example of them, so that people always gave their best and made sure everything was right before it reached him. Whitey assessed people very quickly and was incredibly good at spotting their true talent and then supporting them.'

* * * *

Another notable characteristic of Whitey is his sense of humour. Besides never taking himself too seriously and making jokes at his own expense, he would poke fun at his rivals, suppliers and sometimes government, and over the years his quirky sayings came to be known as 'Whitey-isms'. Among others: 'I always say we put our testicles out there, then people say, "No, that's the wrong word, you put your tentacles out there!"'[20]

Interviews with journalists usually made for entertaining repartee. One asked rhetorically: 'Some say you rule Shoprite with an iron fist.' He replied: 'No, that's not true.' Interviewer: 'So what would you say is your management style?' 'Chaotic,' he quipped.

At times his humour also included a dig at his rivals. 'Shoprite is far ahead of the pack . . . we don't have to import people to run our business,' he remarked on one occasion, with reference to Richard Brasher, a former executive of British retailer Tesco who was hired to head Pick n Pay.

But his jokes often contained a degree of truth. Sean Summers had taken over from Raymond Ackerman in 1999. Nick Badminton, who was appointed in 2007, resigned after five years and was succeeded by Richard van Rensburg. In 2013, Brasher was appointed.[21] So, during Whitey's tenure at Shoprite, his biggest rival had five chief executives. One of Shoprite's success factors was precisely its stable leadership in the form of Whitey and his core team of senior directors, with a single supportive chairman and a stable board that knew retail and could make a contribution to the company. And, ultimately, Shoprite was more than a company. Shoprite's people became Whitey's friends, his family.

In 2010, Whitey's alma mater, Stellenbosch University, conferred on him an honorary doctorate in commerce. The degree recognised his 'outstanding leadership qualities; his excellent achievements as a business leader and job creator; and his continued support of and investment in the development of human potential in the disadvantaged sectors of society'. In his speech, Whitey said that for him, as 'an ordinary guy who sells chickens', this was a great honour, and he affirmed the role his colleagues had played in his life.

'I have always only believed that what you achieve in life must be achieved on merit, and that your principles should never be subservient to popularity. But I am also old enough to know that at certain levels of society there are people who want to be the bride at every wedding and the corpse at every funeral. That is why I am delighted that at a time when popularity plays such a big role, I, as an outspoken man, at least managed to make it.'

Ninety per cent of his doctorate actually belonged to Shoprite, and he therefore wanted to thank his colleagues, chairman, board and friends for always having trusted him to do the right thing, without any sideshows. 'This may have given us more speed than other people who were subject to lengthy meetings and senseless bosberade.'

While 'Doctor' Whitey received congratulations from all quarters, those from employees in particular showed that he was more than just a boss but in many cases a mentor, and also a friend. 'Congratulations on the well-deserved recognition with which the university has honoured you,' wrote Gerhard Kriel, a senior executive of Shoprite. 'I am proud that I have been able to work with you for such a long time, but especially that you call me a friend.' Although he and his family could not give Whitey a degree, they wanted to thank him for the opportunities he had given him and the way in which this had improved their lives. 'We would like you to know we will always remember and appreciate it.'

* * * *

A large part of Shoprite's success can therefore be attributed to the culture Whitey established in the company. When Hanlie Retief from *Rapport* asked him, after his retirement, what had made Shoprite so successful, he replied succinctly: 'Our culture. How we do things.'[22]

Another major factor has been Shoprite's long-term investment in its centralised supply chain. Whitey believed it simply made logical sense for stores to be replenished via the company's distribution centres instead of every supplier having to deliver goods at every store. The benefits of a centralised supply chain include, inter alia, better control over in-store stock availability, the ability to maintain a wider range of stock and supplier base, and cost savings.[23] Continuous improvements of Shoprite's centralised distribution network, supply chain and sourcing models have resulted in greater scale and growth, and ultimately better margins than those of its competitors.[24]

The group has also positioned its trading brands well – particularly Shoprite, Checkers, OK and Usave – to compete in different target markets across income groups. It was the first to expand into Africa, and has done so aggressively. Shoprite still has 'an unmatched footprint' in Africa, and has gained the experience to expand further in the continent.

Whitey always regarded Pick n Pay and Raymond Ackerman as his biggest rival. He also believed you had to know your opponent in order to plan strategically. In 1999 he told *De Kat*: 'At first I thought

332

if I stayed on Ackerman's heels, I was at least beating all the other guys. Now he and I are about the only contestants who are still left in the race. And we're running neck and neck. It makes me feel quite chuffed.'[25]

In November 2019, a senior investment analyst from Sanlam Private Wealth described Shoprite's performance as follows: 'While Pick n Pay, with its philosophy of "consumer sovereignty", pioneered modern grocery retail in South Africa in the 1970s and '80s under Raymond Ackerman, it was Shoprite – under the leadership of Whitey Basson – that led the second phase of modernisation in the sector over the past two decades.'

After the turn of the century, Whitey started showing Ackerman a clean pair of heels. The group not only systematically gained market share – by 2019 its 'leading market share' was 'in excess of 30% of grocery retail in South Africa' – but managed to improve its trading profit margin from 1 per cent in 2000 to nearly 6 per cent by 2017. 'This margin was well above that of competitors, despite the retailer carrying the lowest price perception among consumers – a clear sign of the operational supremacy it attained.

'Over this period, Shoprite's share price outperformed the FTSE/JSE All Share Index by 10% per annum. The better profitability enabled Shoprite to continue reinvesting higher amounts of capital into the business than its competitors to achieve further growth and more efficient operations.'[26]

* * * *

In Wilgenhof, Whitey's old university residence in Stellenbosch, there is a gallery of photos of 'Groot Oumanne', notable alumni who have made their mark, such as the anti-apartheid activist and theologian

Beyers Naudé, the politician Frederik van Zyl Slabbert and the captain of the first Springbok rugby team, Paul Roos. Christo Wiese is there, and above his photo hangs that of Whitey, 'first year 1964'.[27] Whitey is indeed a 'groot ouman'. His ambition propelled him to the top in his business sector, but for him it was essentially about people – his customers and colleagues.

According to Fouché, success should not only be judged by Shoprite's staff and suppliers. 'The more successful you are, the more you can also offer your customers – not only in terms of value for money, but also what you offer in terms of their needs. Your customers are an important stakeholder group in your business. They are the foundation on which your enterprise is built – and without your customers, you are nothing. Whitey knew this only too well, and alongside his employees, his customers were to him the most important stakeholders.'

In 1999, Whitey explained it like this: 'Retail is a living organism. It requires more people employed per rand invested than any other kind of business. The first step in rescuing a retail business is to get the people who work for the company on board. All employees must be proud of it.

'No individual could have turned OK or Checkers around. You had to have the synergistic abilities of a powerful team. Over the last 19 years we have built up a capable team of professionals that is ready, able and eager to do the job. As far as the leader of the company is concerned, you have to ask yourself continually, will they still follow me if I no longer have my title? The position I hold is no longer simply a form of employment. 98% of my friends are around me at work. This is a lifestyle, not a job.'[28]

His ambition meant that his job had become his life, he acknowledged in 2003. 'I'm often away from home – but there are other benefits for my family. By now my children have probably forgotten all the sandcastles we didn't build together. But other things we did do together are now of value to them.'[29]

His dream was to make Shoprite one of the world's twenty largest retailers. 'We're already in the top hundred, so we still need to come down to twenty.' He admitted that he had sometimes overestimated things. 'If you underestimate, you're average – you don't need to worry about losing face or going down in flames. But that's not me – I would rather overestimate.'

He did overestimate Shoprite's eventual size – but it is still the largest food retailer in Africa, and the largest private-sector employer in South Africa. A few years before his retirement, he said: 'In retrospect, I concentrated on building the business, but my legacy isn't in the level of wealth I've accumulated: it's in the number of meaningful relationships I've built over the years. I'd like my legacy to be about the good friends I've had and the people whose lives I impacted. It should be about how many children are professionals because we gave their parents jobs. That's how I want to be remembered.'[30]

Whitey may have left Shoprite, but he has left behind a well-oiled machine, with thousands of trucks delivering stock to more than 2 800 stores in fifteen countries every day. Hundreds of thousands of people will today collect their medication at a Medirite, send precious money to a loved one in another country at a Money Market Counter, and visit a Shoprite, Checkers or Usave branch to shop for their daily needs – their chicken, milk, bread and baked beans.

Epilogue

After reading Niel's text reflectively, I must admit that he has done an excellent job. I am grateful for that, because 40 years is a long period to cover.

Thank you, too, to the people who said and wrote such nice things about me. I don't know whether all of it is true, but the one thing I do know is that no business can be as successful as Shoprite is because of a single individual. A large number of dedicated people have taken the company from 1979 to where it is today.

I have now been asking myself again why a company such as Checkers, which had been so successful under the Herber brothers, could struggle so much under a giant such as Sanlam. And what happened to OK in the period between the era of the Cohens and that of SA Breweries, and to the other smaller companies that had run into difficulties and were then taken over by us? They had not lacked capital or expertise, so somewhere in the process we had to look for the actual problems. Some of the answers follow below.

- **Create basic togetherness.** I want to be so bold as to say it was chiefly the lack of solidarity that comes only from social cohesion and bonding with your colleagues, as Renier van Rooyen had taught me at Pep Stores, as well as a true passion for your business. When enterprises grow and gradually become part of a large conglomerate, they suddenly lose that feature – everyone does something, but they don't do anything together. This was easy to spot when you walked into a company you were taking over and encountered – as Renier described it – little empires instead of cooperation and teamwork.

- **Keep your boards within limits, and your directors and senior management on their toes and involved.** We know that the senior management of controlling companies often try to exercise total control without assuming any responsibility for the business at the operational level. The same goes for today's boards, which consist mostly of professional directors and chairpersons who establish so many subcommittees on which they themselves also serve that their remuneration packages become simply ridiculous. So this consideration is clear: keep your senior executives and your boards on their toes, and keep them involved.

- **Look after your properties.** There was one big common denominator among all the companies we took over and turned around: the enormous losses that arose from bad property portfolios. In Shoprite, we devoted a lot of attention to this aspect – we selected premises with care, constructed new buildings, and rebuilt and refurbished others. When we took over companies with poor property portfolios, we cancelled some lease agreements, sold some buildings, and rebuilt or revamped others.

- **Utilise your spaces.** In the early years I, along with Selwyn Schiff, personally designed the layout of our stores to ensure that no space was wasted. And in the years before I retired, Pieter Engelbrecht would spend every Saturday working only on buildings. This was of cardinal importance to us, and one of the major reasons why we were able to turn around the companies we had taken over. In fact, at one stage we said the stores should pay only about two per cent of their turnover on rent and refer the rest to the head office, where our property division then tried in various ways to settle that which was above that ratio. Otherwise, the poor branch managers would never make a profit and become completely disheartened because most of the time the store itself was not to blame. The majority of the companies that created oversized and opulent spaces did so to stroke the egos of those at the top.

- **Determine your market.** Another problem was that people had not really determined their markets, nor the size of the market. The market strategies of the groups we took over were often a mishmash – aimed at LSM groups that had nothing in common with each other, and with stores that were not necessarily appropriate for their target markets. When you want to start a store, make sure that you know what market you would like to serve, what its size is, and how you intend to go about it. My old saying is still applicable: there may be a gap in the market, but is there really a market in the gap?

- **Maintain financial discipline, and a solid legal practice.** I was not much of a stickler for the finer details of corporate governance, but for any company it is a serious mistake not to have a strong financial discipline and legal practice in the basket. I never did deals without Carel Goosen, our head of finance, and André van Zyl, head of the legal division, working with me. In this way we quickly cleaned up and fixed all the financial weaknesses and legal errors we encountered at the companies, and ensured that there were no skeletons in any cupboards. This had also been the case when I worked at Pep. I did not take a step without the cooperation of Tom Ball, who cleaned up behind me while I negotiated new branches and new business.

- **Give your people a share in the business.** Financial participation is a must. Staff members must be given the chance to share in the company's wealth, preferably by way of shares or bonuses that are linked to the company's growth. This is often opposed, since boards would like to retain everything for the controlling company. And the bigger the company becomes, the further the staff move away from the fire that needs to burn into the future to keep producing better results and make bigger profits for shareholders. So, start with profit sharing from the outset, and gradually give staff members shares in the company.

- **Pay attention to marketing.** Marketing is often neglected. You should never think only of your wife's preferences or your personal preferences: do your marketing for your target market, and define that market carefully. Everything that is beautiful is expensive, and everything that is expensive gives you poor returns unless you make it even more expensive, so guard against imposing your own style on a business and thereby impairing your marketing.

In retail, if you pay attention to these facets and you work hard and purposefully, you will certainly achieve success.

Finally, thank you as well to Baai, Esau and Dappie Tang, my childhood friends in Porterville, who taught me so much about humanity and helped me define my life goals. One of these days we'll buy a new rugby ball.

Greetings, and I miss you.
Whitey Basson, September 2022

Tributes and memories

*What you see is what you get. Whitey doesn't try to pretend
to be someone he's not. He doesn't have 'classes' of friends –
if you're his friend, you're his friend.*

— Jean Engelbrecht, winemaker and
owner of Rust en Vrede

He has been described as 'legendary', but also as 'down to earth', 'un-orthodox', and having a 'no-nonsense' approach – 'Africa's Goliath of retail' who was the 'atomic energy' behind Shoprite and 'the miracle worker' of Checkers and OK Bazaars.[1] But despite his successes, he's still a human being. He was and is as comfortable in the company of world leaders and celebrities as he is among the employees in his stores and the people on his farms.

He is game for fun and horseplay as well. In 2014, the Ice Bucket Challenge swept the globe like an icy tsunami, and in October of that year Whitey was challenged to have a bucket of ice water poured over his head. During the annual Shoprite Checkers Championship Boerewors Competition at Sun City, he was given his 'cold shower' by the singer Kurt Darren. Instead of donating money, Shoprite donated boerewors to the value of R100 000 to several schools in the country and challenged them to make more money from it by using the donations for their own fundraising campaigns, thereby encouraging entrepreneurship.[2]

In 2019, after the Springboks won the Rugby World Cup in Japan, a video did the rounds that showed Whitey and the renowned Bok prop Tendai 'Beast' Mtawarira arm-wrestling at a braai hosted by Richemont chairperson Johann Rupert on his farm L'Ormarins near Franschhoek.[3]

340

Whitey is not only a business leader but also a dad, a husband, a mentor and a friend.

Annalise Basson, spouse

Whitey retained his devotion to Shoprite and his enthusiasm for the business until the end. He had a particular liking for advertisements, and was largely responsible for the concepts of most of them. I can't remember a Saturday or a Sunday when he didn't open *Die Burger* or *Rapport* to the advertisements. Then I knew: here it comes! In the earlier days it was poor Brian Weyers who had to take the flak, and later Neil Schreuder. The criticism would be along the lines of 'It's Easter weekend, and we're advertising rice instead of braai meat . . . the toilet paper is bigger than the cooking oil . . . the opposition's price for maize meal is better . . .' I never ceased to marvel at his eye for detail.

Since his retirement, he has had more time to spend with his grand-children. He is very proud of them. It is blissful for us just to be here at home. Almost every day we drive up the road to Pieter Vlok's restaurant, Mont Marie, which is on our property. It's nice to see how well he is doing, and of course very convenient to have a professional chef virtually on your stoep.

Whitey now also has more time to be involved in all the farming operations – mostly the vineyards and the wine-making process, which he finds very interesting. But Shoprite will always be his first love. He still speaks of 'us' when he talks about Shoprite and continues to keep a close eye on the business. He is extremely loyal towards his people, and always believed in second or even third chances. He had the ability to spot people's potential and would then encourage them to reach the top. He still calls all those with whom he worked closely on their birthday, follows up when he hears of someone who is experiencing problems, and tries to help where he can.

He was a hard taskmaster and expected 100 per cent from his employees, but also gave 100 per cent of himself. He made friends out of his colleagues but didn't hesitate to reprimand them when he thought they had made a mistake – and that requires a special talent.

It is the same in his personal life. I haven't had a single day's worry that I or any of my children would be faced with a problem he wouldn't be able to resolve. That is a huge burden to bear, but I also know that is why he is in our lives. And the same goes for everyone else who has crossed his path.

Christo Wiese, former chairperson of Shoprite

A friendship of 58 years – almost a lifetime. Such a long-standing friendship is clearly special. I count myself lucky to have such a friend in Whitey. Over all these decades, the two of us have shared the sweet and the bitter of life – we experienced great adventures, enjoyed socialising together and had lots of fun. My mother-in-law always said: 'To have a friend, you have to be a friend.' Besides all his other virtues, Whitey certainly knows 'how to be a friend'.

His successes in the business world are legendary. Through his leadership and entrepreneurship he has impacted the lives of literally hundreds of thousands of people: employees, colleagues, suppliers, shareholders, and notably Shoprite's customers. Over four decades, he built Shoprite into the largest retailer in Africa, with close to 150 000 employees. Typically, he never hesitated to share the credit for this massive success with others. As a businessman, it is my conviction that he should definitely be rated as one of the best retailers South Africa has produced to date, and possibly the very best.

For me, however, he is much more than a prized business partner. At the end of the day, he is not only a businessman but also a family man, farmer, fisherman and hunter. He and Annalise raised four children who have given them endless joy and beautiful grandchildren to boot. One of my greatest delights is that Whitey's elder son Adrian and my son Jacob have become close friends over the years.

Notwithstanding his busy schedule, Whitey regularly went on holiday with his family. What impressed me was that even during ski holidays he would make time to visit other stores in Kitzbühel in an attempt to make his own business even better.

I can of course tell many anecdotes about Whitey's sense of humour, his practical jokes, his wonderful ability to appraise people and to get along with everyone. If he has enemies, I am not aware of them. Whitey is an exceptional and gifted South African we can all be proud of.

Patrice Motsepe, mining magnate

Whitey Basson is truly a legend in the formal food retail sector, where he undoubtedly can be considered the visionary leader of this sector over the past four decades.

He notably made his mark by growing Shoprite from a small business into the market leader it is today. This was accomplished by bringing about excellent organic growth after the two big acquisitions, first Checkers and then OK Bazaars, that created a platform for expansion. Both these acquisitions required substantial turnaround strategies, which were masterfully implemented. Following the transition to a democratic dispensation in 1994, Whitey expanded the platform that had been created both locally and in other parts of Africa, and established Shoprite as the trendsetting leader. In 2015, just before Whitey's retirement, Shoprite was ranked as the largest retailer in Africa.

Whitey achieved these accomplishments through his personal dedication, exceptional leadership and attention to detail, with a no-nonsense approach. Throughout, he has retained his distinctive sense of humour. He indeed leaves behind a monument he can genuinely be proud of! I pay homage to him for his contribution to the South African business environment.

It is a great honour and privilege to be able to regard Whitey as a brother.

GT Ferreira, former CEO, Rand Merchant Bank

Whitey Basson must surely be the most successful but also the most underrated retail CEO in the country. If you take into account the fact that he has built a massive retail chain from almost nothing and simultaneously succeeded in turning two large companies (Checkers and OK) around that were in the red – something the giant SAB, with some of the best management, could not even do – you have to agree that he is not getting all the kudos that he deserves.

Whitey also achieved legendary status in the industry through his negotiation skills, not only because of his ability to secure the best prices from his suppliers of groceries and food but also because he could really turn the screws on banks such as RMB and FNB to get the best financing rates and the best prices for Shoprite's transaction business. Of this, I have personal experience. No wonder it is said that Whitey's teeth are the softest part of his anatomy. Despite all the success that Whitey achieved, he remained the same Whitey I got to know at university. Outspoken but never arrogant, sharp but never devious, wise but with a touch of humility.

If I ever had to write an obituary about Whitey (which I hope I will never have to do), I would probably not be able to find better words to describe Whitey than this excerpt from Theodore Roosevelt's famous 'Citizenship in a Republic' speech, which he delivered at the Sorbonne in Paris, France, on 23 April 1910. The speech is popularly known as 'The Man in the Arena':

'It is not the critic who counts; not the man who points out how the strong man stumbles or where the doer of deeds could have done them better. The credit belongs to the man who is actually in the arena, whose face is marred by dust and sweat and blood; who strives valiantly; who errs, who comes short again and again, because there is no effort without error and shortcoming; but who does actually strive to do the deeds; who knows great enthusiasms, the great devotions; who spends himself in a worthy cause; who at the best knows in the end the triumph of high achievement, and who at the worst, if he fails, at least fails while daring greatly, so that his place shall never be with those cold and timid souls who neither know victory nor defeat.'

Hail to Whitey the Legend!

Francois Groepe, banker and former CEO, Media24

Our paths first crossed more than a decade ago when our respective teams – he at Shoprite and me at Media24 – were involved in challenging commercial negotiations. The matter was eventually escalated to the two of us. Knowing that Whitey is a tough negotiator, I decided to appeal to his broader vision of society as opposed to taking a narrow commercial approach. I explained to him that print media is an important institution in any society and that we should do all we can to ensure its sustainability. Whitey immediately saw the merits of my line of reasoning. We successfully concluded our negotiations.

Why is this important? South Africa, as a frontier nation, has had a long line of very successful entrepreneurs. Sadly, however, there are far fewer business leaders. Whitey is one of that scarce breed of business leaders. One who has immensely contributed towards our society.

We subsequently became firm friends. Over the years I had been impressed by his compassion and caring nature, his loyalty, his insightful mind and, of course, his wonderful sense of humour and the twinkle in his eye. A humble human being who could walk with paupers and dine with kings.

I am aware of several instances where he assisted less privileged staff or associates, getting them access to the best private health care at his own expense. There are many people who can attest to his generosity and help, people across all generations, social groups and across the racial spectrum. And this does not even include the generous bursary scheme he set up.

Whitey, despite his soaring success, remained grounded and is, through and through, a family man, and a loyal friend.

Anita van Rensburg, executive personal assistant

The company where I worked closed down, and I did not intend to take up another job. Karin Dippenaar, a friend who worked at a personnel placement agency, called me and asked me to apply for the position of Whitey Basson's secretary, as they hadn't found a suitable candidate. I knew nothing about Shoprite, but then she added that Whitey was a very dynamic person, that he would reach great heights, and that he drove a Porsche, which of course piqued my interest.

Consequently, my journey and career at Shoprite started on 15 February 1990. For the next 32 wonderful years, I was privileged to work for the most dynamic business leader imaginable, and to grow along with him and Shoprite. He believed in me, and I always wanted to give only my best. One thing is certain – a more loyal boss and friend you won't find anywhere.

Ann Crotty, financial journalist

Just hours after he'd finalised the R1 purchase of OK Bazaars from South African Breweries, Whitey was complaining he'd overpaid. He told me a really smart retailer wouldn't have paid any more than 99c.

And then he laughed. He frequently laughed. And almost as frequently he complained grumpily about something or other that was irritating him, sometimes it was a journalist who he reckoned didn't understand the complexities of executive pay, other times it was more serious.

During that OK Bazaars interview Whitey gave no indication of being in any way daunted by the challenge he had just taken on: 157 supermarkets and 146 furniture stores were being added to Shoprite's existing 241 stores. Of course, even if he was daunted by the prospect, it wouldn't have been his style to let on. Whitey's style was rather unique – a mix of scary bluster and resolute determination wrapped in just enough humour to assure you he was one of the good guys.

As it happens, he had reason not to be daunted. He had pulled off an even bigger deal back in 1991 when he acquired Checkers from Sanlam which had taken it over from Natie Kirsh's Tradegro a few years earlier. Checkers was the deal that ensured we all had to take Whitey very seriously. It propelled him into the big league. But more important than size was the fact he'd managed to turn a company around that looked to be beyond saving. For years Checkers had been haemorrhaging money with stories of pantechnicons of goods disappearing in the few kilometres between a distribution centre and a store. At one stage it seemed the level of 'shrinkage' was about the same as the level of sales.

We watched and waited for this swaggering new player to implode under the pressure. Amazingly, and with what must have been superhuman effort by a huge swathe of people, he knocked Checkers into shape within a few years. Equally amazing, given his reputation, in the process he managed to avoid a potentially bruising confrontation with Checkers's militant trade unions. Whitey was well on the way to redesigning the grocery retail industry. Twenty-five years on and Whitey had reached near-iconic status.

And then came the shocking news, announced rather abruptly at the beginning of the annual general meeting in 2016. He was 'weary and gatvol' and so had decided to retire from the group he had built. Given his decades-long energy and passion, not many bought the 'weary and gatvol' story. There was a stunned silence in the room full of shareholders, analysts and journalists; it was the end of an era. The retirement of arguably South Africa's greatest retailer who had built the largest grocery retail group in Africa. He was probably worth every cent he was paid.

Schalk Burger Sr, winemaker and businessman

As I arrived at the new Shoprite Head Office in Beaconvale, I saw this black Porsche 911 to my right and wondered, as a petrolhead, whose car it could be. 'Most probably a rich supplier to Shoprite,' I mused. After announcing myself in the modest reception area, I waited to meet Brian Weyers, their marketing manager and the buyer of wine for their expanding grocer's wine licence stores, something which had just been authorised by Dawie de Villiers, the then minister of Trade, Industry and Tourism. There was a maximum number of grocer's licences that a single retailer could own, and everyone was aware that the Shoprite Group had opposed this limit.

I met with Brian and pitched the concept of a new wine that we – Union Wines, owned by Jan Pickard's Picbel – were launching. It was Culemborg Diamanté. A semi-sweet rosé wine with a little fizz, in a unique bottle. With the launch we were going to put a diamond into one of the bottles for a lucky customer to win. As I was about to finish the sales pitch, in walked the CEO who introduced himself as Whitey and sat down on Brian's desk. I had to run through my pitch again.

Whitey said, 'How much of this have you got? I want all of it! Turning to Brian, he said, 'What is the price?' And as Brian grabbed his calculator to work out the selling price, Whitey said: 'Nee man, hoeveel kos die ding?' I gave him the trade price, saying that we were granting a 10 per cent discount. 'Nou goed,' was the reply. 'Hier is die deal. We will list it on the following conditions: You offer us another 5 per cent discount, you add another diamond into the bottles you sell to us and you make sure Jan Pickard allows us to purchase his grocer's wine licences.

'And by the way,' he said to Brian, 'make the price the same as the trade price and advertise the hell out of it.' To which I protested, anticipating the rest of the retail trade's complaints. Whitey stood up, shook my hand and said, 'Dankie Schalkie, lekker voetbal speel Saterdag.'

Shoprite kept on growing by doing these types of deals by gut feel, knowing the supplier and forgetting about a calculator when the deal felt right! As I walked out, having done the wine deal of the year, I asked the receptionist whose Porsche was outside. Proudly she offered: 'Dis my meneer Whitey s'n.'

Louis Vlok, clinical psychologist and friend

I have known Whitey since 1993 when we met on our sons' rugby tour to Mossel Bay. What immediately struck me was that he travelled with his son on the train and later the bus. He was offered many car rides, but he declined.

Whitey is widely renowned for his ambition, intelligence and drive. But essentially, he is a 'people person'. He shows great compassion towards those close to him, although he sometimes gets overinvolved. However, his intentions are always good. He is a brilliant raconteur, and his stories normally centre around those who supported him in his career.

He is very inquisitive, and, given the amount of information he has recently compiled about the corona pandemic and other related matters, I am inclined to think he should have followed his original impulse and done a medical degree!

Dr Johann Rabie, physician and friend

My friendship with Whitey Basson dates back as far as about 1981, when he still lived in Welgemoed. As time went on, our shared interest in the sea and the fact that we had both been in Wilgenhof led to a close friendship.

Whitey's knowledge of human nature impressed me time and again. He asked me on a few occasions to accompany him when he went to visit employees in the hospital in Malmesbury. During the trips he played a tape of Norman Vincent Peale, and we could listen to words of wisdom about life. Whitey was always very concerned about his employees, especially when it came to their health, and he wanted only the best for them. Over time he acquired the nickname 'Dr Basson'.

Doug Smollan, Shoprite service provider (Smollan Group)

I have known Whitey Basson for more than 40 years. He is man with a strategic vision and enormous drive – one of the very few people who can look at the big picture and the small picture simultaneously. He studied the products in his stores in the finest detail, tracked the supply chain, and then made sure that only the best products were supplied. I don't know any supplier to Shoprite who does not have the greatest respect for Whitey.

In his dealings with suppliers he was always firm, fair and friendly, and he made a lot of money for many people. It was never his aim that people shouldn't make a profit. Unusual for a chief executive, he took an interest in everything that went on in his business. He was tough and probing and scrutinised everything closely, but he always looked after his people, young and old. He searched for bright-eyed people and developed them into champions. He planted acorns that grew into tall oak trees under whose shade many in South Africa and elsewhere have sat.

Kenny Cheng, Chinese supplier and friend

I first met Mr Basson in 1978 when he visited Hong Kong for the first time while he was still at Pep Stores. I was working for another supplier at the time, but started my own company, Kedah, in 1985. According to Chinese tradition, I didn't supply Pep Stores or Shoprite for a few years after I left the previous company.

Mr Basson contacted me in 1990 to ask whether I would supply some items to Shoprite, for which I was very grateful because from then on, my company grew very fast. We built good relationships with the best reliable factories to supply Shoprite with any kind of items, according to their needs.

Mr Basson would regularly travel and work alongside the Shoprite buyers. These trips were always very enjoyable, and we became great friends. Our bond and mutual trust have grown ever since. So much so that Mr Basson convinced me to buy a house in Stellenbosch, which I use on our business trips, and also for holidays.

One valuable lesson I learnt from Mr Basson is how to negotiate properly. Sometimes I would give the suppliers too much information. Then Mr Basson would tell me afterwards: 'Stil mond is 'n heel mond' [A silent mouth means you won't get hurt]. From then on, I always remembered that! It is my great honour to be Mr Basson's friend. He is like a brother to me.

Jo-Ann Strauss, former Miss South Africa and businesswoman

Bono, Madonna, Beyoncé . . . only the biggest stars require a single name for everyone to know who is being referred to. Well, Whitey is on that list. I remember the first time I was introduced to him, at an event for Shoprite at Klein DasBosch. I was quite nervous because as a BCom student at Stellenbosch I'd obviously heard a lot about this legendary character. I had a good laugh, however, because he jumped right in and asked whether I'd given them the best price to act as master of ceremonies, and whether I could perform that role the following year as well, but at a good rate if I was willing to do a 'package deal'. I felt quite honoured that I could have done my first negotiation with Whitey. He always has that sparkle in his eye, and it's the sweetest thing to see how much he loves his family. After all these years he now calls me 'Jo-tjie' – one of the few nicknames that always makes me smile. Yes, Whitey won in that first negotiation, but I was the real winner in that I can now say that legend and his family are part of my life.

Mynie Grové, singer and versatile music personality

I remember walking into Shoprite's head office for the first time and being so impressed by the walnut grand piano in the centre of the reception area, set against the backdrop of an atrium with greenery and amid a restful and elegant atmosphere. Wow . . . a CEO with a grand piano in his foyer had to be quite special . . . In 1999, Shoprite held its first gala event for the Woman of the Year Competition. I was approached to perform as guest artist, to deliver other artists, and to handle the music rights. I booked the best musicians and artists. The other main singer withdrew at the last minute, and I quickly had to find a suitable replacement. I immediately thought of a young student from the University of Cape Town I had helped during a television competition – none other than Judith Sephuma.

I had written a special song titled 'You Are The One', and Judith performed it excellently. This was Judith's big Hollywood moment – it introduced her to the entertainment industry, and the rest is history.

Whitey is a guy with infinite dreams and an audacity I admire. A man who established a giant in Africa, the largest retailer on the continent, had to have a vision that is bigger than yours and mine.

He loves fun and games. The soft heart that melts at the slightest gesture of humanity is like that piano in the reception area – audacious, beautiful, unorthodox and grand.

Jak de Priester, singer, songwriter and television presenter

In April 2012, I was in Oudtshoorn where I was acting in a South African movie for the first time. My wife and mother-in-law, along with our two young children, left for Port Shepstone in Kwa Zulu-Natal on a week-long holiday, but on the way they were involved in a serious car accident.

When I came off set and switched on my phone, everyone was trying to get hold of me. My heart was in my mouth when I called my wife Michelle on her cellphone, and a stranger answered. In the background, I heard the sounds of an accident scene.

Members of the film crew immediately rushed me to George Airport. The fastest way of getting to Durban by plane was to fly via Johannesburg. All I had with me was the clothes on my back, my wallet and my ID document. My driver's licence had expired, and the proof of renewal was with all my other possessions at the guest farm where we were staying, but it would've taken too long to go and collect it.

On my arrival in Johannesburg, I received the news that my mother-in-law had passed away. She, my wife and my children had been admitted to different hospitals. The flights took ages, and the news about my wife and children was uncertain. On the flight to Durban, it struck me that I wouldn't be able to hire a car without a valid licence, and I didn't know a soul in Durban. My younger child was only nine months old at the time. The hospital wanted to know what brand of baby formula she was fed with, but my wife was undergoing an emergency operation and I was stuck on a flight.

353

Whitey had also heard about the accident – and about the formula and my licence crisis. He personally phoned the hospital where the children had been admitted, and then called his people at Checkers. By that time it was already evening. He instructed them to take all the powdered baby formula brands that were on the market to the hospital. Everything was arranged, down to the nurse who would receive the formula. 'All the brands?' was the question. 'Yes,' said Whitey, 'they must try all of them until they find out which one she drinks.'

I landed at Durban at ten o'clock in the evening, still not knowing how I would get to the different hospitals. I didn't know Kwa Zulu-Natal well, it was dark, and the weather was foul. As I walked out into the reception area, I saw my name on a placard. A wonderful man from Checkers, named Frans, greeted me and said Mr Basson had sent him; he was now at my service for an indefinite period and would take me everywhere I needed to go. He had already dropped off the formula at the hospital. At that moment, I collapsed.

Kurt Darren, singer and television presenter

I met Whitey Basson 20 years ago at the Huisgenoot Skouspel music concert, and from that first meeting I realised that this man would play a big role in my life – as mentor and friend. Over the years I have gained so much respect for Whitey – on occasion we hunted together, skied together in Austria, and had deep conversations over a glass or two of red wine. These were special moments in my life that I will always cherish. I have also developed a close bond with dear Annalise, his lovely wife. I love these people very much.

Nataniël, singer and versatile entertainer

One afternoon in 1998 I was in Gordon's Bay, shooting a television programme; we were at the home of Catharina de Bliquy, a lifelong friend and favourite artist. A quiet man and his lovely wife arrived at some point amid the chaos, looked around and then went to wait calmly on a couch for Catharina to make her appearance. Sweet coffee (with whiskey and lots of milk powder) was served in big mugs, some with a paint spot on them, we were introduced to each other, as usual I talked too much, and the friendly couple left after an hour, the man with a painting under his arm.

'Tell me his name again?' I asked.

'Whitey!' Catharina said. 'He comes to buy my art every time when I'm just about to go under. I'm so happy. Someday he'll end up buying the whole town. His world is money and business, but he's a human being like you and me; actually only wants to have a smoke and look at a farm.'

I never forgot Whitey's name again. He was the man who opened the enormous store diagonally opposite Kuils River's library and changed the lives of all of humanity. Years later, my own life too.

The majority of successful, serious, powerful and prestigious people regard me as a joke, a clown in search of his tent. Whitey was either very sweet or very brave; for nearly a decade he trusted me as a face for his business, gave me free rein with speeches, deemed me important enough to cut ribbons at some of his largest stores, and to display my products on his shelves.

We seldom socialised outside work situations, we laughed, and now and then, more or less incidentally, he would teach me a big lesson, about everything from charity to patience to trust.

I hope he knows that he touched lives and is still doing so, especially among artists. I hope there is joy in his heart. I hope he knows how we talk about him. And that he is an abiding example for many. I hope he looks out every morning over his vast lawn and says to himself, F&*%#@!, things are good.

Brümilda van Rensburg, actress

Whitey Basson is a 'gentle giant' and a person of stature. I also came to know him as someone full of fun and merriment, with a razor-sharp sense of humour. It all started years ago with Checkers's Championship Boerewors Competition. He once came to collect me at Lanseria in his private jet to act as master of ceremonies at the Shoprite event, but is a wonderful, down-to-earth human being. One day he told me very honestly: 'Before I met you, I first had to inquire: I've heard of Brümilda van Rensburg, but what does she actually do?' In his hectic life he obviously hadn't had time to watch *Egoli*! Today, we are each other's biggest fans. I treasure DasBosch wines like jewels – they are just as precious to me as Whitey himself.

Rocco de Villiers, pianist and entertainer

Whitey has given me wine, whisky, long conversations with many jokes, and valuable investment advice. But the greatest gift I have received from him is the value of charity. Following a big concert for senior citizens, Whitey invited me to travel the country as representative of Shoprite and entertain senior citizens at old-age homes and retirement villages nationwide. After his retirement as CEO of one of the biggest brands in South African history, I am still visiting old-age homes and retirement homes. After nearly 300 visits, the gift, the value and the return on investment have just kept growing with every visit.

Michelle McLean, Miss Universe 1992 and businesswoman

I always looked forward to acting as master of ceremonies at the year-end functions at Klein DasBosch. Everyone was treated as members of the family when we gathered to celebrate the achievements of the many people who had worked so hard to make the Shoprite Group succeed. I especially enjoyed staying over at Klein DasBosch with my parents (my dad, Athol, had been at high school with Whitey), and my son Luke had great fun running around on the farm, chasing ducks and climbing trees while we savoured the wonderful wines. The way in which Whitey handled every person – whether employees or stars – with patience and kindness astounded and inspired me. He was also my business mentor over the years, and for this I will always be grateful. Everyone – myself included – has only the greatest respect for Whitey. I love Whitey and his family and feel blessed to have them in my life.

The contributions have been edited, and some have been shortened.

Notes

Introduction: The making of a legend

1   Curt von Keyserlink, 'Whitey Basson hou aambeeld warm by OK Bazaars', *Sake-Beeld*, 10 November 1997.
2   Curt von Keyserlink, 'Shoprite koop OK Bazaars vir net R1', *Sake-Beeld*, 4 November 1997.
3   Flip Meyer, 'Basson en sy span moet weer 'n wonderwerk verrig', *Sake-Beeld*, 4 November 1997.
4   Stan Maher, 'The R1 man', *Leadership*, April 2000.
5   Ibid.
6   Sonja Loots, 'Whitey se wil', *De Kat*, February 1999.
7   Ibid.
8   *Succeed SA*, 'The third entrepreneur', Supplement, August/September 1999.

PART ONE: FORMATIVE YEARS

1. Son of the Swartland

1   Wikipedia, 'Maitland-kiesafdeling', at https://af.wikipedia.org/wiki/Maitland_(kiesafdeling)
2   Wikipedia, 'James Wellwood Mushet', at https://fr.wikipedia.org/wiki/James_Wellwood_Mushet
3   At the time, Dasbos was the spelling of the farm's name. It is now DasBosch.
4   Supplement to *Die Burger*, 'Stellenbosser vertel verhaal van Rebelle vader voor sy sterf', 15 August 1998.
5   Wikideck, 'Seepunt (kiesafdeling)', at https://wp-af.wikideck.com/Seepunt_(kiesafdeling)
6   KykNET, *Reis na Gister met Whitey Basson*, 3 February 2015.
7   Ibid.
8   Ibid.
9   *Swartland Gazette*, 'Whitey Basson moedig entrepreneurskap aan', 18 November 2014.

2. Learning from 'the English'

1   Hermann Giliomee, *Die Afrikaners: Verkorte en Aangevulde Weergawe*, Tafelberg, 2018.

3. Taking chances in Matieland

1   Starke died in Stellenbosch in July 2018 at the age of 87. See Rugby 365 [online], 'Loyal James Starke dies', 25 July 2018, at https://rugby365.com/countries/south-africa/loyal-james-starke-dies/
2   *Rooi Rose*, 'Dié man ken 'n winskopie', 24 December 1997.
3   Ibid.
4   *Succeed SA*, 'The third entrepreneur', August/September 1999.
5   Whitey Basson, Letter to Rina Loubser, 24 October 2012.
6   *Die Burger*, 'Sakeleier wil supermarkte van Kaap tot Kaïro sien', 1 August 1997.

4. Whitey finds direction

1 *Sarie*, 'So sê hulle', 21 April 1999.

2 Theo Vorster, *Mind Your Business: Advice from South Africa's top business leaders*, Jonathan Ball Publishers, 2013.

3 KykNET, Oor die kole met Kobus en Toks, MP4 (no date).

5. Whitey meets his better half

1 *Die Byvoegsel*, a supplement to *Die Burger*, (from family scrapbook – no date).

2 *Die Burger Leefstyl*, 'Sakeleier se vrou stel hom eerste', Wednesday 13 August 1997.

3 Ibid.

4 Ibid.

5 Ibid.

PART TWO: THE PEP YEARS

6. Birth of a retail giant

1 Johann van Rooyen, *Renier van Rooyen: Founder of Pep Stores*, Kindle edition, 2018.

2 CapeTalk, 'Whitey Basson on The Money Show with Bruce Whitfield', 19 October 2017, at https://www.youtube.com/watch?v=jJfJM9_KNG0

3 Van Rooyen, *Renier van Rooyen: Founder of Pep Stores.*

4 TJ Strydom, *Christo Wiese: Risiko & Rykdom,* Tafelberg, 2019.

5 Ibid.

7. A baptism of fire

1 Johann van Rooyen, *Renier van Rooyen: Founder of Pep Stores*, Kindle edition, 2018.

2 Ibid.

3 Ibid.

4 Ibid.

5 *Succeed SA*, 'The third entrepreneur', August/September 1999.

6 David Meades, *Afrikaner-Kapitalisme: Van brandarm tot stinkryk*, Naledi, 2019.

7 *Financial Mail*, 'Pep Stores: how high can it fly?' 20 December 1974.

8 TJ Strydom, *Christo Wiese: Risiko & Rykdom*, Tafelberg, 2019.

9 *Pep Nuus*, 'Wellwood Basson', December 1983.

10 Ibid.

11 Strydom, *Christo Wiese: Risiko en Rykdom.*

12 *Succeed SA*, 'The third entrepreneur'.

8. Whitey gets power of attorney

1 Johann van Rooyen, *Renier van Rooyen: Founder of Pep Stores*, Kindle edition, 2018.

2 Pep Stores: How high can it fly? *Financial Mail.* 20 December 1974. From Whitey Basson archives, author unknown.

3 *Financial Mail*, 'Pep's cash', 23 July 1976.

4   Ebbe Dommisse, *Fortuine: Die wel en wee van Afrikaner-magnate*, Jonathan Ball, 2021.
5   TJ Strydom, *Christo Wiese: Risiko & Rykdom*, Tafelberg, 2019.

9. Takeovers and turnaround attempts

1   *Pep Nuus*, 'Pep neem winkels oor', 1976.
2   Ibid.
3   *Cape Times*, 'Pep to sell 43 boutiques', February 1980.
4   Johann van Rooyen, *Renier van Rooyen: Founder of Pep Stores*, Kindle edition, 2018.
5   *Cape Times Business Report*, 'Scott's increase bid and Pep match it', Thursday 13 July 1978.
6   *Cape Times Business Report*, 'Half Price takeover battle reaches climax today', Saturday 15 July 1978.
7   Van Rooyen, *Renier van Rooyen: Founder of Pep Stores*.
8   Ibid.
9   Ebbe Dommisse, *Fortuine: Die wel en wee van Afrikaner-magnate*, Jonathan Ball Publishers, 2021.
10   *Rooi Rose*, 'Dié man ken 'n winskopie', 24 December 1997.

10. The acquisition of Shoprite

1   *Die Burger*, 'Pep Stores neem Shoprite oor', May 1979.
2   *Sake/Rapport*, 'Renier wil dieselfde met kos doen', May 1979.
3   CapeTalk, 'Whitey Basson on The Money Show with Bruce Whitfield', 19 October 2017, at https://www.youtube.com/watch?v=jJfJM9_KNG0

PART THREE: SHOPRITE'S EARLY YEARS

11. Learning on the shop floor

1   Email from Charles Back.
2   A tribute to Mr Basson (Whitey Basson tribute book).
3   *Cape Times*, 'The Shoprite story', October 1979.
4   CapeTalk, 'Whitey Basson on The Money Show with Bruce Whitfield', 19 October 2017, at https://www.youtube.com/watch?v=jJfJM9_KNG0
5   *Sunday Times, Cape Metro*, 'Son of the soil reaps the dividends', 29 June 1997.
6   Johann van Rooyen, *Renier van Rooyen: Founder of Pep Stores*, Kindle Edition, 2018.
7   Ibid.
8   *Cape Times*, 18 October 1979. Cited in Van Rooyen, *Renier van Rooyen: Founder of Pep Stores*.
9   *Pep Nuus*, 'Shoprite sails into Salt River', April 1980.
10   Theo Vorster, *Mind Your Business: Advice from South Africa's top business leaders*, Jonathan Ball Publishers, 2013.

12. Cheaper on chicken

1   Rainbow, at https://rainbowchickens.co.za/
2   A tribute to Mr Basson (Whitey Basson tribute book).

3   News24, 'Consumers to bear brunt of dumped US chicken – Shoprite', 22 December 2015, at https://www.news24.com/Fin24/consumers-to-bear-brunt-of-dumped-us-chicken-shoprite-20151222

13. Refining a winning recipe
1   Sam Walton with John Huey, *Sam Walton: Made in America – My Story*, Bantam, 1993.
2   *Pep Nuus*, 'Shoprite bekyk Transvaal vir uitbreiding', August 1981.
3   A tribute to Mr Basson (Whitey Basson tribute book).
4   *Pep Nuus*, 'Seven new stores for Shoprite', November 1979.
5   Walton, with Huey, *Sam Walton: Made in America*.
6   Spondylitis.org, 'Overview of Ankylosing Spondylitis', at https://spondylitis.org/

14. Full steam ahead
1   *Pep Nuus*, 'Shoprite se tiende', June 1980.
2   CapeTalk, 'Whitey Basson on The Money Show with Bruce Whitfield', 19 October 2017, at https://www.youtube.com/watch?v=jJfJM9_KNG0
3   Theo Vorster, *Mind Your Business: Advice from South Africa's top business leaders*, Jonathan Ball Publishers, 2013.
4   *Pep Nuus*, 'Wellwood Basson', December 1983.
5   David Meades, *Afrikaner-Kapitalisme: Van brandarm tot stinkryk*, Naledi, 2019.
6   TJ Strydom, *Christo Wiese: Risiko & Rykdom*, Tafelberg, 2019.
7   Meades, *Afrikaner-Kapitalisme*.
8   Strydom, *Christo Wiese: Risiko & Rykdom*.
9   *The Argus*, 'Shoprite set to challenge Peninsula stores', December 1983.
10   Ibid.
11   *Pep Nuus*, 'Shoprite bekyk Transvaal vir uitbreiding', August 1981.
12   Ibid.
13   *Marketing Mix*, 'Shoprite opens six new branches', May 1984.

15. The north beckons
1   Netwerk24, 'Vergeet van 2020 – 1986 was veel erger', 4 March 2021.
2   *Pep Nuus*, 'Shoprite volgende', August 1986.
3   *The Citizen*, 'Shoprite forecasts higher earnings', October 1986.
4   *The Star*, 'Shoprite gearing up to lend a hand at Pepkor', November 1986.
5   *Die Burger*, 'Shoprite vandag op beurs', December 1986.
6   *Volksblad*, 'Groep open tak hier', November 1986.
7   *Die Burger*, 'Shoprite se wins 55% op', April 1987.
8   *Vaderland*, 'Shoprite optimisties', June 1987.
9   Shoprite, Annual Report, 1987.
10   *Pep Nuus*, 'Groter deelname vir werknemers in maatskappywins!', May 1988.
11   Tim Cohen, 'Reluctant entrepreneur', in *South Africa's Greatest Entrepreneurs*, compiled by Moky Makura, MME Media, 2010.

12 Ibid.

13 *Pep Nuus*, 'Shoprite belange al wyer en wyer deur Republiek', May 1988.

PART FOUR: THE ACQUISITION YEARS

16. A grand affair

1 Tim Cohen, 'Reluctant entrepreneur', in *South Africa's Greatest Entrepreneurs*, compiled by Moky Makura, MME Media, 2010.

2 *Business Report*, 'Shoprite's Basson clear on how to meet the OK challenge', 7 November 1997.

3 *Financial Mail*, 'Wellwood Basson: substance over style', 31 August 1990.

4 *Cape Times*, 'Survey: Groceries are more expensive', 5 July 1988.

17. Checkers goes downhill – and rises again

1 *Hearing Grasshoppers Jump: The Story of Raymond Ackerman*, as told to Denise Prichard, David Philip, 2004.

2 David Meades, *Afrikaner-Kapitalisme: Van brandarm tot stinkryk*, Naledi, 2019.

3 Stephen Cranston, 'Swallowing the whale', *Financial Mail*, 4 October 1991.

4 *Hearing Grasshoppers Jump*.

5 Ibid.

6 At that stage the name was Pick 'n Pay, but the apostrophe was dropped in 2007. For the sake of convenience, the spelling 'Pick n Pay' is used throughout the text.

7 *Financial Mail*, 'Checkers: You shouldn't pay more'. From Whitey Basson archives (author and date unknown).

8 Radio 702, Whitey Basson on The Money Show with Bruce Whitfield, 19 October 2017.

9 Ebbe Dommisse, *Fortuine: Die wel en wee van Afrikaner-magnate*, Jonathan Ball Publishers, 2019.

10 *Finansies & Tegniek*, 'Hoe Whitey Basson Checkers regruk', 30 October 1992.

11 *Financial Mail*, 'Swallowing the whale', 4 October 1991.

12 Theo Vorster, *Mind your Business: Advice from South Africa's top business leaders*, Jonathan Ball Publishers, 2003.

13 *Die Burger*, 'Sakeleier wil supermarkte van Kaap tot Kaïro sien', 1 August 1997.

14 Radio 702, Whitey Basson on The Money Show with Bruce Whitfield.

15 Tim Cohen, 'Reluctant entrepreneur', in *South Africa's Greatest Entrepreneurs*, compiled by Moky Makura, MME Media, 2010.

16 Vorster, *Mind your Business*.

18. The retail wizard

1 Shoprite staff, *Tribute to Mr Basson*, 2017.

2 Stephen Cranston, 'Swallowing the whale', *Financial Mail*, 4 October 1991.

3 Ibid.

4 *Rapport*, 'Hy is vir sy mense net om die hoek: Ons praat met Checkers se Whitey Basson', 23 February 1992.

5   *Finansies & Tegniek*, 'Hoe Whitey Basson Checkers regruk', 30 October 1992.

6   *Financial Mail*, 'Checkers: You shouldn't pay more'. From Whitey Basson archives (author and date unknown).

7   *Die Burger*, 'Checkers-omskakeling vorder', 18 June 1992.

8   Shoprite, Annual Report, 1993.

9   Tradegro, Annual Report, 1993.

10 *Rapport*, 'Hy is vir sy mense net om die hoek: Ons praat met Checkers se Whitey Basson', 23 February 1992.

11 Shoprite staff, *Tribute to Mr Basson*.

12 *Rapport*, 'Hy is vir sy mense net om die hoek'.

19. Exodus to Stellenbosch

1   *Cape Metro*, 'Son of the soil reaps the dividends', *Sunday Times*, 29 June 1997.

2   Ibid.

3   *Sarie*, 'Omring deur die natuur', 3 December 1997.

4   History, 'Bauhaus', at https://www.history.com/topics/art-history/bauhaus

5   *Die Burger*, 'Sakeleier se vrou stel hom eerste', 13 August 1997.

6   KykNET, Oor die kole met Kobus en Toks, MP4 (no date).

7   TJ Strydom, *Christo Wiese: Risiko & Rykdom*, Tafelberg, 2019.

8   Ibid.

9   *Rooi Rose*, 'Dié man ken 'n winskopie', 24 December 1997.

20. Whirlwind Whitey

1   Letitia Watson, 'Al die Checkerse is steeds net om die hoek,' *Sake Rapport*, 30 August 2009.

2   Shoprite, Annual Report, 1995.

3   Ibid.

4   *Die Burger*, 'Sente tel in stryd om beste supermark', 1 August 1997.

5   *Financial Mail*, 'Still gaining market share', 26 April 1996.

6   Shoprite, Annual Report, 1996.

7   Tim Cohen, 'Reluctant entrepreneur', in *South Africa's Greatest Entrepreneurs*, compiled by Moky Makura, MME Media, 2010.

8   *Finance Week*, 'They Shop so Right', 1 May 1996.

9   Progress Retail, January 1996. From Whitey Basson archives (author and date unknown).

10 *F&T Weekly*, 'Retail's White Knight', 26 September 1997.

11 *Die Burger*, 'Sakeleier wil supermarkte van Kaap tot Kaïro sien', 1 August 1997.

12 *Die Burger*, 'Shoprite wil sy brul laat hoor in die kitskosmark', 25 July 1997.

13 *Die Burger*, 'Sente tel in stryd om beste supermark'.

14 Shoprite Holdings: Confident outlook, 1 November 1996.

15 *Die Burger*, 'Shoprite verkoop versekering', 3 July 1997.

16 *Die Burger*, 'Sakeleier wil supermarkte van Kaap tot Kaïro sien'.

17 *Cape Metro*, 'Son of the soil reaps the dividends', *Sunday Times*, 29 June 1997.

18 *De Kat Bylae*, September 1996. From Whitey Basson archives (author and date unknown).

19 *Die Burger*, 'Sakeleier wil supermarkte van Kaap tot Kaïro sien'.

20 *Rooi Rose,* 'Afspraak met Pa', 11 June 1997.

21 *Die Burger*, 'Sakeleier wil supermarkte van Kaap tot Kaïro sien'.

22 *Die Burger*, 'Dinamiese Whitey troon uit', 1 August 1997.

23 Ibid.

24 Ibid.

25 Ibid.

26 Letter from Bernhard Andrag. From Whitey Basson archives (date unknown).

27 *Die Burger*, 'Afrika-renaissance lok talle', 1 August 1997.

21. The R1 transaction

1   Gert Blij, email to Anita van Rensburg, 10 September 2002.

2   Radio 702, Whitey Basson on The Money Show with Bruce Whitfield, 19 October 2017.

3   KykNET, Oor die kole met Kobus en Toks, MP4 (no date).

4   OK Furniture, 'About us', at https://www.okfurniture.co.za/about-us/

5   SA History Online, The first OK Bazaars opens on the corner of Eloff and President Street in Johannesburg, at https://www.sahistory.org.za/dated-event/first-ok-bazaars-opens-corner-eloff-and-president-street-johannesburg

6   John Stretch, 'The Strange Story of OK Bazaars', at http:// www.johnstretch.com/strange-story-ok-bazaars

7   *Business Report*, 'Talks may be OK for Shoprite but there's a sting in the tail', 12 September 1997.

8   Tim Cohen, 'Reluctant entrepreneur', in *South Africa's Greatest Entrepreneurs*, compiled by Moky Makura, MME Media, 2010.

9   *Cape Argus*, 'It's no longer OK for stores to be in the red'. From Whitey Basson archives (author and date unknown).

10 KykNET, Oor die kole met Kobus en Toks, MP4 (no date).

11 Trevor Cohen, in Shoprite staff, *Tribute to Mr Basson.*

12 *Finance Week*, 'Shoprite/OK – Wants to be where the nation shops ', 18–24 September 1997.

13 Cohen in *South Africa's Greatest Entrepreneurs.*

22. Everything is OK again

1   *Sunday Times*, 'Shoprite plays role of knight in armour to struggling OK', 9 November 1997.

2   *Finance Week*, 'Changing step in high street', 13–19 November 1997.

3   *Sake-Beeld*, 'Basson en sy span moet weer 'n wonderwerk verrig', 4 November 1997.

4   Peter Galli (ed.), 'Business Watch' *Business Report*. From Whitey Basson archives (author and date unknown).

5   Tim Cohen, 'Reluctant entrepreneur', in *South Africa's Greatest Entrepreneurs*, compiled by Moky Makura, MME Media, 2010.

6   *Business Report*, 'Shoprite plays role of knight in armour to struggling OK', *Sunday Times*, 9 November 1997.

7   John Stretch, 'The Strange Story of OK Bazaars', at http://www.johnstretch.com/strange-story-ok-bazaars

8   *Financial Mail*, 'How Whitey pulled OK out of the hole', 28 August 1998.

9   Ibid.

10   *F&T Weekly*, 'How Basson will Shoprite the OK', 14 November 1997.

11   *Financial Mail*, 'How Whitey pulled OK out of the hole'.

12   Interview with Jannie Holtzhausen.

13   *Business Report*, 'Shoprite's Basson is clear on how to meet the OK challenge', 7 November 1997.

14   *Financial Mail*, 'Moving ahead to Number One', 7 November 1997.

15   *Business Report*, 'Shoprite's Basson is clear on how to meet the OK challenge'.

16   *Sake-Beeld*, 'Whitey Basson hou aambeeld warm by OK Bazaars', 10 November 1997.

17   Ibid.

18   Shoprite staff, *Tribute to Mr Basson*.

19   *FAS Retailer*, 'OK Bazaars – have Shoprite stopped the bleeding?', March 1998.

20   *Financial Mail*, 'Moving ahead to Number One', 7 November 1997.

21   *Hearing Grasshoppers Jump: The Story of Raymond Ackerman*, as told to Denise Prichard, David Philip, 2004.

22   *Finance Week*, 'Changing step in high street'.

23. Full steam ahead

1   *Leadership*, 'The R1 man', April 2000.

2   *Huisgenoot*, 'Die man wat die OK vir R1 gekoop het', 2 November 1997.

3   Ibid.

4   *The Star Business Report*, Poster, 26 August 1998.

5   Radio 702, Whitey Basson on the Money Show with Bruce Whitfield, 19 October 2017.

6   Ibid.

7   Fin24, 'SAB wins Shoprite case', 20 September 2007.

8   *Financial Mail*, 'Everything's still not OK', 24 July 1998.

9   Fin24, 'SAB wins Shoprite case', 20 September 2007.

10   *Rooi Rose*, 'Dié man ken 'n winskopie', 24 December 1997.

11   Marcia Klein, 'Huge theft tarnishes Basson's Superman image', *Business Times*, 29 August 1998.

12   Shoprite, Annual Report, 1999.

13   Tim Cohen, 'OK's R1 sale haunts Basson', *Business Day*, 30 August 1999.

14   *Finansies & Tegniek*, 'Shoprite vs Pick n Pay', 27 August 1999.

15   Klein, 'Huge theft tarnishes Basson's Superman image'.

16   *Leadership*, 'The R1 man'.

17   Klein, 'Huge theft tarnishes Basson's Superman image'.

18   *Sake-Beeld*, 'Whitey bekend as regrukker', 20 December 1999.

19   *Sake-Beeld*, 'Verdienste van Shoprite tuimel meer as 50%', 25 August 1999.

20   Tim Cohen, 'OK's R1 sale haunts Basson', *Business Day*, 30 August 1999.

24. Africa beckons
1   Shoprite, Annual Report, 2000.
2   ACNielsen Customised Research. From Whitey Basson archives (author and date unknown).

PART FIVE: THE GOLDEN YEARS

25. Making his mark in Africa
1   Tim Cohen, 'Reluctant entrepreneur', in *South Africa's Greatest Entrepreneurs*, compiled by Moky Makura, MME Media, 2010.
2   *Finansies & Tegniek*, 'Basson hou van uitdagings', 26 September 1997.
3   Tribute Book for Whitey Basson, 2018.
4   Ibid.
5   Shoprite, Annual Report, 1997.
6   *Enterprise*, 'Great Trek of the Grocers', February 1998.
7   Laura Hartzenberg, 'How Shoprite trailblazed trading in Africa', bizcommunity Africa, 28 May 2018, at https://www.bizcommunity.africa/Article/410/182/177400.html
8   *YOU*, 'Whitey – light in Africa's gloom', 7 July 2002.
9   *Finansies & Tegniek*, 'Whitey in Afrika', 31 August 2001.
10   *Business Times*, 'African safari brings the lure of prize game for Shoprite', 8 December 2002.
11   *Finansies & Tegniek*, 'Whitey in Afrika'.
12   Ibid.
13   *Business Report*, 'Shoprite lists in Zambia today', 19 February 2003.
14   Ibid.
15   *De Kat*, 'Whitey se wil', February 1999.
16   Cohen in *South Africa's Greatest Entrepreneurs*.
17   Hartzenberg, 'How Shoprite trailblazed trading in Africa'.

26. Global dreams are tempered
1   *Rooi Rose*, 'Klatergoud laat hom koud', January 2001.
2   Femi Adewunmi, 'How *The Economist* changed its tune on Africa', 11 December 2011, at https://www.howwemadeitinafrica.com/how-the-economist-changed-its-tune-on-africa/14001/
3   Shoprite, Annual Report, 2011.
4   Shoprite, Annual Report, 2000.
5   *Leadership*, 'The R1 man', April 2000.
6   Laura Hartzenberg, 'How Shoprite trailblazed trading in Africa', bizcommunity Africa, 28 May 2018, at https://www.bizcommunity.africa/Article/410/182/177400.html
7   *De Kat*, 'Whitey se wil', February 1999.
8   Tim Cohen, 'Reluctant entrepreneur', in *South Africa's Greatest Entrepreneurs*, compiled by Moky Makura, MME Media, 2010.
9   *Sake-Rapport*, 'Shoprite: Tyd om te baljaar in Indië', 24 August 2003.
10   Walmart, 'South Africa', at https://corporate.walmart.com/about/south-africa
11   CNBC Africa, 'Captains of Industry – Whitey Basson Part 1', at https://www.youtube.com/watch?v=y_rUQ7rPdm0&t=35s

12 IOL, 'Cambridge Food captures commuters for Massmart', 2 March 2009, at https://www.iol.co.za/business-report/companies/cambridge-food-captures-commuters-for-massmart-702060

13 Anathi Madubela, 'Game and Makro owner sells some of its businesses to Shoprite in R1.3bn deal', fin24, 20 August 2021, at https://www.news24.com/fin24/companies/retail/game-and-makro-owner-sells-some-of-its-retailers-to-shoprite-in-r13bn-deal-20210820

14 Hanlie Stadler, 'Dié Massmart-winkels gaan Shoprite of Usave word', Netwerk24, 7 September 2021, at https://www.netwerk24.com/netwerk24/sake/maatskappye/die-massmart-winkels-gaan-shoprite-of-usave-word-20210907

15 Promit Mukherjee, 'Walmart enters deal to buy remaining stake in SA's Massmart', 1 September 2022, at https://www.moneyweb.co.za/news/companies-and-deals/walmart-enters-deal-to-buy-remaining-stake-in-sas-massmart/

16 *Financial Mail*, 'Shoprite: Not so bulletproof anymore', cover story, 7–13 March 2019.

17 Ibid.

18 Shoprite, Annual Report, 2018.

19 Tim Cohen, 'Reluctant entrepreneur', in *South Africa's Greatest Entrepreneurs*, compiled by Moky Makura, MME Media, 2010.

27. Wine, meat and Gordon Ramsay

1 Shoprite, Annual Report, 2001.

2 PWC, *South African retail and consumer products outlook 2012-2016*, October 2012, South African edition.

3 Shoprite, Annual Report, 2000.

4 KykNET, Oor die kole met Kobus en Toks, MP4 (no date). DVD from Whitey Basson archive.

5 *Business Report*, 'Revived Checkers to join Hyperama', 5 September 2001.

6 *Supermarket & Retailer*, 'Best boerewors by far', September 2002.

7 Marklives.com, 'More than just agency lore – Mad Advertising gets real', at https://www.marklives.com/2015/06/not-just-agency-lore-mad-advertising-gets-real/

8 Figures supplied by Charlotte Hassan from Shoprite Meat Markets and Neil Schreuder.

9 Shoprite, 'Shoprite Group is first retailer to stock certified natural lamb', 1 September 2007, at https://www.shopriteholdings.co.za/articles/Newsroom/2007/shoprite-group-is-first-retailer-to-stock-certified-natural-lamb.html

10 Checkers, 'All wine routes lead to Checkers', at https://www.checkers.co.za/wine-route

11 Nompumelelo Magwaza, 'No-name brands "slowly changing face of retailing"', IOL, 23 March 2012, at https://www.iol.co.za/business-report/economy/no-name-brands-slowly-changing-face-of-retailing-1262148

12 Figures for the 2021 financial year, supplied by Neil Schreuder's office.

13 *Perpetua Perspectives*, 'The shift to private label in food retail', Spring Edition, 2021.

14 Netwerk24, 'SA hou ál meer van produkte sonder handelsmerk', 8 September 2021.

15 Figures for the 2021 financial year, supplied by Neil Schreuder's office.

16 Shoprite Holdings, Sustainability Report, 2021.

17 Shoprite, Annual Report, 2002.
18 Shoprite, Annual Report, 2003.
19 Shoprite, Annual Report, 2006.
20 Santando Thukwana, 'Shoprite's Money Market account is now fully fledged – how it fares against some low-cost peers', 31 August 2022, Business Insider South Africa, at https://www.businessinsider.co.za/how-shoprites-money-market-bank-account-compares-to-tymebank-bank-zero-fnb-easy-zero-standard-bank-mymo-2022-8
21 Ibid.

28. Building for the future

1 Ebbe Dommisse, *Fortuine: Die wel en wee van Afrikaner-magnate*, Jonathan Ball Publishers, 2021.
2 Motivation Ark, 'Jeff Bezos 15 Minutes for the NEXT 50 Years of Your LIFE', at https://www.youtube.com/watch?v=WRUqXZx5EUM&list=RDLVyCEX_Q5O0CI&index=2
3 Goodreads, 'Jeff Bezos > Quotes > Quotable Quote', at https://www.goodreads.com/quotes/966699-i-very-frequently-get-the-question-what-s-going-to-change#:~:text=It's%20impossible%20to%20imagine%20a,'%20Impossible
4 Shoprite, Annual Report, 1998.
5 Tim Cohen, 'Reluctant entrepreneur', in *South Africa's Greatest Entrepreneurs*, compiled by Moky Makura, MME Media, 2010.
6 SLT Architects, 'The Whitey Basson Distribution Centre: A credit to the architects and the whole professional team', 24 August 2021, at https://www.linkedin.com/pulse/whitey-basson-distribution-centre-credit-architects-whole-?trk=organization-update-content_share-article
7 Andrew Thompson, 'Take a look: Inside Shoprite's massive warehouse – which operates in near total silence', Business Insider South Africa, at https://www.businessinsider.co.za/shoprite-high-tech-warehouse-2019-12
8 Shoprite Holdings, Sustainability Report, 2021.
9 Figures for the 2021 financial year supplied by Neil Schreuder.
10 Shoprite, Annual Report, 2000.
11 Ibid.
12 Theo Vorster, *Mind Your Business: Advice from South Africa's top business leaders*, Jonathan Ball Publishers, 2013. The book was an offshoot of KYKnet's popular television show 'Sakegesprek met Theo Vorster'.
13 Tribute Book for Whitey Basson.
14 Average quantity per year over the past five years (end of June 2022), figures supplied by Freshmark.
15 Shoprite, 'Freshmark', at https://www.shopriteholdings.co.za/group/brands/freshmark.html
16 Shoprite website at https://www.shopriteholdings.co.za
17 Shoprite, Annual Report, 2005.

18 Cadiz Asset Management, 'Shoprite – Quality on Sale', November 2019.

19 Shoprite, Annual Report, 2009.

20 Shoprite, Annual Report, 2018.

29. An aversion to rules

1 *Finansies & Tegniek*, 'Basson hou van uitdagings,' 26 September 1997.

2 Shoprite, Annual Report, 2003.

3 Investopedia, 'Enron Scandal: The Fall of a Wall Street Darling', at https://www.investopedia.com/updates/enron-scandal-summary/

4 Werksmans Attorneys, 'A Review of the King IV report on Corporate Governance', at https://www.werksmans.com/wp-content/uploads/2013/05/061741-WERKSMANS-king-iv-booklet.pdf

5 CapeTalk, 'Whitey Basson on The Money Show with Bruce Whitfield', 19 October 2017, at https://www.youtube.com/watch?v=jJfJM9_KNG0

30. The Shoprite family

1 *Rooi Rose*, 'Klatergoud laat hom koud', January 2001.

2 *Leadership*, 'The R1 man', April 2000.

3 Tribute Book for Whitey Basson.

4 Shoprite, 'From Till Packer to Branch Manager at Africa's largest retailer', 21 February 2022, at https://www.shopriteholdings.co.za/articles/Newsroom/2022/charity-malope-till-packer-branch-manager.html

5 Theo Vorster, *Mind Your Business: Advice from South Africa's top business leaders*, Jonathan Ball Publishers, 2013.

6 Tribute Book for Whitey Basson.

7 *Maksimum*, 'Witwarm Whitey', March 2002.

8 Tim Cohen, 'Reluctant entrepreneur', in *South Africa's Greatest Entrepreneurs*, compiled by Moky Makura, MME Media, 2010.

9 Tribute Book for Whitey Basson.

10 Johann van Rooyen, *Renier van Rooyen: Founder of Pep Stores*, Kindle Edition, March 2018.

11 Marklives.com, 'More than just agency lore – Mad Advertising gets real', at https://www.marklives.com/2015/06/not-just-agency-lore-mad-advertising-gets-real/

12 Shoprite, Annual Report, 2004.

13 Shoprite, Annual Report, 2007.

14 *finweek,* 'The birth of a cycling legend', 9 February 2017.

31. Virgin Cola and Madiba

1 CapeTalk, Whitey Basson on The Money Show with Bruce Whitfield, 19 October 2017, at https://www.youtube.com/watch?v=jJfJM9_KNG0

2 *Mail & Guardian*, 'Starry, starry night', 19 September 1997, at https://mg.co.za/article/1997-09-19-starry-starry-night/

3 Correspondence between Whitey Basson and Richard Branson, Tribute Book.

4   Wikipedia, 'Virgin Cola', at https://en.wikipedia.org/wiki/Virgin_Cola

5   Tribute Book for Whitey Basson.

6   *Supermarket and Retailer*, 1 July 2004. From Whitey Basson archive.

7   Tribute Book for Whitey Basson.

8   Shoprite, 'Whitey Basson on the passing of Nelson Mandela', 6 December 2013, at https://
     www.shopriteholdings.co.za/articles/Newsroom/2013/whitey-basson-on-the-passing-of-
     nelson-mandela.html

9   *Mail & Guardian*, 'Mandela funeral closure cost Shoprite about R260m', at https://mg.co.
     za/article/2014-01-20-mandela-funeral-closure-cost-shoprite-about-r260m/

10   Shoprite, Annual Report, 1996.

11   *Rooi Rose*, 'Klatergoud laat hom koud', January 2001.

12   Figures for the 2021 financial year, supplied by Neil Schreuder.

13   CapeTalk, 'Whitey Basson on The Money Show with Bruce Whitfield'.

14   Shoprite Holdings, Sustainability Report, 2021.

PART SIX: THE RECENT YEARS

32. Whitey hands over the reins

1   Hanlie Retief, 'Hanlie Retief gesels met Whitey Basson,' *Rapport*, 6 November 2016.

2   Fin24, 'Retiring Shoprite CEO Whitey Basson: "I am tired"', Fin24, at https://www.fin24.
     com/Companies/Retail/retiring-shoprite-ceo-whitey-basson-i-am-tired-20161101

3   Ibid.

4   Ann Crotty, 'Hush-hush Shoprite deal stuns investors', *Financial Mail*, 11 May 2017, at
     https://www.businesslive.co.za/fm/money-and-investing/2017-05-11-hush-hush-shoprite-
     deal-stuns-investors/

5   SABC News, 'Shoprite CEO Whitey Basson announces his retirement', 31 October 2016,
     at https://www.youtube.com/watch?app=desktop&v=n8eX6f_bP9E

6   Moxima Gama, 'Looking to recoup its losses', *finweek*, 10 September 2021.

7   Jacques Bartleman, 'One South African retail CEO crushed his competitors in shareholder
     returns', Daily Investor, 7 September 2022, at https://dailyinvestor.com/retail/2002/one-
     south-african-retail-ceo-crushed-his-competitors-in-shareholder-returns/

8   SENS announcement from Shoprite Holdings Limited, 31 October 2016.

9   Ibid.

10   Fifi Peters, 'Whitey Basson on Steinhoff, Ramaphosa, and Life after Shoprite', CNBC
     Africa, 18 October 2019, at https://www.youtube.com/watch?v=CseWABsXHds

33. The Steinhoff debacle

1   AmaBhunghane, *Steinhoff's Secret History: How Markus Jooste's scam began*, eBook, Vol. 1
     No. 3, March 2021.

2   Steinhoff International, '50 Years of Steinhoff', 26 February 2018, at https://www.youtube.
     com/watch?v=xa3U2BKKeNk

3   James-Brent Styan, *Steinhoff: Inside SA's biggest corporate crash*, LAPA, 2018.

4   Ibid.

5   Christo Wiese's testimony before Parliament's Standing Committee on Finance, 31 January 2018.

6   SENS announcement from Steinhoff International Holdings, 25 November 2014.

7   Reuters, 'South Africa's Steinhoff expands discount offer with $5.7 billion Pepkor buy', 25 November 2014, at https://www.reuters.com/article/us-pepkor-m-a-steinhoff-int-idUKKCN0J919I20141125

8   Bloomberg, 'Why billionaire Christo Wiese's retail vision faces hurdles', 19 February 2017.

9   Shoprite, Annual Report, 2016.

10 Reuters, 'South Africa's Shoprite cuts chairman Wiese's voting influence', 18 April 2019.

11 CNBC Africa interview. 'Whitey Basson on Steinhoff, Ramaphosa & life after Shoprite'. Interview with Fifi Peters. 18 October 2019.

12 Rob Rose, *Steinheist: Markus Jooste, Steinhoff and SA's biggest corporate fraud*, Tafelberg, 2018.

13 Ibid.

14 Ibid.

15 Ibid.

16 SENS, Joint detailed cautionary announcement relating to the establishment of an African retail champion, 14 December 2016.

17 SENS announcement, 20 February 2017.

18 *Financial Mail*, 'Rise and fall of a retail star', 14 December 2017.

19 Reuters, 'Wiese misses out as South Africa's Steinhoff and Shoprite scrap merger', 20 February 2017, at https://www.reuters.com/article/us-shoprite-hldgs-m-a-steinhoff-intlnl-idUSKBN15Z1WV

20 *Financial Mail*, 'Why Shoprite is better off without Steinhoff', 2 March 2017, at https://www.businesslive.co.za/fm/features/cover-story/2017-03-02-why-shoprite-is-better-off-without-steinhoff/

21 Ann Crotty, 'Why Whitey quit,' *Financial Mail*, 4 November 2016.

22 Businesslive, 'Rejecting Steinhoff has paid off for Shoprite', 6 February 2018, at https://www.businesslive.co.za/bd/companies/2018-02-06-company-comment-rejecting-steinhoff-has-paid-off-for-shoprite/

23 Nellie Brand-Jonker, 'Shoprite-hoof oor Steinhoff: "Die waarheid wen altyd"', Netwerk24, 2 March 2018, at https://www.netwerk24.com/Netwerk24/shoprite-hoof-oor-steinhoff-die-waarheid-wen-altyd-20180302

24 SENS announcement, Steinhoff International Holdings, 30 November 2017.

25 Marcia Klein, 'Why would I take my life's work and gamble with it?', *finweek*, 5–18 July 2018.

26 SENS announcement, Steinhoff International Holdings, 4 December 2017.

27 TJ Strydom, *Christo Wiese: Risiko & Rykdom*, Tafelberg, 2019.

28 SENS announcement, Steinhoff International, 6 December 2017.

29 *Financial Mail*, 'At 78, can Wiese start again?', cover story, 30 July – 5 August 2020.

30 Rose, *Steinheist*.

31 Brand-Jonker, 'Shoprite-hoof oor Steinhoff: "Die waarheid wen altyd"'.

32 Editor, 'Christo Wiese wins back dollar billionaire status', Biznews, 9 February 2022, at https://www.biznews.com/sa-investing/2022/02/09/christo-wiese-billionaire-status

33 Gareth Cliff, Interview with Christo Wiese, cliffcentral.com, 15 November 2016.

34 Ibid.

35 Oor die Kole met Kobus en Toks (recording of conversation with Whitey Basson). No date available.

34. Farmer, investor and family man

1 *Rooi Rose*, 'Klatergoud laat hom koud', January 2001.

2 Pieter du Toit, *The Stellenbosch Mafia: Inside the billionaires' club*, Jonathan Ball Publishers, 2021.

3 Vriesenhof, 'Once upon a wine', at https://vriesenhof.co.za/the-farm/

4 KykNET, 'Hannes aan Huis met Whitey Basson', at https://www.youtube.com/watch?v=E-uomU_wwQk&ab_channel=kykNETArgief

5 Ebbe Dommisse, *Fortuine: Die wel en wee van Afrikaner-magnate*, Jonathan Ball Publishers, 2021.

6 *Die Burger*, 'Sakeleier wil supermarkte van Kaap tot Kaïro sien', 1 August 1997.

7 *Rapport-Tydskrif*, 'Whitey moet tuisvoel en ontspan', 21 May 2000.

8 *Rooi Rose*, 'Klatergoud laat hom koud'.

9 *YOU*, 'Whitey – light in Africa's gloom', 7 November 2002.

10 KykNET, 'Reis na Gister met Jak de Priester', 3 February 2015, at https://m.facebook.com/kyknet/videos/10153006531824827/?locale2=fr_FR

11 Dominique Herman and Brett Florens, *Perfect Weekend*, Art Publishers, 2010.

12 Ibid.

13 *Baba en Kleuter*, 'Jou werk, jou kinders?', June 2003.

14 *Die Burger Leefstyl*, 'Sakeleier se vrou stel hom eerste', 13 August 1997.

15 *Rooi Rose*, 'Klatergoud laat hom koud'.

16 *Rapport*, 'Shoprite kry jong bloed', 25 September 2005.

17 Hungry Lion, at https://www.hungrylion.co.za/about

18 *Sarie*, 'Bekende pa's se dogters bring hulde', 6 June 2011, at https://www.netwerk24.com/sarie/ons-wereld/sarie-blogs/bekende-pas-se-dogters-bring-hul-hulde-20170914

35. Whitey's success factors

1 Shoprite staff, *Tributes to Whitey Basson*, 2017.

2 Ibid.

3 Ibid.

4 Johan Marx, quoted in Shoprite staff, *Tributes to Whitey Basson*.

5 Shoprite staff, *Tributes to Whitey Basson*.

6 Robbie Stammers, 'Mighty Whitey: Basson's brilliant business acumen', *Leadership*, 304, May 2010.

7 *Maksiman*, 'Witwarm Whitey', March 2002.

8 Theo Vorster, *Mind Your Business: Advice from South Africa's top business leaders*, Jonathan Ball Publishers, 2013.

9   Shoprite staff, *Tributes to Whitey Basson.*

10 *Maksiman,* 'Witwarm Whitey'.

11 *Finansies & Tegniek,* 'Basson hou van uitdagings', 26 September 1997.

12 *Rapport,* 'Whitey het Afrika klaar getem', 14 September 2003.

13 Jannie Mouton, *And then they fired me,* as told to Carié Maas, Tafelberg, 2011.

14 Vorster, *Mind Your Business.*

15 Shoprite staff, *Tributes to Whitey Basson.*

16 KykNET, Reis na Gister met Jak de Priester, 3 November 2015, at https://m.facebook. com/kyknet/videos/10153006531824827/?locale2=fr_FR

17 *Rooi Rose,* 'Klatergoud laat hom koud', January 2001.

18 Jane Steinacker, 'Ackerman vs Basson – A tale of two giants', 3 October 2009, at https:// www.leader.co.za

19 Tim Cohen, 'Reluctant entrepreneur', in *South Africa's Greatest Entrepreneurs,* compiled by Moky Makura, MME Media, 2010.

20 Zeenat Moorad, 'From jokes to stats', *Financial Mail,* 24 August 2017, at https://www. businesslive.co.za/fm/opinion/shop-talk/2017-08-24-zeenat-moorad-from-jokes-to-stats/

21 Ray Mahlaka, 'A "remarkably transformed" Pick n Pay is CEO Richard Brasher's farewell legacy', *Daily Maverick,* 25 April 2021, at https://www.dailymaverick.co.za/article/2021-04-25-a-remarkably-transformed-pick-n-pay-is-ceo-richard-brashers-farewell-legacy/

22 Hanlie Retief, 'Hanlie Retief gesels met Whitey Basson', *Rapport,* 6 November 2020.

23 Renier de Bruyn, 'Shoprite: A falling knife, or food for thought?', 6 November 2019, at https://sanlamprivatewealth.sanlam.com/resources/investments/Shoprite-a-falling-knife-or-food-for-thought/

24 Marco Barbieri, 'From the analysts: equities – Shoprite', Northstar Market Report Q2, 2019.

25 *De Kat,* 'Whitey se wil', February 1999.

26 De Bruyn, 'Shoprite: A falling knife, or food for thought?'

27 KykNET, 'Reis na Gister met Jak de Priester'.

28 *Succeed SA,* 'The third entrepreneur', August/September 1999.

29 *Rapport,* 'Whitey het Afrika klaar getem'.

30 Mzo Witbooi, 'Right on, Mr Shoprite!', *Destiny Man,* 28, January – February 2014.

Tributes and memories

1   KykNET, 'Hannes aan Huis met Whitey Basson', 1 June 2022, at https://www.youtube. com/watch?v=E-uomU_wwQk

2   Whitey Basson Ice Bucket Challenge, at https://youtu.be/dX-ZEosCFYI

3   'Beast "arm-wrestles" Whitey Basson as Boks braai with Johann Rupert and friends', at https://www.youtube.com/watch?v=B3oo6x-PLlo

Index

About the author

Niel Joubert is communications manager at Momentum Investments. He started his career as an accountant and auditor, after completing a bachelor of accounting degree at Stellenbosch University. He later completed BPhil Honours (journalism) at the same university.

Niel was a financial journalist and associate editor of Sake24 on Netwerk24, the digital news platform for Media24. He also wrote for *finweek*. In 2012, Niel won the Consumer Education category of the Citadel Words on Money journalism awards; in 2013 he won PriceWaterhouseCoopers's Tax Journalist of the Year Award as the best newcomer, and in 2014 he was named Media24's Business Journalist of the Year.

After helping OUTvest with their content strategy, he joined Hill+Knowlton Strategies, where he was a content editor and account manager in the financial services and investor relations division.

Niel also holds an MBA degree from Stellenbosch University, and a Postgraduate Diploma in Financial Planning from the University of the Free State. This is his first book.